BOB FLANAGAN:

In a bizarro, alternative universe kind of way, I sort of resemble Superman. Look, up in the sky, suspended by his wrists and sporting a huge erection—it's me. Yes, it's me, and most of the time I feel as though I come from another solar system. And despite my skinny physique and frail sensitivities, I possess certain powers and abilities far beyond those of so-called normal human beings. I was born with a genetic illness that I was supposed to succumb to at two, then ten, then twenty, and so on, but I didn't. And, in a never-ending battle not just to survive but to subdue my stubborn disease, I've learned to fight sickness with sickness.

SUPER-MASOCHIST

PUBLISHERS/EDITORS:	Andrea Juno & V. Vale
PRODUCTION MANAGER:	Elizabeth Borowski
PRODUCTION STAFF:	Mindaugis Bagdon, Mason Jones & Stacy Wakefield
PUBLICITY/FOREIGN RIGHTS:	Ira Silverberg, NYC, Tel: 212-226-6580
SPECIAL THANKS TO:	Black and Color Photo Lab (Los Angeles), Dennis Cooper, Margaret Crane, Kevanne Kirkwood, Sam Lax, Tom Rhoads and The Santa Monica Museum of Art, Ira Silverberg, Bill Sine, Christopher Trela, Donna West, Judy West, Megan Williams
CHIEF CONSULTANT:	Ken Werner
BOOK DESIGN:	Andrea Juno & Stacy Wakefield
ALL PHOTOGRAPHS BY:	Sheree Rose (unless otherwise noted)
COVER DESIGN BY:	Rex Ray (from photo by Bob Flanagan & Sheree Rose)
PHOTO CAPTIONS WRITTEN BY:	Bob Flanagan

Chapter Head Design (crown of thorns): originally drawn by Jill Jordan (used as tattoo for Bob Flanagan)
Back Cover: Bob Flanagan's chest X-ray photographed by Sheree Rose
End Papers: "Wall of Pain" by Bob Flanagan & Sheree Rose

Copyright © 1993 by Re/Search Publications
ISBN: 0-940642-25-5

BOOKSTORE DISTRIBUTION: Subco, PO Box 160 or 265 So. 5th St, Monroe OR 97456.
  Tel: 503-847-5274 or 800-274-7826. Fax: 503-847-6018.
NON BOOKSTORE DISTRIBUTION: Last Gasp, 777 Florida St, San Francisco, CA 94110.
  Tel: 415-824-6636. FAX: 415-824-1836.
U.K. DISTRIBUTION: Airlift, 26 Eden Grove, London, England N7-8EL.
  Tel: 071-607-5792. Fax: 071-607-6714.

Send SASE for catalog:
  RE/Search Publications, 20 Romolo #B, San Francisco, CA 94133, (415) 362-1465

Printed in Hong Kong by Colorcraft, Ltd
Type service bureau: Fotolithics, San Francisco
Photostat service: Northern Lights, San Francisco

10 9 8 7 6 5 4 3 2 1

WARNING: Do not attempt any of the body modifications or practices described herein. If you insist on doing any, go to a professional. Neither the contributers nor the publishers will assume responsibility for the use or misuse of any information contained within this book.

TABLE OF CONTENTS

INTERVIEW ONE	10
INTERVIEW TWO	30
"WHY"	64
INTERVIEW THREE	66
INTERVIEW FOUR	84
INTERVIEW FIVE	94
SHEREE ROSE	102
INTERVIEW SIX	110
BIOGRAPHY	112

BOB FLANAGAN  SUPERMASOCHIST

 # INTRODUCTION

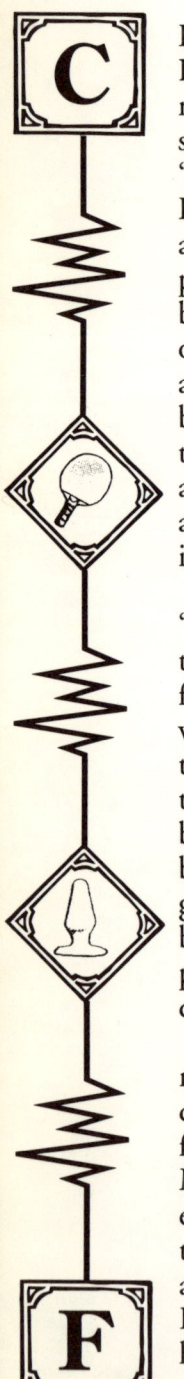

For the first volume of our *People Series,* we selected Bob Flanagan, a complex and fascinating performance artist, poet and "Super-Masochist." We first saw Bob in two 1989 performances (both titled "Nailed"). At the second performance at Southern Exposure Gallery in San Francisco, after mounting a scaffold constructed for his personal masturbatory practices, Bob attached 50 clothespins to his unclad body in an endurance ritual; slowly, they snapped off. Then he sewed up his scrotum with a needle and thread, and nailed what was left of the skin to a block of wood. What was amazing was: during all this shocking activity, Bob was standing in front of an audience naked and unashamed, talking with wit and intelligence—actually cracking jokes while nailing his scrotum to a board!

In the background, a recording of Bob's poem "Why" (listing reasons for his sado-masochistic activities) yielded deep resonances and meaning. Far from being a freak with "weird" sexual practices, Bob was addressing universal issues about guilt, our relationship to our bodies, and our sexuality. Even though his sexuality is on the extreme edge of the bell curve, what was most illuminating was the link between that sexuality and his growing up with a genetically-inherited, always-fatal disease: Cystic-Fibrosis. As a child Bob had to experience extremes of pain, frequent hospitalizations and repeated near-death encounters.

We had not seen anyone so comfortable with their nakedness in public, so transparently and honestly disclosing extreme masturbatory acts in a matter-of-fact way, completely purged of shame or pretension. Most people (ourselves included) don't engage in such extreme sexual experimentation. But Bob brought to the foreground conflicted and unresolved issues around Sex and The Body. Most "enlightened," post-Dr Ruth, literate people intellectually espouse a healthy acceptance of their bodies, sexuality, and masturbation. We would actually view someone who has *never* masturbated as "repressed" or "sick" and in need of therapy. Nevertheless, how many of us would not feel a pang of guilt or shame if someone accidentally walked in on us while we were masturbating . . . doing what we espouse as natural?

We are still under the tight, insidious grip of the past thousands of years of Judeo-Christian brainwashing that runs like an unconscious river through all of our myths and belief systems, setting the tone for our unanalyzed narratives. This patriarchal belief system (whose foundation rests upon the inferiority of the feminine) views the human body and sexuality as sinful and evil. Life on earth is envisioned as a purgatory wherein we ascend from the revered "foetus" stage into longed-for *death* (and thence to a sterile, bodiless heaven—or hell, if you actually *do* masturbate!). In this construct, death is more revered than life. Bob Flanagan's performances (and being) force seldom-expressed conflicts such as these into discussion. Particularly noteworthy is his attitude of fully living his life in the present, accepting the body he was given, and not only accepting all his desires but *owning* and *living* them. Onstage, Bob unabashedly does in public what most people do in private. Of course, with his fully articulated masochism, his activities are more extreme than most.

In our book, *Modern Primitives* (1989), we had already included Bob Flanagan's long-term partner, Sheree Rose, but had not yet interviewed Bob. What sealed our decision to devote an entire book to him was a viewing of his installation/performance at the Santa Monica Museum of Art. Not only was the show extremely moving, but it had an important (and unexpected) side-effect: while Bob was sitting in a hospital bed amidst a display of his sexual and medical artworks and videos, countless individuals (most of whom didn't know Bob) began conversing with him. The responses varied, but there was a surprising amount of tolerance and an unprecedented level of intimacy—many strangers became confessional

is fairly "normal"—he goes grocery shopping, attends art events, sees movies and visits friends.

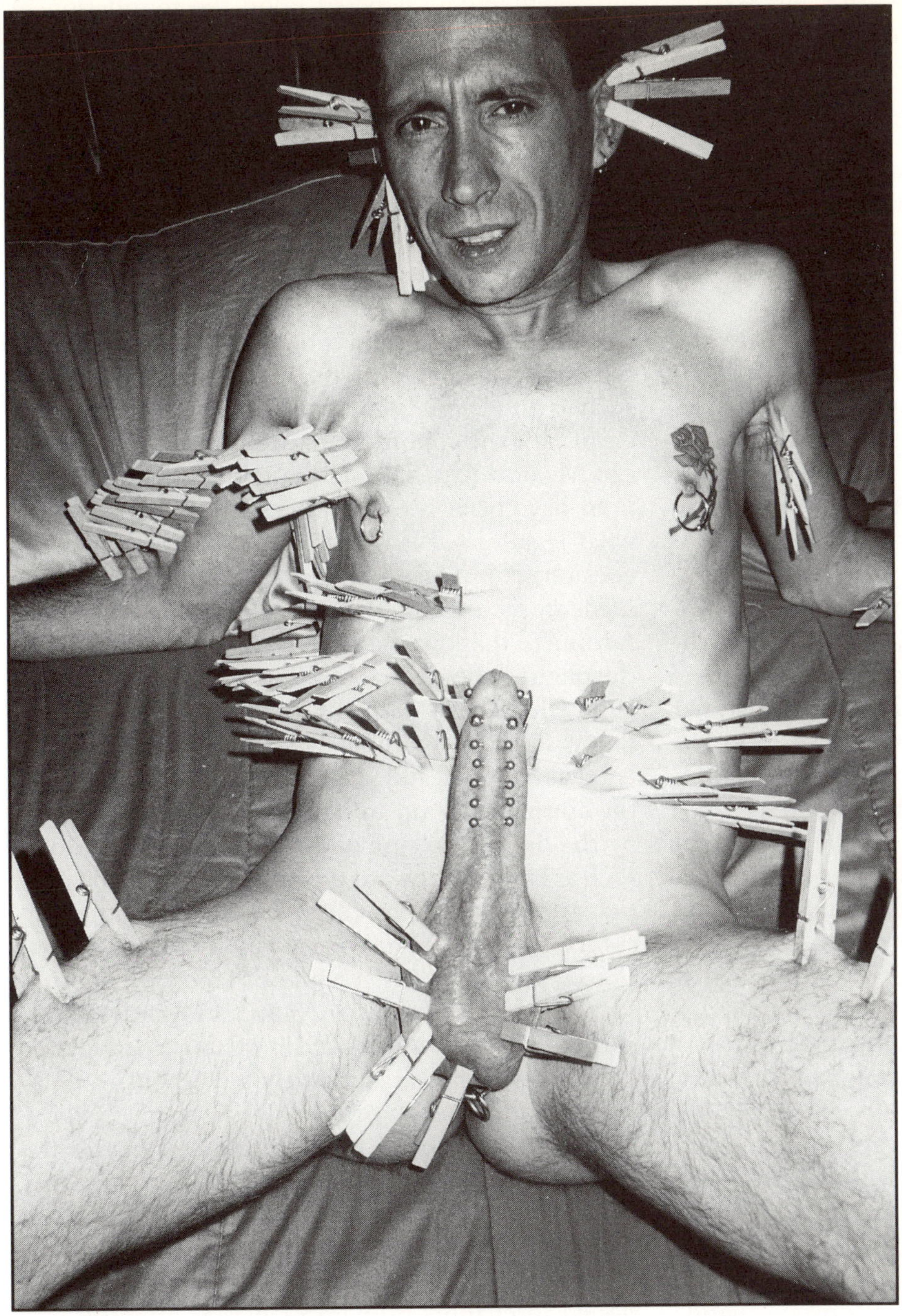

Bob does not flaunt a dark, Svengali-like *persona* when describing his SM activities (an adolescent "I'm going to shock you" affectation of superiority). What he does is openly disclosed and expressed. He has a clarity of self and a tap onto his unconscious, from whence springs his unique creativity. Bob seems fully integrated with his desires and all the parts of himself—purged of guilty self-judgment. Most refreshing is the humor and irony which accompanies his disclosures. Even a potentially "humiliating" photo of him covered with pelted food reveals no defensiveness: it's just Bob, his body and his penis—*and* he's laughing.

This volume contains many photos of Bob naked. After viewing photo after photo of Bob unabashedly revealing his genitalia, a strange *de-eroticization* takes place: the penis becomes demystified. After seeing so many views of Bob's penis tied up, pierced, weighted down, and just lying out in the open, the penis becomes mere bodily tissue whose eroticism is reserved for Bob himself and Sheree, not specifically for *our* gaze. Repetition has functioned to neutralize a charged icon. In our culture, advertising and mass media usually present *women's* bodies as objectified images, while the phallus is rarely glimpsed—thus it retains the aura of power and mystery. Even in "pornography" it is mainly the female genitalia which are permitted to be on display (gay pornography excepted, but gay pornography is not dominant in our homophobic society). And in TV movies and advertisements which are becoming increasingly sexualized and fetishized, one now can see naked women's bodies and breasts—yet the penis remains off-limits. That which is veiled

about their deepest quandaries and fears. It's rare to see "installation art" in a gallery function to create a community forum wherein crucial (yet taboo) subjects such as death, cancer, illness and sexuality could be freely discussed.

Upon meeting Bob, we found him unpretentious, good-natured and kind-hearted. Bob lives in a stable home with his long-term partner, photographer Sheree Rose; their relationship to date has lasted 14 years—longer than most mainstream heterosexual couples. Aside from the fact that he has to deal with Cystic-Fibrosis and practices masochism, his daily life

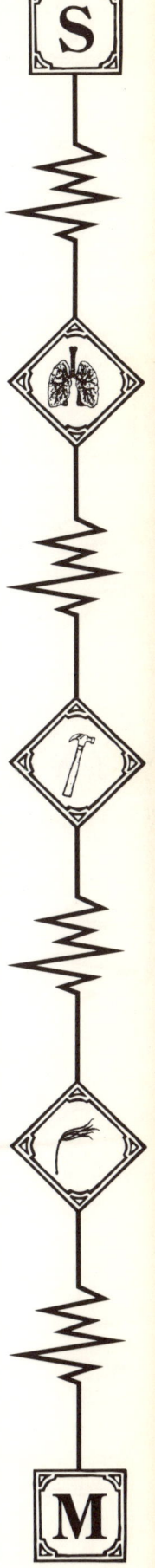

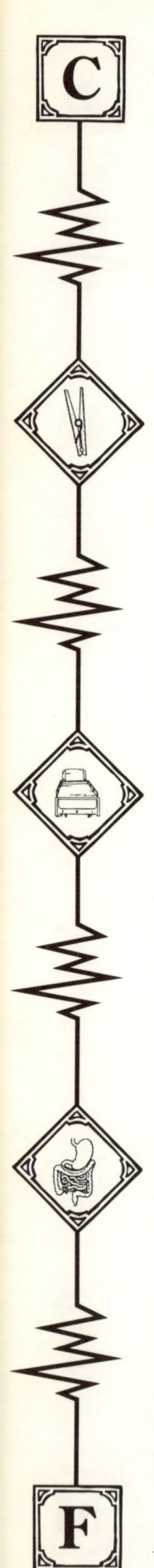

or put in the shadows builds up power—just as parts of the psyche which are buried and repressed become that much more forceful. Bob *un-conceals* not only his body but his desires, thus defusing power which is based on mystery and shrouding-in-darkness. As Bob throws light upon his desires and body, he produces a very liberating feeling in the beholder: we see shame transformed through creative disclosure into art.

Unlike most persons in our society, Bob Flanagan has a unique and emancipating connection to the eroticism of his personal childhood experiences. With a rare clarity of analysis, he has unraveled the complex origins of his extreme forms of masochism. Everyone's eroticism, all of our desires and repulsions (what we like and don't like), and all of our erotic preferences stem from unique experiences in childhood and adolescence. Our family situations, enjoyable and traumatic experiences, smells, certain foods, etc, all mingle to form synaesthetic memories which, upon recall, stimulate an erotic bodily response. However, most people keep their formative sexual experiences unconscious and un-analyzed. Bob has reclaimed his fascinating sexual past, and brought a full scrutiny of consciousness to bear upon it.

Since each person's eroticism is unique unto themselves, this book is not promoting an SM lifestyle, masochism, or *any* form of sexuality that is not personalized. This book is calling for *tolerance* and deep analysis of one's very personal desires and sexuality. This book is also about: being able to suspend judgment (which usually derives from un-analyzed, societally-imposed prejudices) long enough to truly perceive the depth of someone like Bob. Hopefully, we will enter an Age of Liberation where humans will actually possess the maturity to look deeply into their own desires. In an evolved culture, individuals will actually feel free to talk openly about sex, death and illness without puerile derision and hypocrisy pushing such vital issues into the dark shadows . . . and, hopefully, have the clarity to express their desires under the explicit rule of *consensuality* with other consenting *adult* humans.

The SM community which Bob describes is adamant about the *rule of consensuality*. Its practitioners only interact with conscious, *willing* ADULT partners—people who ultimately derive pleasure from their various activities. Bob Flanagan strongly emphasizes this, noting that rapists, serial killers, and child molesters don't *want* to become involved in the SM community because they aren't interested in *consensual* activities. Criminals derive pleasure at the *expense* of another person: depriving another person of their power and will. (Of course, the history of heterosexual activity is based upon the foundation of sexism, where the woman has no power. Basic heterosexuality provides many ever-present examples of non-consensual SM—without the benefit of being named as such!). Bob points out the hypocrisy of people who feign being shocked at SM play, while in real life acting despicably and sadistically with non-consensual power-plays toward others.

Widespread abuse of power, on every level, is one of the most shocking and salient characteristics of this society. In fact, one could reasonably argue that our society is literally *based* upon power inequities such as child abuse—perhaps the most flagrant and despicable use of non-consensual power. The American Medical Association admits that 1/3 of all children have been sexually molested as children, and what is admitted is but a fraction of what actually goes on. If physical beating, neglect and abandonment are factored in, the statistics climb even higher. Adding to that the relative poverty levels of children, the plight of homeless children, dwindling funds for child education—and you have a social foundation that is shockingly brutal. This underlying culture of child abuse replicates itself; abuse becomes a cycle—the abused grow up to be abusers. This is reflected by the flagrant misuse of power in our institutions, such as by police toward the more powerless, by politicians, by the rich, by corporate entities to the consumer, by powerful nations toward those less powerful, by whites against people of color, by men towards women and children, humans towards animals and the Earth. . . a daisy chain of abuse perpetrated by those with power against those without.

Bob and Sheree propose that their ritually-eroticized SM power-playing channels aggressive, potentially destructive desires into safe (and for them, pleasurable) outlets, in the privacy of their own bedroom with their full will and consent as adults. Throughout the ages, theater and the arts have functioned to channel humanity's darker impulses into safe creative expressions, and to expose social problems. An oft-cited example is the Balinese, a very peaceful people who stage violent, trance-like theatrical rituals involving all members of the community. Outlets such as these more *consciously* release aggressive or sexual impulses (this is infinitely preferable to the alternative: pretending these urges don't exist). And this is exactly what Bob is doing when he transforms his personal life into performance art and thus communicates his unique views and experiences to a wider community. Art has always functioned in the service of liberation and revelation—to grant a glimpse into the human character on all levels, including the dark side. At best, art can help involve us in a community catharsis, and just because we appreciate Shakespeare's *Macbeth* does not mean we will then go out and commit murder. Similarly, a well-made horror film can exorcise our fears rather than incite us to commit mayhem; and a rap song can transform anger and outrage into poetry and political insight.

Not only does Bob deal with his sexuality, but ever-present in his equation is: *nearness of death*. Our language has always associated sex with death: the phrase "petit mort" (little death) for orgasm is just one example. Motivated by uncertain health, Bob is enjoying his life fully and is truly *in* his body—rare even for healthy people. Most people do whatever they can to *not* experience the full intensity of feelings and emotions: from overworking at mindless jobs, to not delving into personal creativity and desires. A common mid-life crisis occurs when people (finally comprehending their mortality) realize they were only doing what their parents or society told them to do: sacrificing their inner urges and negating their opportunities for a fully-dimensional and creatively satisfying life.

To be able to talk honestly with somebody about death is a rare experience. Since Bob has survived Cystic-Fibrosis far longer than he expected, he has had to face sooner then most what we will all experience: death. All too often people employ defense mechanisms of denial, or turn to pseudo-religions, metaphysical systems, or cults in an attempt to escape the inevitable. Bob does not try to evade death by championing a pseudo-religious escape hatch; he does not reify his desires to avoid responsibility for who he is.

It is ironic that as we are genociding indigenous peoples all over the planet, a number of mostly white Americans are romanticizing and aping certain rituals torn out of other cultural contexts. One must be conscious of the naivete of aping other cultures defined as "primitive"—this merely replicates the imperialism and colonization that white western cultures have always indulged in. It is pretentious and arrogant to think that if a Westerner does a Kavandi dance (a Hindu ritual with thin spears pierced into one's body), he is participating in an "authentic" ritual . . . that this has anything to do with the actual community of Indian fakirs who originated the ritual, or that it will somehow illuminate consciousness in some mystical way. When a Lakota Sioux does a sun dance, this act is an integral part of a bonding with other members of a community, but for a white American male to do this is quite different. This is not to say that the smorgasbord of human ritual, past and present, can't be our palette for a theater of the future. However, to claim that the re-enactment of some "authentic" ritual will lead to "enlightenment" is inexcusable. In his interviews, Bob Flanagan addresses issues such as these, and his clarity of insight is refreshing—*he* links what he does to his American childhood and films such as Jerry Lewis's *Cinderfella* and Porky Pig! He does not "metaphysicize" his experiences; his is a stark clear existential acceptance of his desires, his body and his impending death.

Bob was born with a disease that set him apart. As a child he was frequently sick and isolated; he had stomach and intestinal problems, so the other kids made fun of him. He had a masochistic sexuality, and all these factors set him apart from his peers. In the process of having to deal with his "difference" he had a choice: to accept himself for who he is, or let others define him. Since death was so close by, he chose to accept himself. Bob speculates that ironically, perhaps *because* of his SM practices, he is one of the oldest survivors of the disease. His masochism kept him physically active, it developed his will, and was an area he could control—whereas his disease was beyond his control. (Perhaps his SM activities gave him *kundalini*-like energy which regularly recharged his body to fight the disease—who knows? Certainly, the doctors don't.)

Not long ago the cover of the *NY Times Magazine* featured a controversial photo of the model/artist Matuschka displaying her mastectomy—scar tissue had replaced one of her breasts. Despite the obvious disfigurement, she looked beautiful, defiant and *alive*. How many of us can look into the mirror with total self-acceptance—with love, and without judgment? One of the problems in our society, particularly with women, gays, drag queens and racial minorities, has been a constant "putting away" of the parts of the self that society does not deem acceptable. In this regard, Bob's unashamed display of his body with an IV-catheter in his lungs and his penis in bondage underscores the necessity for a widespread societal transformation of *shame* into *disclosure*.

As Bob and his partner Sheree disclose their life, their moral and political beliefs become illuminated. The outlet for their deep concerns for a better world is their fully committed lifestyle. For them, their relationship is the embodiment of the truism *the personal is political*. Bob's integration of his home life, artistic process, and sexuality is an example giving us a glimpse of a more tolerant, more responsible and more conscious society where creativity is no longer fettered by censorship, sexist repression, and denial of one's past.

—Andrea Juno & V. Vale
September 6, 1993

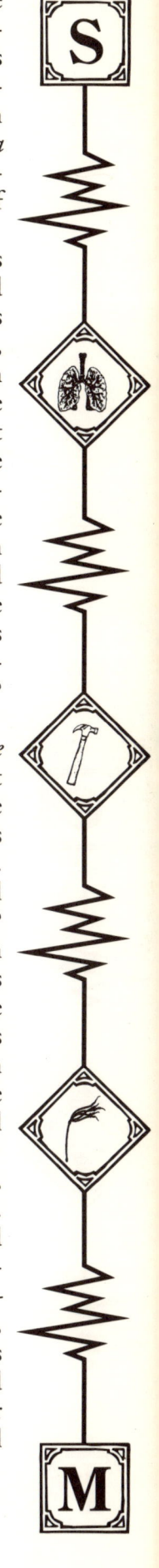

BOB FLANAGAN SUPERMASOCHIST

Interview One

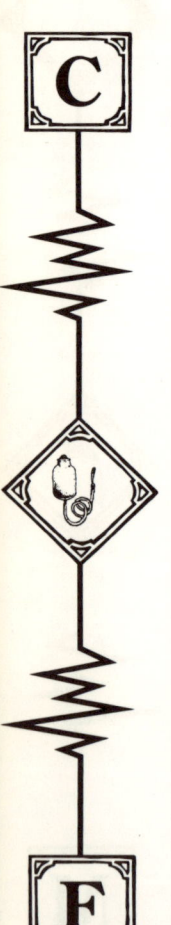

♦ **VALE: Can you start from the beginning, and tell us about your life, your philosophy, your ideas and your experiences. Your cystic fibrosis affected everything in your life . . .**
♦ BOB FLANAGAN: I'm the oldest in my family. I was born in New York City in 1952, and as an infant was always sick with something. I was always crying, had stomach-aches, and was in and out of the hospital with different symptoms. Back then no one knew what the problem really was. The doctors accused my parents of mistreating me, they said I had colic, they said my parents were worrying too much . . . but they knew I was sick.

Two years later my brother, Tim, was born, and he was healthy. But a few years after that my sister, Patricia, was born, and she was even sicker than I was. Again, the doctors said my parents didn't know what they were talking about: she had a cold, she had colic, she had pneumonia—*anything* but the right diagnosis. My parents were young and panicky and didn't have any money—
♦ **V: You grew up in an Irish family?**
♦ BF: Yes; my mother grew up in a family of ten kids. Anyway, finally my parents talked to a doctor on the phone who recognized my sister's symptoms—that she was dying—and he paid for the cab ride to the hospital, diagnosed her with cystic fibrosis and got her through the worst of it. Then he diagnosed *me* as having cystic fibrosis, which in 1952 was still relatively unknown. Previously, people had just died and the cause had been attributed to pneumonia or something else. Most "cystics" rarely lived past infancy anyway, and there were no tests for it—even today, only the larger hospitals test for it. And back then the tests were more complicated; today it's a simple sweat test.

This doctor suggested that because of the air and the extreme weather, we leave New York and move to California or Arizona. My parents flipped a coin and we moved to L.A.—
♦ **ANDREA JUNO: —wrong choice!**
♦ BF: We moved to the San Gabriel Valley which as far as air quality goes is even worse than L.A.; it's more inland. Then we moved to Orange county, which at the time wasn't too bad.
♦ **AJ: Were your parents attentive to you?**
♦ BF: Yes. They always had money problems, because at the time there was no MediCal or insurance to pay for this—they had to pay for it all by themselves. They had me, my sister, my two brothers (who were both healthy), and another baby sister who died in infancy (probably of CF; she was never tested). My sister who survived died at the age of 21 in 1979. She did a lot in her life, but still had a really hard time.

It's been a real effort for all of us. Since the age of 18 I've worked at a summer camp for kids with cystic fibrosis as a director, assistant director and all round camp fool. I've done that for 21 years now, so I've seen a lot of kids die. In the beginning I used to sing camp songs at their funerals but it started to become expected of me, by parents and funeral directors—it started to feel like a sick night-club act, so I had to stop. I remember one funeral director asking me, "Oh, do you do this for a living? Because we could *really* use your services." I said, "No, I don't do this—ever again!"

♦ *AJ: What's the treatment for CF?*
♦ BF: I see a physical therapist who pounds on my back and chest for an hour, upside-down and sideways, to dislodge all the mucus—
♦ *V: Exactly what is cystic fibrosis?*
♦ BF: Basically, the body produces too much mucus. Mucus is normal for most people; usually it's pretty thin and functions to keep the airways lubricated in the lungs. With cystic fibrosis there's a defective gene which causes the body to produce far too much mucus, and this mucus is thick and sticky—it looks like a dark- (or light-) green pudding. It just sits there in your lungs until you cough it up or have somebody pound it out of you. There are drugs you can take to dilute the secretions and expand the airways. This mucus gets into the tiniest parts of the lungs where it never leaves, and furnishes a great breeding ground for bacteria, viruses, pneumonia, etc. That's why I'm always in the hospital, because I always have bacteria growing there; the mucus provides a really fertile area. After years of this you get a lot of scar tissue building up from all the infections.

♦ *AJ: When you grew up, did your mom pound you?*
♦ BF: They didn't have to do that much when I was growing up; I was pretty lucky. Then, when I was ten years old I went into the hospital for a month and almost died. After that, I had more stomach problems, because the other part of cystic fibrosis is: the pancreas gets all screwed up and doesn't produce enough enzymes to properly digest food. Because of this, I've always had to eat a lot, but I stay thin.

When I was a kid I was in a lot of pain from stomachaches. But because I didn't get a lot of the major infections that my sister got, my lungs didn't deteriorate as quickly as hers. Her lungs got scarred early; this caused difficulty in breathing and strained her heart. But I didn't have those problems . . . although I'm having more problems now as I get older.

♦ *AJ: You've found a link between the medical world and the SM world—*
♦ BF: —except the SM world is more fun, and you can choose it. I was *forced* to be in the medical world, so I turned that into something I could have control over instead of something that was controlling me.
♦ *V: Didn't you last longer than most CF sufferers?*

Bob's (second row from the top, far left) First Communion, St. Francis Church, Azusa, CA, 1962

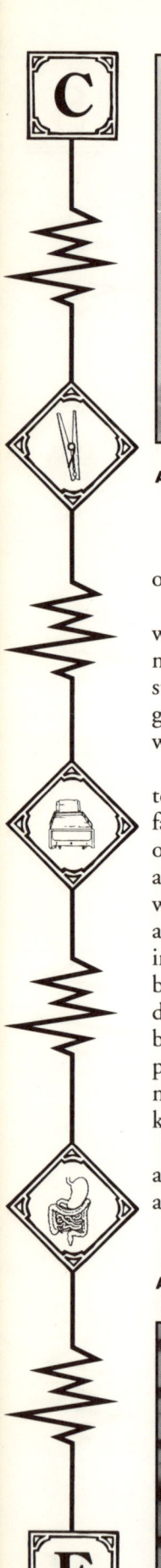

Age 10

♦ BF: Yeah, I'm one of the oldest. There's a few people in their early '60s who are still alive.

♦ **V: Were there any early harbingers of your later SM life?**

♦ BF: My mother said that when I was a baby and really sick in the hospital, they had to stick needles in my chest to draw fluid out. I was always thrashing around and fighting (I was in pain), so the doctors tied my hands and feet to the bed so I wouldn't hurt myself. And that's still one of my favorite positions to be in: flat on the bed, tied up.

Because of my early, really horrible stomach-aches, I would rub against the sheets and the pillows to soothe my stomach and this became more and more erotic—I started to masturbate that way; slowly it all blended together. One way of taking control of the stomach-ache was to turn it into an orgasm.

For one whole year I didn't go to school; I had a home teacher and was mostly in bed. I had a lot of time to fantasize, to watch TV, and to become increasingly aware of my body in one sense or another. On top of that, I had a cousin two years older than I and we started playing what he called the "Slave/Master" game. This was right after we moved to California, in the first house we lived in in El Sereno. It's such a strong memory that I've driven back to that house just to look at it and recall what we did. He was nine, his sister was my age (seven), and my brother Tim was five, so we were all pretty young to be playing this erotic "slave/master" game. I label it "erotic" now, but I don't know what we called it then; we just knew it felt good.

I remember being locked in a tool shed with cobwebs and spiders (I still get turned on by dark confined spaces and the smell of wood). At some point he pretended to whip us with a belt as we swung back and forth on a swing set. It wasn't hard enough to hurt, but I remember wanting it to be harder and wanting it to hurt. At the end of the day when it got dark, he passed out these paper tickets and said, "Be sure to bring these back with you tomorrow or else you will be punished." The first thing I did when I got inside was rip them

Age 12

up and toss them away—I was thrilled at the thought of being punished! I have no idea where this thrill came from; I didn't see it in movies or magazines (I was too young).

We didn't play these games very often—only every few months or so—but every time we played, it got more intense. As we got older and reached puberty the games involved more nudity and touchy-feely stuff, although that's as far as it went—we got caught. One day my cousin and I were blabbing away about how much fun we were having, and of course my mother overheard us.

♦ **AJ: What did your mother do?**

♦ BF: She threatened to put us in a home if we ever did that again. It was one of the things she said to scare us, but it didn't stop us. We continued to play from time to time as we got older, and the game got sexier. That was the first "high" I got from SM and I've always tried to pursue that in one form or another all the way into my adult life. During high school, while the rest of the family was watching TV, I'd be in the bathroom whipping myself with the ping-pong paddle or suspending myself by the wrists in the garage. When Friday night came and I didn't have school the next day, I'd be doing all kinds of bizarre things to myself all night long.

♦ **AJ: What was your first *conscious* SM act?**

♦ BF: At the age of seven, in the first house we lived in, I got naked (which was a bizarre thing for a kid to do) and—I don't know what possessed me, but I wanted this feeling of being *mummified,* so I laid a blanket on the floor, held on to one end of the blanket and rolled myself up tighter and tighter until I was rolled up ("mummified") inside this blanket. I really liked the feeling of not being able to move my arms or legs or anything—that was so exciting. I stayed like that for awhile and finally I couldn't breathe, so I unrolled myself.

Afterwards, I was always doing weird things like that around the house. In high school I got my first drum kit and learned how to play. It came with this giant canvas bag for the bass drum, and one of the things I liked to do was roll myself up into a ball and zip myself in. I just barely fit; I'd be in this bondage position where I couldn't breathe very well and I'd remain there until all the oxygen ran out. Then I'd unzip the bag, panicky and hyperventilating, and get outta there.

As kids, whenever we said something nasty my mother would say, "I'm gonna wash your mouth out with soap!" Again, this was just an idle threat, and she never made good on it, but it got me thinking and fantasizing and finally I had to see what it was like. So I went into the bathroom, soaped up a washrag and washed my mouth out with soap and got real turned on by it. It *still* turns me on to think about it!

♦ **V: Did any of your ideas come from movies? In Cleopatra *there's a scene where a huge carpet is unrolled, revealing her inside it—***

♦ BF: Lots of movies provided inspiration, but I think the bondage goes back to being tied up as an infant—it could be something as simple as that. I'm sure that while I was tied up as an infant in the hospital my parents felt really sorry for me and were overly (or justifiably) concerned, trying to comfort me as much as possible. While horrible things were happening to me, I was getting extra love and attention, so the two contradictory feelings probably fused together . . . the horrible things happening to me were made into something better; a sweetness was overlaid. When I'm the most turned on by SM, there's a sweet sensation felt—a candy-kind of feeling, no matter how brutal it might *look*.

There are lots of layers . . . one layer after another. I didn't go to Catholic school but I went to catechism until junior high school—I got to experience Catholic guilt and confession, the Stations of the Cross, and the saintliness of suffering. I think I related my suffering and illness to the suffering of Jesus on the cross—the idea that suffering in some way was kind of holy. As I got older and still believed in god, I felt guilty when I actually started tying myself up in positions that looked like the cross . . . but I purged *that* in the '70s when *Jesus Christ, Superstar* came out. My parents bought the album for us as a pre-Christmas present, and while they were out Christmas shopping, I took a belt (I didn't have whips in those days), and put the record on (specifically the "Trial Before Pilot" track, which includes the full 39 lashes, complete with dramatic counting and sound effects), and there I was naked in the living room giving myself the full 39 lashes along with the record—feeling *somewhat* guilty and stupid . . . but if it was good enough for Jesus, it was good enough for me!

♦ **AJ:** *You're more Nietzschean: negating Christianity while making a positive affirmation—*

♦ **BF:** I can't get past the fact that the things I do are on some level enjoyable. One good thing about my parents: there wasn't much criticism about our lifestyles or what we wanted to do with our lives, so I didn't come to SM with the baggage of "This is a horrible thing to be doing." We have a weird family: I'm into SM, my brother two years younger is an actor and gay, and I don't know what my sister would have become but she was artistic and made things and did puppet shows and was very creative. My youngest brother is a fundamentalist Baptist who works with kids and preaches sermons on Sunday—he's the *white* sheep of the family!

♦ **V:** *What did your father do for a living?*

♦ **BF:** He did a lot of things. Most of the time he worked two or three jobs at once just to keep ahead of the bills. He worked at Winchell's donuts, he worked at an orange juice factory, but mainly he worked with computers—he was into computers in the '50s. Now he's a systems analyst. Both my parents are alive and healthy; my mom does medical transcribing. She's worked with computers and has been a waitress—she did any kind of job she could.

♦ **AJ:** *Does she know about what you do?*

♦ **BF:** She's starting to get the idea. My parents have been very supportive of all our careers; they paid for art lessons and drama lessons and loved the fact that we were into the arts. I think there's art in our genes; my grandfather was a frustrated artist, and several uncles were, too. My dad started out to be an actor; he was on the Ted Mack Amateur Hour (that's like *Star Search*) but when he started a family that ended.

All my work before I wrote *Fuck Journal* was about my illness and family; it was clean. Because it was poetry, it was hard for my parents to understand, but they liked the fact that people were getting to know who I was. After I started my autobiography, the *Book of Medicine*, I didn't show them anything anymore—I thought, "This is too explicit. They won't *get* it; they'll be afraid for me and feel bad about how they raised us." When I did a performance at the *RE/Search Modern Primitives* series of events at Southern Exposure Gallery [San Francisco, 1989] I did it under the pseudonym of "Bob F" because I had a comedy career and didn't know how far I was going to go with SM work, and how open that would become . . . but it all just *exploded* after that.

My parents and I started having little talks. Now they know that my work is sexual, that it has something to do with fantasies, and they're getting more comfortable with that. As a matter of fact, last year I saw Annie Sprinkle's performance at *Highways* [performance art space] in Santa Monica, which HBO was filming that night. Annie did her usual bit with the speculum and invited the audience to come up and look inside to see her cervix, and like a lemming I went along with the crowd. Well, months later my brother the Baptist is flipping the channels on TV and naturally he stops at HBO and the Annie Sprinkle show: "Hey Mom!" he yells. "I think I just saw Butch on TV looking up some lady's legs on this sex show." (*Butch*—that's what they call me; I was given that name by my uncle who's a dwarf—well, he *was* a dwarf; he died. My dad's sister married a dwarf; he came to the hospital when I was born and snarled [nasal voice], "His name is *Butch!*" Nobody wanted to argue with him, so that's what they called me, to this day.) Anyway, HBO actually showed this Annie Sprinkle show on TV. I was sitting in the front row with my nose ring on and I got up and took the flashlight and peered at her cervix—that was shown on the air!

♦ **V:** *Can you go back and*

Age 12

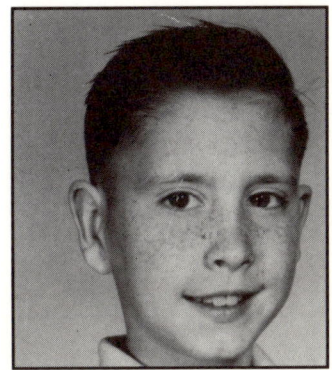
Age 14

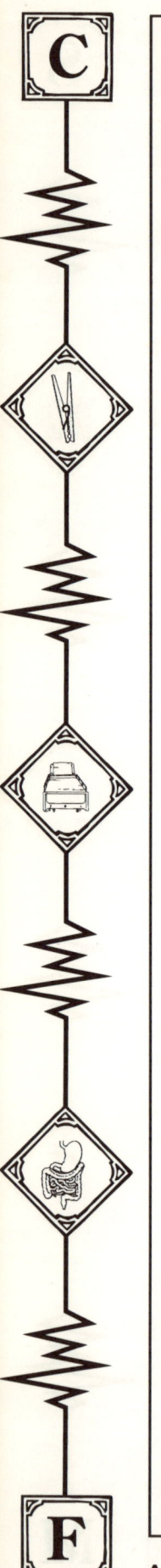

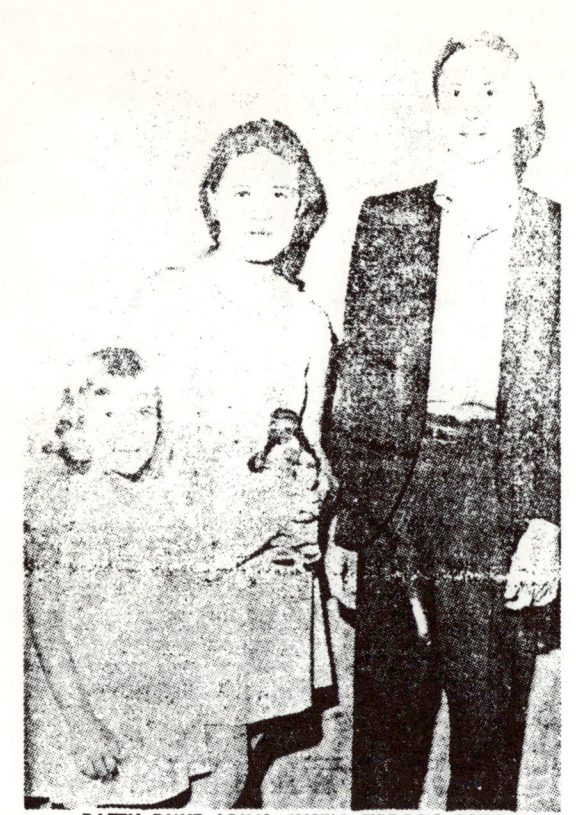

PATTY DUKE JOINS CYSTIC FIBROSIS DRIVE
Lisa Huff   Patty Duke   Robert Flanagan

Cystic Fibrosis Drive Scheduled Saturday

ANAHEIM — "Give Them a Run for Their Lives" is the theme for the annual door-to-door campaign for funds sponsored by the North Orange County Chapter of the National Cystic Fibrosis Research Foundation scheduled Saturday and Sunday.

According to chapter president Mrs. John P. Kaiser of Anaheim, thousands of young volunteer canvassers from Los Angeles, Ventura and Orange county will join in the two-day campaign to raise money to combat the hereditary lung disease.

Contributions will be used to help support a network of 38 regional centers throughout the U.S. and to help finance a basic research program into the cause and control of the disease which parents can pass on to their children.

Climax of the 1967 campaign is expected to be an "Op-Hop" featuring many popular recording stars at the Hollywood Palladium on Sunday evening.

Those wishing to contribute to the campaign by mail should send their contributions to the North Orange County Chapter. NCFRF, PO Box 3204, Anaheim.

Article in local paper, 1967

trace more of your early evolution—

♦ BF: It all just steadily grew. I played more mummification games with the blanket, and played more games with my cousins. It started to go in the direction of fraternity games where you have to run a gauntlet and go under each other's legs and get spanked. At the time I never gave any of this much thought; I knew that it was nasty but *fun*. I also knew it was weird, and since I didn't want to get caught and get into trouble, I didn't tell anyone about it. I never felt guilty until well into my '20s when I told someone about it and it developed into a bad experience. I was with this woman and she said she wanted to try all these things and she did—then she felt really guilty about it, and that guilt transferred onto me. That relationship only lasted for about a week. I *stopped* the guilt by talking about it; I told my best friend and he just thought it was funny and great and crazy that I was doing these odd things, because I'd exhibited a completely different persona to the world. My friend's acceptance made me think, "Okay, this is *right.* This is a good thing."

I didn't blab about any of this too much, but I always looked for that intimate moment (whether it was a female I was dating, or whoever) when I could talk about what I was doing. When I started meeting poets like Dennis Cooper who were so openly and brazenly writing about what they were doing . . . once they found out I was this *freak,* then they became much closer to me, and that was good for me.

♦ *AJ: The act of disclosure is so liberating; society wants you to keep everything inside where it festers, and then you're more controllable through your guilt—*

♦ BF: Actually, with most of the girls I dated since high school, it would get to the point where I'd say, "I'm into *this;* I've been doing this," and often they wanted to try it or play around with it.

♦ *AJ: You've broken through to the other side of guilt—*

♦ BF: To me, it's just: "This is the person I am. I'm not afraid of *any* aspect of what I am. I'm just exploring and I want to explore all of it and feel *all* of it." It seems so silly to feel guilty about any of it or think that it's wrong, because that would mean condemning everything that I am—all the feelings I have.

♦ *AJ:* **Perhaps** *because you've explored your deepest feelings and desires, you've managed to stay alive so long—*

♦ BF: I think that has a lot to do with my longevity. Disclosure purges a lot, and these activities kept me a lot more physically active than I probably would have been.

♦ *AJ: Maybe your activities summoned up something akin to kundalini energy, and brought about a sexual recharging of being—*

♦ BF: While in high school, on Friday nights, late at night I would open the window when it was cold and lie naked on the floor and let the cold air blow across me. For whatever reason I'd take white glue and smear it all over my body and let it dry; in the morning I'd have to peel it off. I did anything to cause a weird body sensation, usually around the genital area.

When I started tying myself up with belts, I'd read about

GRADES CLIMB
Phone Hookup Makes Invalid Boy Live Wire

By ALLAN GAUL
Tribune Staff Writer

Voices crackled through the small box on the wall of the Glendora home.

"Goodnight, Bobby," came calls from several dozen children.

"Goodnight, everyone," a handsome 12-year-old boy answered from the confines of his bedroom.

Another school day had ended for Bobby Flanagan. It is due to that little box on the wall, that he is still a member of the sixth grade class at Drendel School.

Bobby, a bright, intelligent boy with a cheery smile, is too ill to attend classes. He tried for a long time, but his illness forced him to leave school.

Where other children come down with colds, Bobby's illnesses quickly become pneumonia.

On the surface, Bobby looks a picture of health. An oxygen tank beside his bed and rigging for an oxygen tent are a constant reminder this is not so.

According to his parents, Mr. and Mrs. Robert C. Flanagan, 19040 Rimview Dr., Glendora, Bobby has a lifelong history of illness.

"He was in the hospital more than half of the time prior to his second birthday," his father said. "Since then he has missed a lot of school because of bad spells."

The family used private tutors for several years, but Bobby started to lose interest last month when it became evident he would not be able to return to school for some time.

That's when Earl Edelbrock, business assistant for the Azusa Unified School District, stepped in and made a major difference in Bobby's life.

Two weeks ago a special direct telephone line was hooked up linking the Flanagan home with the school, which is a part of the Azusa Unified District.

Every word spoken in the class is audible in the Flanagan home. When Bobby wants to talk, he pushes a button and recites his lesson, which is then heard by everyone in the class.

The proudest moment of Bob's young life came the other day when he read a book report he had done on the life of Jules Verne.

As he finished, the entire class stood and applauded.

Although he missed three months of school this year, the direct telephone line has enabled him to catch up on his schoolwork.

He has confided to his parents that the telephone hookup has renewed his interest in school, and in his favorite subjects, mathematics and science.

Bobby has a vivid imagination, as reflected by "monster" models he has constructed which rest atop several dressers.

For kicks, he has decided to become a motion picture writer-producer-director-makeup man.

Using his own motion picture camera, he stages movies (monster type, naturally). He applies makeup to friends and then they act out the parts to his direction.

Next step in his mind is to show the pictures for profit.

"We have a garage where we'll show them," he said happily.

"We'll charge 10 cents for admission. If all goes according to plan, we'll make $3 on popcorn, $2 on candy and another couple of dollars on admissions."

Despite his illness, Bobby is active and has a deep-seated pride in being self-sufficient.

He is a Tribune carrier boy and boasts that in the year he has had his route he has only had "one complaint."

Mom, dad, brother Tim, 11, and brother John, 5, help him on his route.

VITAL LINK—Bobby Flanagan, 12, bottom photo, keeps up with his schoolwork at Azusa Unified School District's Drendel School through direct telephone hookup from bedside to his sixth grade classroom and teacher, Mrs. Neilen Zimmerman, top photo. A rare illness keeps the lad from attending classes, but this link keeps him up with his classmates.

Tribune Photo by John Duricka

The Flanagan family is a close-knit group, but it has to be.

In addition to Bobby's illness, the family is faced with the fact that the couple's fourth child, Patricia, 6, has the same illness as Bobby.

A fifth child died at the age of 6 months.

Now the Flanagans are faced with another hardship. The home in which they are living is doomed. It must go to make way for the Foothill Freeway.

They have until the last of June to move. They have hopes of finding a home close to a junior high school so that the same telephone arrangement can be rigged for Bobby.

If the junior high school officials want recommendations about the program, they just have to consult with Drendel School Principal Jack Swords.

"Bobby's participation has lifted the morale of the whole class," he said.

Bobby is best described by his proud father.

"He can't do many of the things which other kids do . . . So those things he can do, he does with all his heart and soul."

The San Gabriel Valley Daily Tribune, 1964

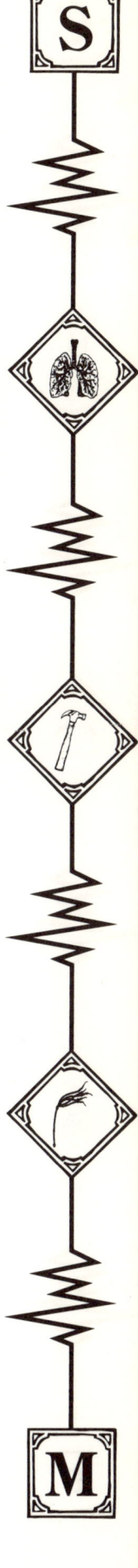

---

a father who was arrested for abusing his kids—articles like that always turned me on. My parents didn't abuse *us,* but hearing about what happened to other kids always got me excited, especially when things got creative or bizarre. I read one article where the father took the kids and hung them up by their wrists in the garage for *four hours* at a time as punishment. I started doing the same thing. This was in 1970 when the Beatles' "Let It Be" came out; I had a '60s bedroom with black light posters on the walls and a weird lamp hanging from a hook in the ceiling. In the middle of the night I would take this lamp down and suspend myself by the wrists with a belt and swing back and forth. Before that, I would go inside closets and hang from the doorways, but after awhile none of the closet doors would close and nobody could understand why: "This door doesn't close anymore!" While my parents were shopping or at work, I'd be hanging from the doorway jacking off on the doorknob or something.

I got a little more sophisticated and started hanging from the hook in the ceiling until the hook broke, and I scared the hell out of myself falling to the floor. The one thing about suspending myself: I couldn't do it for very long, yet these kids were tied up for *hours*—I couldn't do it for more than a minute or so.

♦ **AJ:** *Why can't you hang by your wrists for more than a minute?*

♦ **BF:** It hurts too much. If you're doing this to yourself, it's too easy to jump off and get down, so you need a little more "persuasion": somebody else who's in control. Your arms feel like they're being ripped out of their sockets, plus your wrists start getting cut (at the time I didn't have bondage cuffs; I wasn't that sophisticated). I was doing all this years before there were clubs and equipment specifically designed for this kind of activity. When I found out, I couldn't believe it: every bizarre thing I was doing (involving urine, etc) other people were doing too; and you could *buy* things for each activity.

♦ *AJ: How old were you?*
♦ BF: A sophomore in high school; 15 or 16. It took puberty to hit before everything started to coalesce into really wild acts, like getting naked as often as possible and sneaking into the backyard in the moonlight while everybody was sleeping inside the house. The thrill involved *fear of getting caught:* at any moment my parents could look out their bedroom window and see me. I'd leave my clothes on the back porch and then just creep around the yard. I took a shit behind one of the bushes and that was a real thrill; I lay down on the grass and squirmed while the dog was all over me; I was whispering: "Go away! Go away!" The dog had no idea what I was doing there. I would be looking around nervously to see if anybody would catch me while I masturbated; then in a frenzy it would all be over and I'd think, "What the hell am I doing here?" almost like I were coming out of a trance, then I'd sneak back into the house as quietly as possible.

I was so amazed that I was never caught. Once I was hanging from a hook in a weird bondage position and my parents woke up at 3 in the morning and walked past my room to the kitchen (at the time I didn't have a lock on the door; eventually I got one). I thought they might just walk in, and I'd have no explanation for the fact that I'm all tied up. I had a sofa bed which I could unfold and tie myself up to in different bizarre ways with ropes. I got pretty inventive; it's easier to tie yourself up than get yourself out of things. Sometimes I'd be really stuck, especially after I grew up; as an adult I got myself into some pretty funny situations.

I remember in history class being really turned on by the thought of the California Indians going into their sweatlodges; the men would heat rocks and go into them for hours (or days) and just sweat. That idea stuck in my head.

Speaking of school, I remember getting excited about SM during summer school around the fifth grade. The class staged a little play about Pocahontas and I played Captain John Smith—the Indians tied him up and were going to cut his head off. The chopping block was a chair, and the kids tied me down and put my head on the chair and I got so excited (I don't know if I had a hard-on or not) but there was this moment of intense excitement at the thought of being controlled by somebody else—this memory never left me.

I tried to do some fasting during high school. I'd bring the lunch my mother made for me and put it in the locker and try to force myself not to eat until I went home. Sometimes it worked and sometimes it didn't. Also, out of the blue I would go to the refrigerator and force myself to eat foods that I absolutely hated. I hated mayonnaise, so I would take a spoonful and force myself to eat it and retch; I was into force-feeding in high school! I'd make myself eat a raw egg; I don't know where I came up with that idea, but now people do that as part of an SM scene.

♦ *AJ: Was the idea to reach an altered state of consciousness . . . jar the body out of its complacency?*
♦ BF: Yes. I saw *The Pit and the Pendulum* and was inspired to make a pendulum out of an old saw tied to a string; again, this was while everyone was watching TV in the living room. I was in the bathroom lying in the tub with the saw above me suspended from the shower rod. The saw was old and rusty; I thought to myself, "This isn't really going to cut you open," so I taped sewing needles along the edge. I was lying there—one hand was lowering the saw while the other was making it swing back and forth—and my stomach got all scratched up.

I got into other blood rituals involving piercing, although I didn't know it was "piercing" at the time. I had been whipping myself with a belt for a long time before I realized that wasn't *enough,* so I turned the belt around so the buckle would hit me. Then I attached a needle so that a little pinpoint protruded, and started whipping myself with that. I started really *going at it,* and then opened my

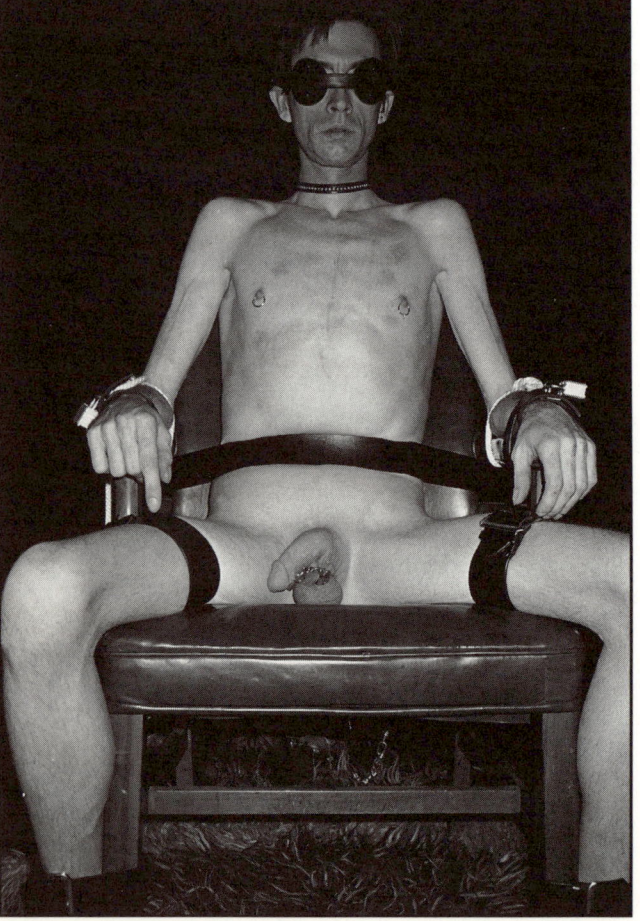

Early experiments in virtual reality. Obviously way ahead of my time. Los Angeles, 1983

eyes and the tiles were all splattered with blood! That was kind of scary—only because I thought somebody might catch me: "Ohmigod, I gotta clean this up!"

Once I was in the bathroom spanking myself with a ping-pong paddle and there came a knock on the door: my brother said, "Our cat's dead!" I said [nervously], "Uh—what do you mean?" "This neighbor kid just found him." Here I am naked, with a ping-pong paddle: "Oh— I'll be right out!" My parents weren't home, so I had to get dressed and deal with this dead cat . . .

♦ **V: What were you thinking?**
♦ BF: If things go wrong, you think, "Oh, this is telling me I shouldn't be doing these things." I had my first girlfriend right out of high school; we moved in together. I was 19 and she was 18. At least twice we threw away all the equipment we'd collected, because if we had a fight I'd say, "Okay, we'll give this up and maybe we'll get along better." But that was stupid.

♦ **V: You didn't have relationships with girls before then?**
♦ BF: Just my cousin. She was submissive, playing the slave role to her older brother, and was definitely important when we started touchy-feely look-at-each-other-naked games—she was the only girl, so that was important. In high school I was such a nerd that I just had normal dates, until I met a girl who liked me because she thought I was a drug addict (she was pretty wild herself). She was the first girl I "told all" to, and we lived together for a couple years.

♦ **AJ: A lot of creative, thinking people are social outcasts—**
♦ BF: Right. I think I managed to stay relatively "balanced" because the other side of me was so nerdy. I was a good student, never did anything wrong in school and didn't give my parents any trouble (except by being sick a lot). I was the oldest, so I was "in charge of the house." I did a lot of the cleaning, I cooked dinner, and took care of the rest of the kids. My parents could depend on me from a really early age, because they both worked at two jobs. So while I was doing all these weird things, I was also the one in charge.

In other respects I was completely normal. My brother who was two years younger was the one who experimented with drugs, was gay and came out—he was much more *out there* doing things than I ever was. I was a sick little kid. In the fifth grade I had a teacher who was really into biographies of famous Americans: legends of Ben Franklin, Jeb Stuart, Thomas Edison, etc. It turns out that it was all a bunch of lies, but I read about these "heroes" and started to identify with them and felt I had this "grander" purpose in life. Also, for a while I was into science fiction and read Jules Verne. In high school Bob Dylan and Van Gogh were my big influences—I wanted to be a painter then.

Actually, *art* provided a centering for me. When I was sick I was alone a lot, so early on my parents gave me coloring books and tracing paper—it was always understood that I was going to become an artist. While watching TV I'd be sketching portraits of people like Bobby

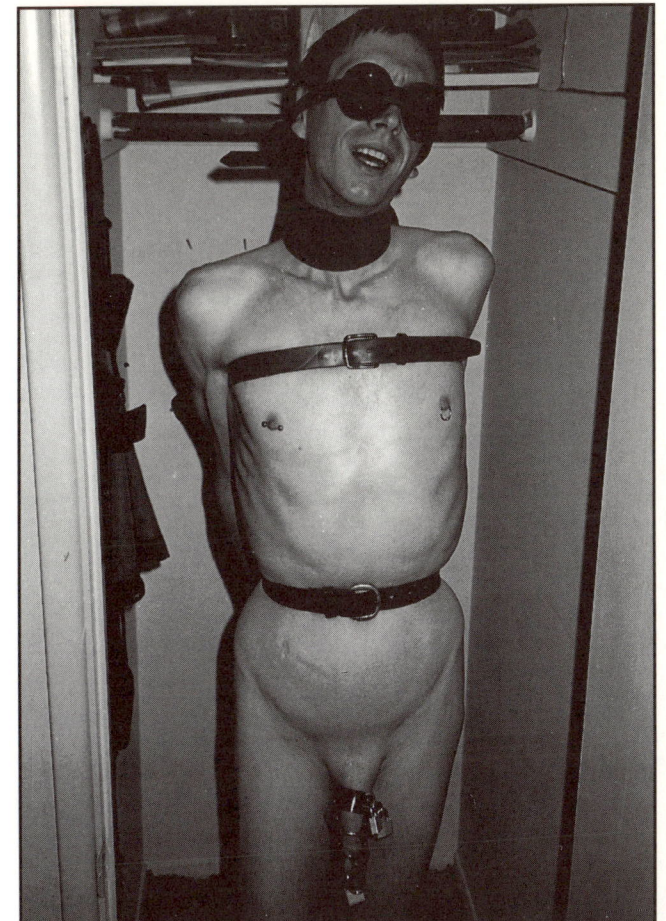

Los Angeles, 1982

Sheree had gone to a dance class with Amy, and before she left she blindfolded me and tied me to the post in the back room. It was awful and wonderful to wait for her like this. It was difficult to stand in one position for so long (two hours). And the straps were tight around my feet, stomach, chest, and neck. The handcuffs dug into my wrists, which were behind my back. I did whatever I could to pass the time. I counted. I listened to my breathing, I rocked back and forth—what little I could rock. I wiggled my dick until I became hard and it started to hurt because of the cock cage in which it was encased. Finally, I just started moaning and whimpering, listening to the sound of my voice and waiting for Sheree to leave her message on the tape machine. Finally it came. I heard the beep and then her voice: "Hi, Bob. It's your mistress talking to you. I know you must think it's been a long time by now. I want you to know that I'm fine. No accidents. And Amy and I had a very nice time together. And I'm on my way home. And I expect to find you waiting for me. And I'll look forward to seeing you and feeding you a very very good dinner. I'll be home in just a few minutes. Bye." Bliss. Relief. The "very very good dinner" was a collection of the worst stuff she could find: canned okra, canned meat by-products, hot chile peppers. She fed me blindfolded and I had no idea what I was eating. I expected to be eating worse things and I wanted it to be more fun, but by this time her son had called and it was all over.
—Journal entry, June 3, 1982

Kennedy. My parents paid for art lessons, and during high school I got lots of special attention for my art; that's what saved me. That's why this girl thought I was a drug addict: because I was an *artist*—and because I was so pale

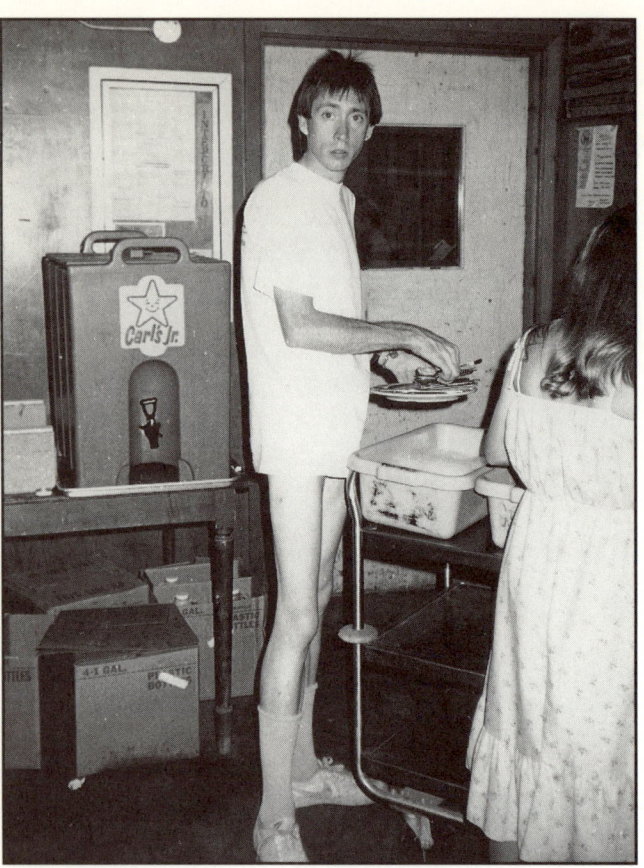

Scraping dishes at cystic fibrosis summer camp: once a slave, always a slave. San Juan Capistrano, 1982

and thin. She was an actress; there was a group of about twelve people that everybody hated: the "parlor people" consisting of the drama people and the art people, and I wound up in that group. We made some movies; my brother was an actor, my girlfriend was an actress . . . we all thought of ourselves as artists and outcasts. This gave us a lot of freedom to be strange and think strangely and do weird things.

When I left home and first had an apartment, the neighbors would look at me strangely: "Why isn't he at work?" but I was staying home being an artist. My drawings were totally "straight." Then I started doing more abstract work, but didn't really know what it meant or what I was doing. At the time, what was big was conceptual art—this was the early '70s: a bad time for art and a bad time to be going into art. My high school teachers were pretty conservative, especially compared to what art is really about. I applied to Cal Arts and probably would have become completely different if I'd gone there, but they turned me down. I definitely had a lack of education, which may have worked to my advantage—I don't know.

I didn't go to college right away. I thought that since I was an artist I didn't need college (this was *after* Cal Arts turned me down). Then I started writing. I knew that the art I was doing wasn't contemporary at all; I couldn't go on painting like Van Gogh and be happy (my mother might be happy; and I sold every one of my paintings out of high school, but . . .). I did collages and mixed-media paintings: huge portraits with dripping paint and splashed-on things, but always rooted in a subject. At the time nobody was painting subjective work, it was all abstract and conceptual: blank canvases with slight variations in tone. I knew people were excited about that, but I didn't know what it meant—

♦ *AJ: Very few people do.*
♦ BF: Right. People like Jim Shaw and Mike Kelley, who kept drawing the same way I did in high school, are what it's all about now. I remember I entered some painting festivals in shopping malls and won a few ribbons, but I thought, "These aren't the people I want to attract." So then I started writing these horrible rhyming love poems, imitating '60s singer-songwriters like Bob Dylan and Simon & Garfunkel. I didn't discover Bob Dylan until '68 and then I had to backtrack and get all his early protest albums, so I was even late in *that*—that wasn't a very good role model for poetry, although it inspired me to play the guitar and sing.

As a final art project I created a book of poems and drawings. The first song I wrote was for a radio contest (the winner would have his song recorded by the Beach Boys), so I wrote this song: "Time Is Drifting By" [sings]: "Time is drifting by/spring flowers are starting to die/winter is coming on/and thoughts of the past are gone." My first girlfriend in high school played the guitar and sang (she came from a Catholic family with ten brothers and sisters) and we became the Bob Dylan and Joan Baez of high school—we were *terrible!* But we gave little performances in the school theater (this was my freshman year) and I was too embarrassed to even kiss her; I was just a total nerd. She was a nerd too and eventually became a nun—then she quit the nunnery. A year ago she contacted me and revealed that she was a lesbian—something I was not surprised to hear at all (because of how our dates went); it seems very logical. I knew she became a nun because she was very confused about boys and dating itself, as was I. So I revealed to her my life (the SM stuff) . . . and haven't talked to her since! Hmm . . .

During our Bob Dylan and Joan Baez phase I wrote mostly song lyrics like: "Eighteen years passed by so fast/times when I knew how to laugh/Times when I knew how to play/Taking advantage of each day/Eighteen years . . ." I came up with a crapload of stuff, mostly unpublishable, like "Ballad of a Hippie": "Man, I don't wanna be a hippie no more/I'm gonna cut my long hair . . ." All my teachers thought I was really great, and I breezed through every English class by having it have something to do with my writing, or I'd analyze a Simon & Garfunkel song: how "I Am A Rock" has to do with loneliness. In fact, the class was called "Loneliness in '60s Lyrics." My high school did this "grand experiment": classes would only last six weeks, so every six weeks the classes would change. I picked classes like "Writing Children's Song Lyrics" and that's how I started writing song lyrics as poetry.

I put out a little book of these lyrics, and this one teacher was the first one to *not* like it—my first "critic" ("What do you mean you don't like it?!"). He gave me *Trout Fishing in America* by Richard Brautigan and *Post Office* by Bukowski—two great books to give to a high school student—well, Brautigan was a good *transition* to Bukowski. Brautigan was very easy to copy; he gets you out of writing rhyme (if you're writing rhyme) and makes you think of concrete styles; immediately I got every Brautigan and Bukowski book I could find—I had done the same with Dylan and Van Gogh. So I found my niche; I found a style that was "me" and "contemporary" . . . people would accept this as my place in literature.

I have a lot of really bad Brautigan poems, like: "Seagulls were flying around at the airport/Snickering at their silver imitations." There's a record of Brautigan reading his work and I still imitate it: "It's so nice to wake up in the morning all alone and not have to tell someone you love them when you don't love them anymore." Or "Xerox Candy Bar": "You're just like all the candy bars I've ever eaten." So I had tons of poems very similar to that. Luckily, this teacher had also given me Bukowski—that was a good balance; a little dose of reality. And that's how I got into writing poetry and teaching poetry in schools. As soon as I got out of high school a "Poets In The Schools" program started coming around to Orange county. I already had a reputation for writing poetry (I thought I was already *there),* so I got to know some of the teachers and met a few poets from L.A.

"Someone's singing, my Lord, Kumbaya . . ." Cystic Fibrosis Summer Camp, San Juan Capistrano, 1982

♦ **V: You didn't go through a phase reading erotic books like** *Tropic of Cancer*—
♦ **BF:** No, because I was really square. I didn't even relate my secret activities to sex or pornography; if I were caught I thought people would think I was crazy more than some kind of sex fiend. I don't remember what my actual thoughts were, but it didn't seem like they were related. Later on I saw some magazine my mother had with some photos of boys tied up burning each other with cigarettes (the pornography was usually hidden under my mother's mattress, and it was mostly dirty romance novels). Irish *shyness* rather than guilt prevailed; my grandfather thought *Reader's Digest* was dirty—*literally*—he'd say to my mother: "That's dirty, Kate. That's dirty." Now in a performance I can do almost anything, but I still get shy in conversation about certain things. I remember being in a car with other kids and we'd pass somebody sexy walking on the street and they'd go, "Look!" and whistle or shout something, but I'd be too embarrassed to look, or even let on that I was looking.

As far as pornography and art goes, well—that's why I attended life drawing classes as much as possible—that was a free license to see "sex" right in front of you. And you could draw it! My high school art teacher got in trouble for giving us a book with some g-string models in it; he told us, "Painting comes from below the waist as much as it does from above the waist." My girlfriend Becky, the first one who got involved in SM, started out as my model—she'd come to my bedroom and model nude for me, and I'd try to draw her. And my parents always knew; I'd say, "Becky's coming over to model," and they'd say, "Fine." Then they got worried: "Hey, Becky's underage. We could get into trouble!" (and they could have). One day my dad walked in while she was nude ("Oh—hi, Becky!" "Hi, Mr Flanagan!"—embarrassment, quickly closes the door) but soon after that we didn't paint anymore; we just had sex. But we were very careful; we didn't have intercourse until she was on the pill (but we did everything *else* we could). And my parents still thought I was painting.

♦ **AJ: How long before you moved in together?**
♦ **BF:** Very soon thereafter. During one of those painting sessions I told her about the things I had been doing: tying myself up and whipping myself. It wasn't long before she was tying me up to the sofabed. As soon as high school ended we moved to a house in Long Beach. I started getting sick again, and I remember my doctor trying to teach her how to give me an antibiotics shot in the ass and she couldn't do it! She hated needles; she didn't like getting them and definitely couldn't give them. But she was a willing playmate. We did golden showers together (another forerunner)—she would pee on me in the bathtub and I thought, "Wow, this is great!" But we stopped it when she said, "You know, Hitler was into this"—she got freaked out after reading this in a biography (actually, Hitler was more into shit). I don't know where the golden shower idea came from; I don't remember previously fantasizing about this.

Becky was more into drugs; she smoked a lot of dope and started doing acid and other drugs. I never smoked because of my lungs. And I hated the taste of alcohol and

BOB FLANAGAN

Published by Bombshelter Press, 1978

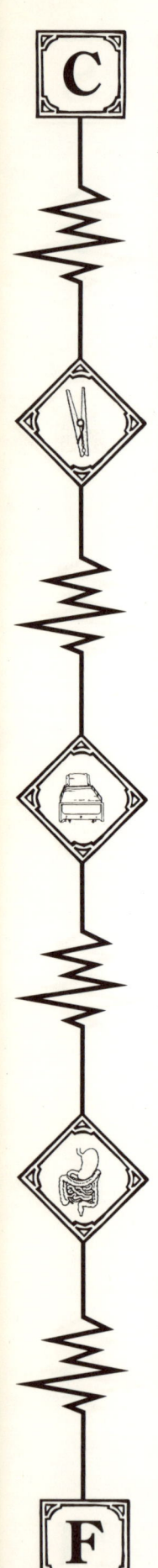

didn't start drinking until I started working at summer camp. I didn't do acid or mushrooms until later, when I met Sheree and she "ordered" me to do them. So there was this rift between Becky and I, because she was stoned a lot and I couldn't get involved in what she was laughing at—plus I was still a nerd. She'd get drunk and go out driving; I'd be running down the street shouting, "You can't drive; you're drunk!" (Again I was a nerd before my time: "Just say No!") This is probably why I lasted forty years; I had a bizarre yet *cautious* lifestyle!

♦ **AJ: You take enough risks in your art.**
♦ BF: In that respect I was a lot older before my time. However, it wasn't long before I started getting drunk and realized how much fun it was. Most of the time I did this in a pretty controlled way; I always had friends around while I had fun drinking tequila. But I was already an adult by then.

♦ **AJ: Did you ever have a problem with drinking?**
♦ BF: Where I couldn't stop? No. Now I hardly drink at all.

♦ **V: When did you start writing about your secret life?**
♦ BF: In the early '70s I started writing about what it felt like to be suspended, but I couldn't be honest about it. I was too veiled, trying to cover it up with weird, oblique references. Nothing was honest until after I met Sheree. I think it took being influenced by people like Dennis Cooper in the early '80s for me to "come out."

♦ **V: You missed the punk rock movement—**
♦ BF: Because I was still living in Long Beach playing country-western things and studying literature at Cal State. By then I knew I was going to be a writer. I'd met Exene and John Doe [from the band, X] at the *Beyond Baroque* poetry workshop, but I didn't know what punk rock was about. After I met Sheree and Dennis I started going to shows; I went with Dennis a lot.

♦ **AJ: When did you get more actively involved in the poetry scene?**
♦ BF: After Becky and I split up (we had more terrible times until it was time to call it quits). I moved back with my parents for a little while. Since the age of eighteen I'd always been on SSI [supplemental income for the disabled]; I'd worked odd jobs teaching workshops or doing something else for extra money. I was watching *Good Morning, Los Angeles* (a local 8 AM TV program) and some guy came on and announced the "Andrew W. Thornhill Poetry Symposium" in downtown L.A. Thornhill had managed to rent the top floor of a new high-rise building (before the offices were rented) and he turned it into this three-day poetry fair, with booths. It's hard to believe he had that much money and that much interest in poetry, but he invited everybody in L.A. who had anything to do with poetry to attend. I was sitting on the couch feeling sorry for myself, doing nothing, when I saw this announcement on TV—I got in the car and went to it *that* morning. For three days I drove back and forth, and met everybody there was to meet at that particular time: 1976. I wrote in my journal the names of different places and poetry journals; I met several poets and started hanging out with them. I was taking a class at UC Irvine, and as soon as that was over I started going back and forth to *Beyond Baroque* and other poetry workshops and have done that ever since.

♦ **AJ: Was exciting, wild work being done?**
♦ BF: I don't know about the work, but it was an exciting place to be, especially for a nerd like me from Orange County. At the time I thought, "These are working poets"—*then,* being in a little xerox 'zine meant being published: "This is it!" The workshop was good; it was feisty and fiery; people were arguing and there was a lot of excitement in the air—which I loved. Shortly after John Doe and Exene started attending, Dennis Cooper started appearing, the punk scene was growing, and all this worked as a magnet for meeting other people. *Beyond Baroque* itself was always good, in terms of attracting people. In the early '80s they had punk concerts until the neighbors complained.

Basically, that's how I met Sheree Rose—she was going to punk concerts there and I was going to poetry readings, and I met her when there was finally a party for all the *Beyond Baroque* people. She had gone out with Jack Skelley, a poet and friend of mine who worked there; we were just starting to write songs together and form a band. I drove up from Long Beach to the party with some friends; Sheree came with some friends, and when she rang the bell I happened to answer the door. I was dressed like a zombie from *Dawn of the Dead* with a hand in my mouth, looking half-dead, and she was dressed as Jayne Mansfield with a blond wig and big tits—I had no idea what she really looked like. She asked the woman whose house it was: "Who's that guy?" and the woman replied, "Oh—he's a poet; he's a great poet!" (I just had one dorky book out.) She showed Sheree the book, *The Kid Is The Man*, published by Bombshelter Press. It included about three years' worth of work (or about ten poems) written up until 1978; I write *very* slowly. So that's how we met; I got her phone number and we started dating the week after that.

♦ *AJ: Were you already in an SM scene?*

♦ BF: Let's go back to how I got from Orange county to L.A. After I got involved with the poetry scene at *Beyond Baroque*, I realized, "Now I've got to move to L.A." I was living in Costa Mesa, an hour away. I was used to driving to L.A. because I was a movie buff, and in L.A. there was The Silent Movie Theater on Fairfax where for a dollar you could watch silent movies. There was also the Fox Theater in Venice where for a dollar you could watch classic movies and foreign films. So I was already driving up every weekend to see these movies.

With Sheree on Halloween, our 10th anniversary, recreating the costumes we wore on the night we met, Halloween, 1980. We might be perverts, but we're romantic perverts.
Los Angeles, 1990

In 1976 I got a small apartment in West L.A. by myself. I was living alone and could do anything I wanted, so I started piercing myself. At the time I started buying *Fetish Times*, which is a really bizarre SM newspaper—most of what's in it are fantasies that people make up. I preferred stories which seemed like they were by real people doing real things to themselves or having real things done to them. I didn't see *PFIQ [Piercing Fans International Quarterly*, edited by Jim Ward; see *Re/Search #12: Modern Primitives]* until the '80s, and I didn't know anything about *The Gauntlet* [a piercing studio run by Jim Ward with branches in Los Angeles, San Francisco and New York]. But in *Fetish Times* there was an ad for genital piercing rings, and I don't know if I'd seen it or where I got the idea, but I'd already put a needle in my nipple (just a sewing needle) and it had been hard to do—I'd failed a couple times and couldn't get it through. I got obsessed by this; I'd wake up in the middle of the night and think, "I *gotta* do it; I gotta get it all the way through." It was like an endurance test, and the "high" was more just in the ability to actually *do* it: start to pierce, not mind the pain, and actually get the needle all the way through.

I tried to do the same thing with my penis, but I couldn't do that at all because it hurt too much, and I wasn't knowledgeable about the structure of the penis. It felt like if I did it, something horrible would happen: maybe it wouldn't stop bleeding. I didn't have a cork, I just tried to jam the needle right into the shaft (I didn't know what I was doing). At the time I was into photography; I had an enlarger, and I put my dick on the base and attached a needle to the lens and started cranking it down. As soon as it started to puncture I went, "Ohmigod," got scared and pulled it back up. It wasn't until years later that I got up the nerve to actually pierce my penis. But I pierced my nipples a lot, and pinched parts of my skin and parts of my ass—I figured I couldn't

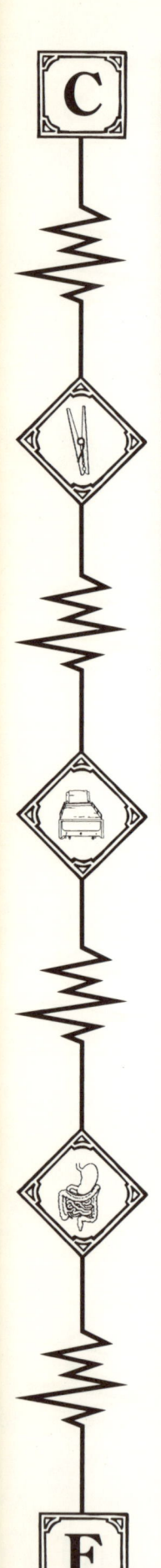

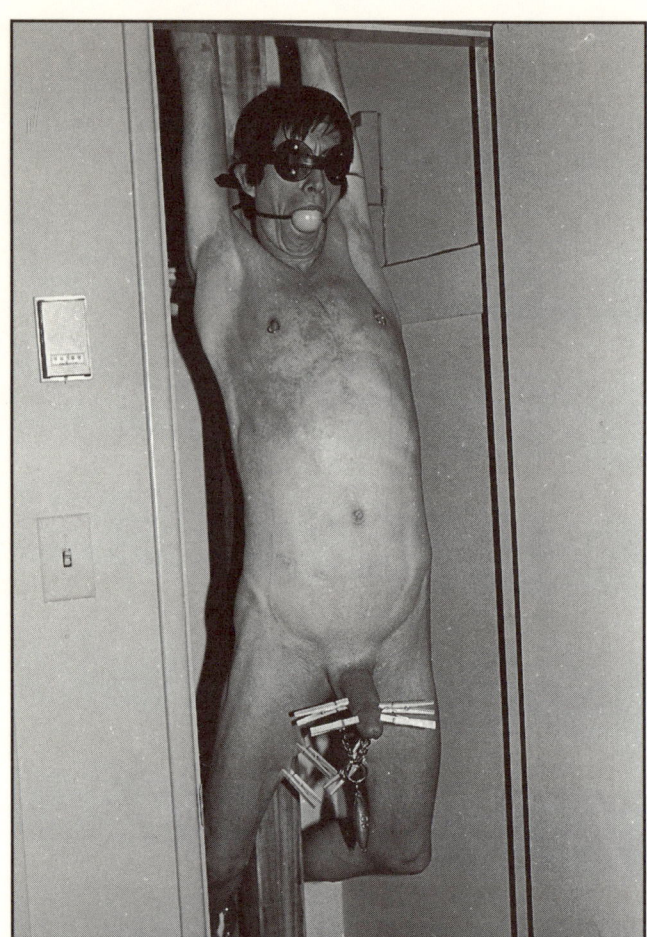

I may be "out" as a masochist, but I still love being in the closet. Los Angeles, 1983

hurt anything there. Again, I was doing these bizarre things—but being overly cautious in many ways, which was good.

Then—I think I read about this in *Fetish Times*—I got the urge to nail my scrotum to a board. I leapt out of bed at 2 in the morning, got a hammer and nails and stretched my scrotum on the bread board—it was the perfect height. The first couple of times I couldn't do it, but then the satisfaction of actually doing it and seeing my scrotum spread out like a butterfly was pretty exciting!

♦ *AJ: At the time you knew this was "okay" to do?*
♦ BF: No, I didn't know anything. I didn't have sterile equipment; I just boiled the nails (which is silly; that doesn't do *anything*—you need an autoclave). I must have read about this; I don't think I would have thought of it on my own. Years later I read another story about a mistress who nailed the head of her slave's penis to a board, and I started obsessing on it until one day I had to try it myself. That was a big event. I wrote in my journal about that, and it became part of a piece. What happened was: I missed the nail and hit the head of my dick and it blew up into this giant knob—all these horrible things happened!
♦ *V: Tell us—*

♦ BF: I was alone in my apartment; for a week I had been doing all kinds of things. I was going to Cal State Long Beach and a lot of this happened during finals; to release tension I would get obsessed by SM activities. Anyway, I decided to nail my dick to a board. I set a board on some bricks, kneeled in front, and again I boiled the nails (nothing was really sterile). I whacked it, and the nail went through—the urge *not* to do it was overcome by the urge to do it—and then I went to give the nail one more whack (to make sure the nail was really *in* the wood) and that's when I missed the nail and hit the tip of my dick as hard as I could: "Ohmigod!" Immediately it turned darker than a grape—purple, really dark—and I thought, "Ohmigod, what's happening? When will it stop swelling?"

♦ *AJ: It turned purple? Does that mean all the blood vessels broke immediately?*
♦ BF: Yeah, and there's lots of blood there. I don't remember the pain; *fright* is all I remember. It was too sudden for pain. The pain didn't matter; it was already over. It was probably throbbing a lot. So I got the nail out of the wood; I was walking around with a big purple dick and a nail in it, still. I had to get the nail out. I went into the bathroom and with the claw of the hammer pulled the nail out and naturally a lot of blood gushed out. I was bleeding all over the bathtub; I turned the water on and bloody water was swirling down the drain just like in *Psycho*. I *felt* like Tony Perkins: "What's going on here?" I peed and it came out red; I thought, "Oh no—I guess I nicked the urethra also. I'm really fucked up!" I wondered if my pee was always going to be red; I was scared I'd have to go to the doctor.

Finally the bleeding stopped, the throbbing stopped, I peed again and it was yellow. Then I got turned on and excited. Everything was cleaned up, and I started getting hard. Instead of a bed I had a mattress on the floor; I laid down some towels and started masturbating against the sheets in a real frenzy; now I was really turned on by what had just happened to me! I had a really good orgasm . . . then I looked down and there was all this blood all over the towels; it had soaked through into the mattress. I got scared all over again, but within a few days everything had healed up. The penis heals fast.

That night I had a date. In those days most of my dates consisted of going out to dinner and a movie and then just going home alone. This was with a new person I hadn't been with before, and she wanted to fuck! I thought, "Ohmigod." She'd already heard rumors about me; by this time I was talking pretty openly about my lifestyle. So I told her, "Well, we can fuck, but I'll have to show you *this* now; it's kind of weird!" She was an odd person; she always *pretended* that nothing was shocking to her, but I think that secretly she was really shocked by a lot of things. We dated a few times but just ended up having horrible fights. She wound up being very judgmental. One time I hadn't seen her for awhile and she said, "I'm joining this group, 'Women Against Violence Against Women.'" And somehow she related what I was doing to this. Even though what I was doing was to *myself*, she tied it all together.

♦ **AJ: *That must have been a funny scene—***
♦ BF: It was hilarious. I had to show her my penis, plus I guess I was not-so-secretly proud of it: "Look what *I* did!" I like shocking people, too—that's part of it. It's always fun to show people things that you've done, otherwise what's the point of doing them? I was keeping a journal at the time, and every detail of what I did is recorded; there's even bloodstains on the page, because I was writing at the time I was bleeding!

♦ **V: *How did you stop the bleeding?***
♦ BF: I just let it run its natural course and kept hoping it wouldn't last too long. I sat in the tub until the blood stopped dribbling out. You can pierce the dick with just a little pinprick and it'll bleed a lot. I already knew that; I'd already pierced the loose skin on the shaft. At that time I used to go to professional houses, and I think a woman might have once pierced the head of my dick and it bled for a long time. So I already knew that it bled a lot, but it wasn't serious—that's just what it does. I wasn't worried about the blood so much as the pounding sensation.

♦ **AJ: *You had started going to professionals?***
♦ BF: I had found out about them before I moved out of my parents' house. My brother Tim was getting the *L.A. Free Press* and circling the gay ads—this is sort of how he came out of the closet: he left these papers around for our parents to pick up and go, "What's this?" He had circled all these ads—either he was drunk and careless, or more than likely he was drunk and unconsciously left these out to show them. So he "came out" quite early, which was really brave of him.

I saw the ads too, but I also saw next to the gay ads, "House of Dominance" and "School of Discipline"—big, full-page ads for these SM houses. I couldn't believe it; I had no idea these places existed! And reading the personal ads describing what people wanted to do to each other—for me that was a phase of my life that was like heaven, in a weird scary way. It's sad, because you can never replace that feeling of *first* doing anything. These places were nothing, but that first feeling of living out these fantasies with a person who was being paid (of course, I had done it previously with the girlfriend from school) and who was *really* dominant—actually they never *really* were, but they *dressed* the part!

The first place I went to was on Santa Monica Boulevard, the School of Discipline. At that time there were all these massage parlors; they hadn't yet been closed down so it looked like Las Vegas or North Beach. There were barkers yelling, "Come on in!" and sexy women standing in the doorways—that's all been cleaned up, and it's too bad because I used to love driving down that street looking at everything. Anyway, I drove around the block for an hour before I actually got the nerve to go in—I had already canceled my first appointment and then made this appointment. My first experience was just silly, but I still remember the feeling: this woman had all these chains and a bed and she whipped me a little bit and did things

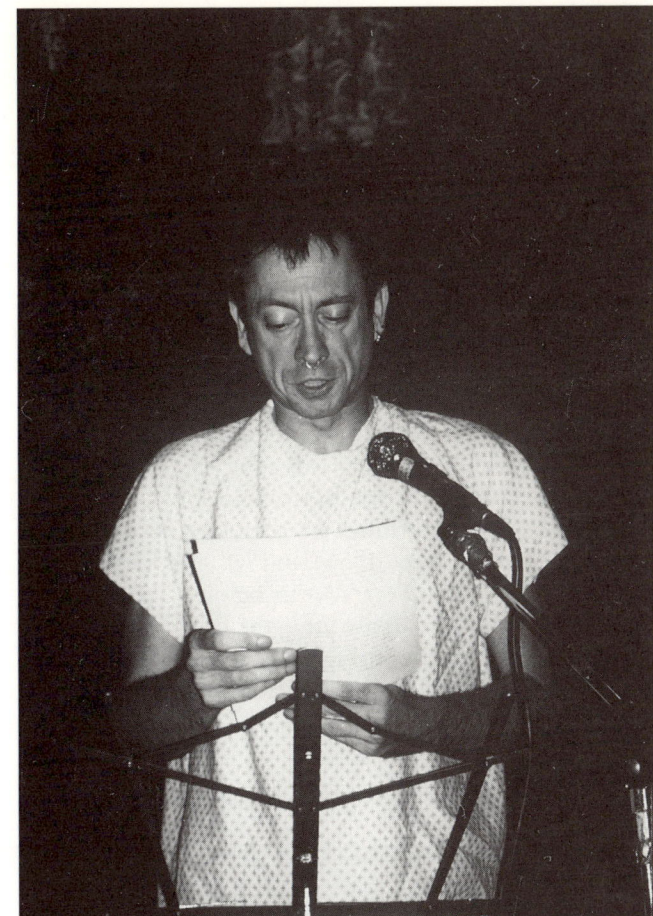

Poetry reading in my hospital gown. Los Angeles, 1991

to me. It always felt kind of unfulfilling when you went home. I did that a few times.

♦ **AJ: *Who can afford to go—especially if you're a working person?***
♦ BF: If you're a working person you save every little bit, then when you get enough money, you go. I had a camera I would hock; back then the going rate was $60 an hour (which was a lot for me); now I hear it's $150-$200. Usually it's wealthy people who go. At that time I had no concept of an "SM community"; the first people I met who were into SM were people who went to these houses. There was a place called the Chateau which is also in San Francisco; I went there a few years before I met Sheree. They had the most professional set-up, so I started going there—the other places wound up closing, anyway. There were places advertising every Thursday night as "B&D Party Night," and you'd pay $30-$60 to attend. They'd serve food, and sometimes it was "Swingers' Night"—you'd see people fucking on a mattress, or they'd give demonstrations. I got involved in a couple of demonstrations and felt excited about having people watch me getting spanked or something in public. Sometimes it felt good, sometimes I felt like I was being ripped off—which I was. But I never talked to anybody; there was no socializing (by *me*, anyway; some

people socialized, but most people didn't).

When I first met Sheree I took her to a couple of these parties. It seemed like a good way to give her a quick introduction to the SM scene—one aspect of it, anyway. But by this time we were already in a real SM relationship together and these parties just seemed kind of stupid; professional parties are a waste of time, but at the time they were all we had. Doing SM alone, Sheree felt isolated. She thought we were the only two people in the world doing this stuff.

♦ *V: Let's back up a little. When you first met Sheree, how did you know whether to trust her . . . to confide in her?*

♦ BF: By that time I had told a lot of people about what I was into. Since I knew this was a big part of my sexuality and that regular sex just didn't interest me, whenever I dated somebody and things started to get sexual, I tried to bring up the subject of SM and let it be known what really turned me on. Several years before I met Sheree, I met the first real love of my life—the first person I fell in love with since Becky in high school. After being with her for three weeks I said, "There's something I have to tell you," and told her about this "thing" [SM]. She loved me, so she wasn't turned off that much by it, although typically (with these kind of relationships) she got annoyed by it afterwards: "Oh, stop talking about it!" I'd make jokes about it and try to get her more interested in tying me up or just talking about it. Even though I was involved in an affair with her, I was still going to professional people—with her blessing; she even lent me the money to do it, because she knew there were things she couldn't give me, or didn't want to.

At the time I was totally convinced that this relationship was more important than the SM lifestyle, so I thought, "I'll do what I can with SM, but I won't blow this relationship because of it." It would have been disastrous if it had lasted, but she ended it—maybe because of those reasons, but I think a lot because of my health, and also because her parents, when they met me, disliked me on sight. I'd been a secret for nine months, because she had a weird sick relationship with them and couldn't be honest or grown-up about her own life; she was already 27 when I met her (I was 23 at the time). So when her parents met me and didn't like me, everything cooled immediately, even though we had this really great romantic relationship where we went to all the poetry readings. Papa Bach's bookstore was big at the time; it was right down the street from where I lived and she worked on their magazine for awhile. I was so upset about losing her that I lost a whole year; I couldn't accept the fact that it wasn't working and that she wanted to break up. For a whole year I was a wreck—that's when I moved to Long Beach. It took that long to get over that relationship.

I dated several people before I met Sheree, and a few people got involved with SM and a few people didn't; it wasn't a big deal. But by that time all my close friends knew about my kinky interests.

♦ *V: Who were your close friends?*

♦ BF: They were mostly people involved with poetry or writing: Jack Grapes, Dennis Cooper, Jack Skelley, Amy Gerstler. My best friend since I was

Why do I do this? Because I can. Los Angeles, 1988

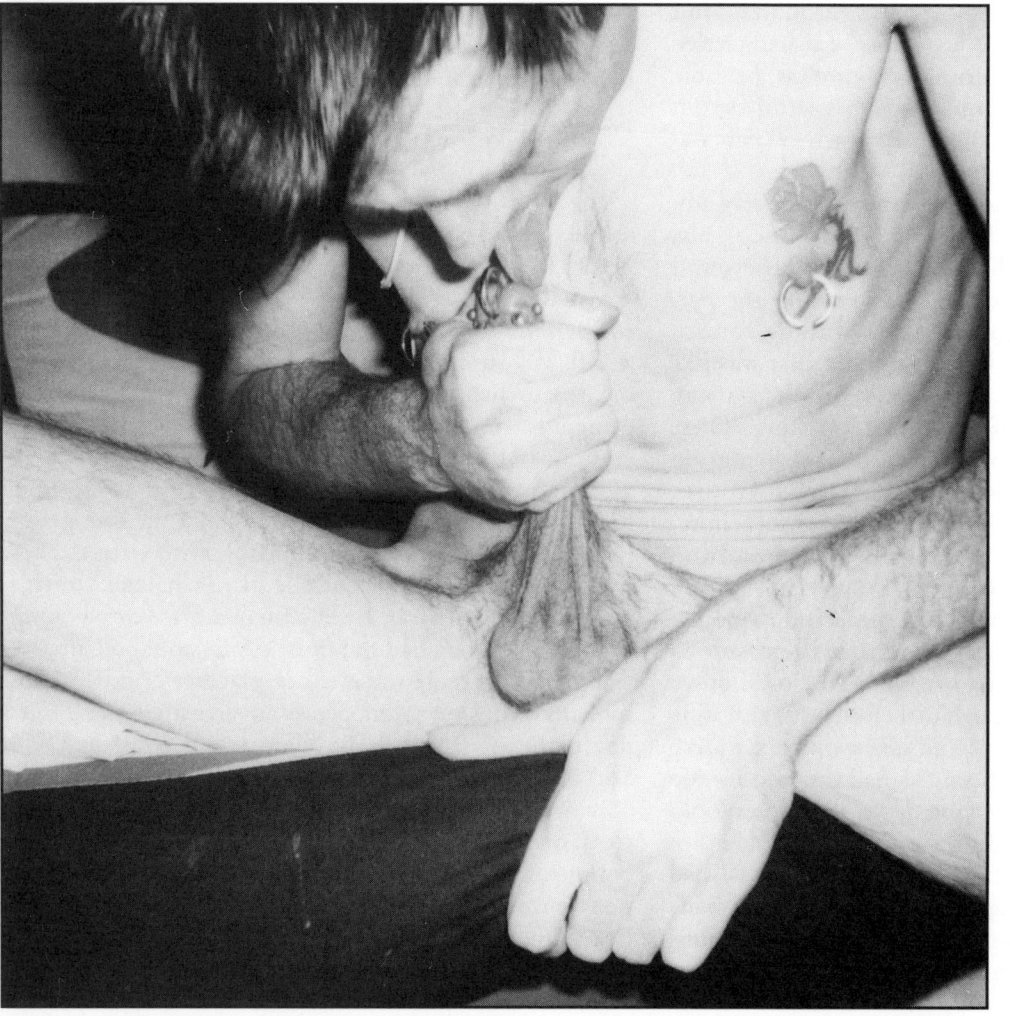

eighteen was Bob, the director of the cystic fibrosis summer camp. He didn't have CF; he was just doing this as a summer job, and we just hit it off. He was the first close friend (besides Becky) that I had ever opened up to about all the SM stuff. I had this depressing moment after a disastrous one-night affair with a poet from the *Beyond Baroque* poetry workshop. She was older than I, and it was sort of a black widow/poetry kid relationship for a night. She was also really into Bob Dylan. I went to her house and she made spaghetti and I sang Dylan songs on the couch and then it was time to go to bed and she was smoking pot (I think that's the only time I ever tried to smoke it; I just couldn't, it stabbed my lungs). I was so nervous I couldn't get hard enough to fuck; I was trying and trying and she was getting more and more frustrated.

We were just lying there; she's smoking and drinking wine, and she says [high voice], "*Bob?* Have you ever done anything *kinky?*" By this time I had already been to the House of Dominance, and I'd already burned myself with a hot glue gun, and nailed my balls to a board—I'd done quite a few things by myself, plus there were a lot of other things I'd been *thinking* about doing. So I told her the whole story, and I don't remember what she said in response, but it was supportive. Before I knew it she had gone; then she returned with all this macrame—she'd taken all these plants out of their macrame and wanted me to tie her to the bed! She said, "I've always had these fantasies, too." She had been in a few abusive relationships where her boyfriends beat her up. So I sort of *half-ass* tied her up to the bed—then I started getting a hard-on (not a great one, but a little one, enough—this took me out of my head a little bit). Then she said, "Hit me!" and now I'm on top humping her while trying to hit her on the thigh with one hand, and she yells, "Harder!" It was a really bad fuck; I came really fast—it was like, *nothing*—and I got off and I guess untied her.

Then there was just *silence.* She's smoking another joint and drinking more wine and finally says [high voice], "*Bob?* You know what I'd like?" "No . . . what?" "I'd like to take a bath and play a game of double solitaire." I didn't know what double solitaire was, but I knew it didn't include *me* (this was like at four in the morning) so I said, "You mean you want me to go?" [high voice] "Yes." This was the first time I ever felt really guilty and horrible about SM. I thought, "Oh, no!" My first girlfriend Becky had ended up really crazy, and I finally tell somebody else (this is the second person I'd ever told), and it's all over. That's when I felt like total absolute shit; I went home and wrote this awful, Dylanesque song about her [sings in Dylan-like voice], "Please, babe, let us try again"—I actually recorded it and sent it to her and it was *really bad.*

So after weeks of depression, moping around, feeling like a total freak and more of an outcast than ever, I told Bob about the whole thing and my short but sordid history. To my surprise all he did was laugh, and then I realized how silly it all was. After that I didn't mind telling people about it and they just loved it; they had no idea I was doing these things. They'd go: "No! What *else* did

My parents give me a surprise birthday party at Chuck E. Cheese—talk about sadistic! Merced, 1990

you do?" "Oh, I pierced myself with a needle—" "No! Come on!" "Yeah, I did that." Now I've been working at this camp for 21 years, and every summer Bob asks me, "What did you do this year?" Sometimes I never see him; our lifestyles are so different that we rarely see each other, but when we do get together it's: "So . . . what did you *do?*" "Well, I did this and I did that . . ."

♦ *AJ: What did you do with that hot glue gun?*
♦ BF: I had this hot glue gun for art projects. A couple of times I tried to burn myself with it—just burn little marks on my skin. But I didn't have the nerve; I needed someone else (or another force) to take control because I couldn't hold it on very long. One night I taped it to a belt, strapped it to my waist, laid the tip against my ass, plugged it on and started masturbating as it was heating up. That was a really *hot* time! I got into a frenzied orgasm, not even feeling a thing from the glue gun—I looked and discovered I'd gotten a really serious burn; I still have a big round scar from it. Yet I hadn't felt a thing—I was experiencing such an intense orgasm. I knew something was going on, but it was all "high"—it wasn't a painful sensation. I had a black scab for over a year and a big red mark for two more years; now it's just a white blemish.

♦ *AJ: That's like an altered state—*
♦ BF: That's what it was. Of course, that happens when it's all *new;* trying to repeat them is harder. The first time is usually the best time; you have to work harder and harder to get to that level of excitement. By then you know the secret of how it works. Now, there's no thrill in nailing my scrotum to a board all alone, but doing it in front of an audience on command—that's still an extra thrill. That's why I still do that when I can. But for me it's too easy to do that now. I guess there's nothing left but to just get old and watch TV and talk about your past glories. [laughs]

♦ *AJ: That's the process of living: there's always that blush*

Smoking my daily brew of bronchial dilators and mucolytic agents to try and keep my lungs clear, but it's a never-ending battle. Los Angeles, 1993

I'm a factory of mucus as thick as pudding. The faucet is always on and it drips this gooey mess like "flubber." Like "The Blob," and just as deadly. Sometimes I just swallow it, but usually I explode into these body-wracking coughs, spitting the loose phlegm into paper dixie cups, sometimes two cups per treatment. I'm a human Foster's Freeze machine making sundaes of sickness. —"Body," *The Book of Medicine*

of youth with the first discoveries you make. Then you evolve to a more mature level where you channel your efforts into your art and into larger public arenas—
♦ BF: When I share the things I've experienced, in a way I re-live them through that process. Also, I re-evaluate them, too: try to discover what it *was* that was exciting. If it had another context, what was it? I discover this through writing or talking about it, not through doing it.
♦ *V: But if there weren't some common ground for your activities, other people couldn't relate to what you do—*
♦ BF: There's definitely a collective consciousness at work here. Just by the fact that I was doing and thinking these things at such an early age, and then I discover that other people are doing and thinking them as adults—so many common experiences have no explanation, they're just *there*. It's unfortunate that especially in Western society, we've labeled a lot of things "wrong," so that early on a lot of people just negate them and shove them aside.
♦ *AJ: Tell us about more of your earlier activities . . . did you ever get enemas as a child?*
♦ BF: Yeah, but I never eroticized that until I met Sheree. She started doing professional dominance at an enema clinic and came home with all these ideas. Maybe I'd read about enemas, but I don't think I'd ever fantasized about them being *erotic*. Because of my cystic fibrosis and the constant stomach problems I'd had several barium enemas for x-ray purposes, but never at home (the fantasy you always read about I never had—darn it!). Enemas were something new that I incorporated later on; they're still something I like to do because they don't take a lot of energy.

I did a lot of pioneering things in my apartment in West L.A. Then I moved to Long Beach where I built a whole dungeon after I met Sheree. I painted the walls black and built all the equipment: crosses, stocks, a great bondage table—I wanted to use the table for an art show but the person I sold it to said it broke and she threw it away. By reading and going to parties I got the dungeon idea. I've always been turned on by dungeons in movies and dark rooms that are foreboding and scary to go into; I love that. I wish I still had a room that was just a fantasy room; in order to go into a closet you have to take everything out and put everything back, and by the time you do all that (with all the energy it takes) you're not in the mood anymore! And if you *are* in the mood, then you don't have the energy to put it all back, so it sits around and makes you feel like you're living in a mess. If I ever get enough money, I'll have a place big enough where I can do that again.

In Long Beach I started doing more *involved* suspensions: hanging myself by the wrists, nailing myself, and doing a lot more piercings involving needles in my penis and nipples. I still only had one little permanent piercing (I didn't get professionally pierced until I met Sheree): one little ring in the frenum, the skin under the head of the penis, that I did myself. I sent away for the jewelry from an ad in *Fetish Times* (the *Gauntlet* was around but I didn't know about it yet); this couple in Oklahoma made stainless steel jewelry and needles. Before I did that, I finally was able to pierce the head of my penis with a sewing needle. I'd read in an article to put some thread through it to keep the hole open while it healed, so I used dental floss. I went to Sears' jewelry counter and bought a little pearl earring stud—that was the first jewelry I put into the frenum. I was all excited about this first tiny little piercing.
♦ *AJ: Had you connected with the gay underground?*
♦ BF: Not at that time. I probably had a lot of fears about the gay world; I didn't know anything about it. I knew my brother was gay, but we didn't talk about that or about SM—he didn't know anything about me, then. He was traveling a lot and we didn't see each other very much during these years. I didn't know any gay people until I started hanging out at *Beyond Baroque* with Dennis Cooper. Then I met his friends from the writing scene in New

York—it turned out all the writers I liked were gay.

♦ **V: In the SM scene, who else were your friends?**
♦ BF: Nobody. After I got involved with Sheree, I met other people, but I knew nobody who would admit being into SM—you see, early on, people didn't admit to doing these things. They loved hearing the *stories,* but . . . And even now not that many people are involved. You meet them at parties specifically for that, but the average person reserves their SM for intimate relationships, and doesn't talk about it very much. So I didn't know anybody else who was doing these things.

For years a lot of the artists in the arts community looked down on us for writing about this. When SM became my subject matter, and when our lifestyle became better known, we'd go to parties and certain people wouldn't talk to us. But now it's become much more fashionable to be open about SM, and more performance artists are doing SM shows. A lot has happened since AIDS; a lot's going on now. SM is a subject that excites people, so it's easy for people who can't do art to do this kind of stuff—*uh oh,* I hope I'm not included in that!

In my new show, "Visiting Hours," SM is referred to, but the show is almost all about my being sick. The other shows were more about SM (although they also referred to my being sick), whereas now it's more about me being sick and *also* referring to SM. This mirrors my life more than anything else at the moment.

♦ **AJ: What do you think of the juxtaposition of metaphors: being sick equals SM?**
♦ BF: My last show in New York and L.A. was titled "Bob Flanagan's Sick." I purposely used that title, and there were three different meanings: 1) Bob Flanagan's sick in the head [mentally], 2) Bob Flanagan's sick [physically], and 3) This is Bob Flanagan's show called "Sick."

♦ **V: Did you have a radical political background?**
♦ BF: Not a bit. During the Vietnam war I started going to poetry readings in Laguna Beach. I was draft age but 4-F so I didn't have to worry, but I felt guilty because all my contemporaries were getting drafted and writing poems about it and talking what I thought was "crazy talk" about how the CIA was funding the war and smuggling

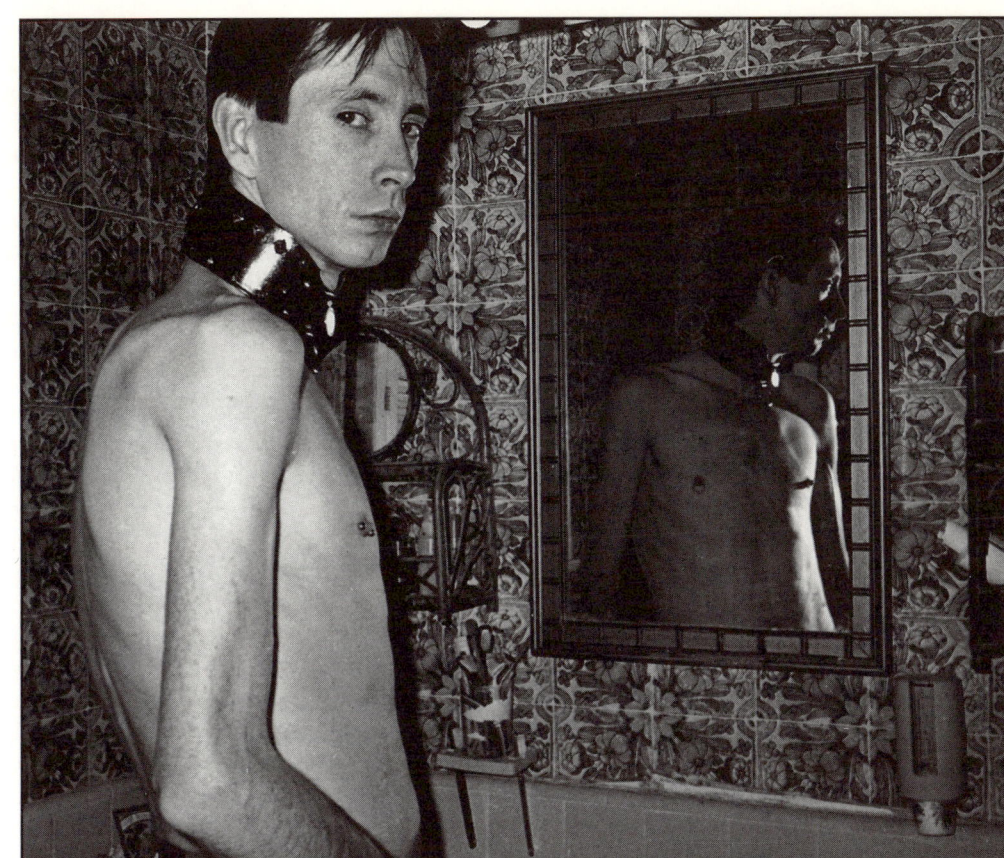

Admiring my brand-new slave collar. Los Angeles, 1983

heroin back in body bags and how it's all tied into big business. One night, instead of a poetry reading there was nothing but talk about this. I wrote a poem describing everything in my wallet (including my 4-F card which I had to carry around), and that was the extent of my "political poetry." I had the hippie '60s mentality but was totally apolitical.

♦ **AJ: When did you realize you weren't going to lead a "normal" life?**
♦ BF: I was always different because of being sick, different because of being an artist, and because *I* knew how different I was! With Beverly, the girl I split up from, I was going to get married. I was never going to have kids because of cystic fibrosis (99% of all males are sterile—I've never actually checked it out, but I have a pretty strong feeling that I probably am sterile). Aside from that, I wouldn't want kids because I pretty much know that because of my illness, *I* need all the attention! I have to constantly think about myself and take care of myself, so I know I couldn't be a good father. Every now and then I see a father-son or father-daughter relationship that kind of gives me a *pang,* but it doesn't last very long!

My whole family is different. My parents weren't rich and they had to work really hard just to put food on the table, and because of CF they had to rebel against bill collectors and the medical world. And they'd rebelled against their own families which were very abusive, so it

Sheree and Bob. Santa Monica, 1984

was a whole family of people used to being different and unusual.

♦ **V: Were you part of the hippie movement?**
♦ BF: I was too young for that. What was going on had filtered down into my high school, but it was all *imitation hippie.* Bands like the Doors and Jefferson Airplane had finally filtered down to the high school level—every week bands like the Strawberry Alarm Clock and the BeeGees would play the Anaheim Convention Center. I saw the Monkees at the Hollywood Bowl; those were the groups I went to see. This was before the '70s when people like Elton John took over.

♦ *AJ: You never took any psychedelics?*

Blindfolded, on my 40th birthday, on route to a surprise party at The Magic Castle. Los Angeles, 1992

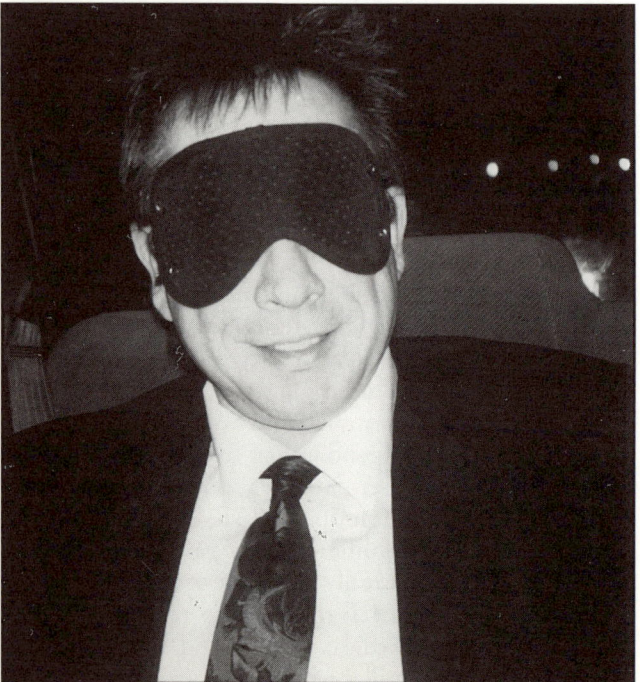

♦ BF: Not until I met Sheree—then she practically *demanded* that I take acid: "It'll change your mind forever!" I protested: "But I like my mind the way it is!" She persisted: "You *have* to take it." So I did.
♦ *AJ: Did it make you more "normal"? [laughs]*
♦ BF: In some ways, *yes:* it made me worry a lot more, and made me much more paranoid and "on edge." I also took mushrooms; for a couple years we'd periodically "do" something. I stopped when I realized how long the recovery time was—it takes a week to recover, and I just don't have that kind of time. If only I could just be fine the next day . . . but I can't.
♦ *AJ: Also, life has gotten worse. These days you have to work so much more just to stay in the same place; it's not like life is getting better and better—*
♦ BF: Now I'm forty years old and the doctors are talking about selling me new lungs. For me the SM thing is in limbo-land, yet people expect it in my art now. I'd love to go back and be involved with it in other ways, but I just haven't found the way. I don't have the health, the time and the energy to do what Sheree and I used to do in performance. Now I'm working on developing images from my past. This is the biggest change in my life: I'm forty, sicker than I've ever been, and it's time to *review.*

L.A. Style did an article on me which describes the Olio show [a show I did that Amok Bookstore put on for the release of *Re/Search #12: Modern Primitives*]. It describes me hanging by my wrists, talks about CF, and basically talks about sex and sickness. It starts out saying, "Bob Flanagan should be dead by now of cystic fibrosis." The writer talks about the disease, about my sister, and describes some of the things I've done to myself, some of the shows, and talks about SM. A lot of people have seen that article; at summer camp a CF kid came up to me and said, "Hey—saw you in that magazine, *man!*"[laughs] I asked him, "Where'd you see it?" "In the Cystic Fibrosis Foundation office in Orange county." I couldn't believe it. It turned out that they have a clipping service, and the woman who runs the foundation office was so pissed that she was running around the office screaming, "This isn't good for CF! This isn't good for CF!" The foundation depends on cute little dying kids . . . those posters of kids with big eyes and sad faces saying "I'm going to die—we need money for research." And I'm like the poster child from *hell* saying, "*Don't* give us money because we'll grow up to do things like *this!*"

This year kids at camp were asking me, "Where'd you get your nipples pierced? Do you have anything else pierced?" [squirms] "Yeah, but . . ." Tattooing has really caught on among teenagers; the son of the friend of mine who runs the camp (I've known him since he was born) just showed me all this black tattoo work he'd gotten from Leo Zulueta, who has a shop called Black Wave in Los Angeles. Here I am, this old guy with one little tattoo and a couple of nipple piercings, and here are all these young "whippersnappers" with their faces tattooed, their eyebrows pierced, their tongues, and their noses . . . ■ ■ ■

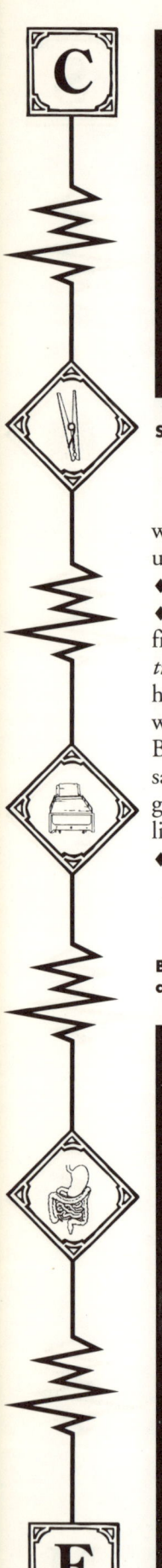

CYSTIC FIBROSIS POSTER BOY
... Robert Flanagan Jr., 14, of Costa Mesa

Mesa Teenager Poster Boy for Cystic Fibrosis

By JOAN GEYER

Robert Flanagan Jr. 14, Costa Mesa — one of two children stricken by cystic fibrosis in his family — has been named as first poster child for the newly organized North Orange County Chapter, National Cystic Fibrosis Research Foundation.

Cystic fibrosis struck alternate children in the family of Mr. and Mrs. Robert Flanagan Sr., 3093 Loren Lane, Beginning with their handsome, talented eldest son, Robert. It skipped Timothy, 12, to strike Patricia, 9, then spared next son, John, 8.

A hereditary disease, believed carried by a recessive gene, C-F is variously called "fibrocystic disease of the pancreas," "pancreatic cystic fibrosis" and "mucoviscidosis."

It affects glands with ducts, sometimes by causing excessive secretion, sometimes causing obstruction by thick mucous, and sometimes by excessive loss of sodium and sodium and chlorine.

Its victims typically suffer chronic respiratory infection, pancreas insufficiency and susceptibility to heat prostration.

It strikes one in every 1,000 newborn infants. But often it is not diagnosed immediately. Mrs. Flanagan recalls that Robert had been a "sickly baby, who wheezed as he fought for breath, and suffered pneumonia at two weeks." But it was not until the family moved from New York to California that the true nature of Robert's difficulty was diagnosed.

A doctor who found Patricia, then 6 months, had C-F examined Robert and found he also had cystic fibrosis, said Mrs. Flanagan.

She said, since diagnosis and treatment, both children have been in improved health.

The treatment includes antibiotics, pancreas extract, massage to dislodge accumulated chest fluid, and, sometimes, sleeping in a mist tent, she said.

Robert's improved strength has made it possible for him to sketch, paint portraits; play drums (he hopes to organize his own band); and tinker in his workshop, where once he built a four-foot robot with eyes which lit up when the robot walked.

But if medical science has extended and made more comfortable the life of a cystic fibrosis victim, it has as yet found no cure. That's why the national association is seeking funds for research.

As C-F poster child, Robert will help the North Orange County Chapter of NCFRF with its September fund drive. Part of the funds will go to help support the C-F outpatient clinic at Childrens Hospital of Orange County.

Robert will take part in a cystic fibrosis walk-in Sept. 9 and 10 and in the Op-Hop at Hollywood Palladium Sept. 10, which will be brightened by such luminaries as Ben (Run for Your Life) Gazzara; Patty Duke, film and TV star; and Casey Kasem, KRLA disk jockey and TV Shebang personality. Kasem is 1967 chairman of the Southern California cystic fibrosis campaign.

Citizens who wish to help in the fund drive are asked to call Mrs. John P. Kaiser, Anaheim, at 535-1470.

Article in local papers in Orange County, July 23, 1967

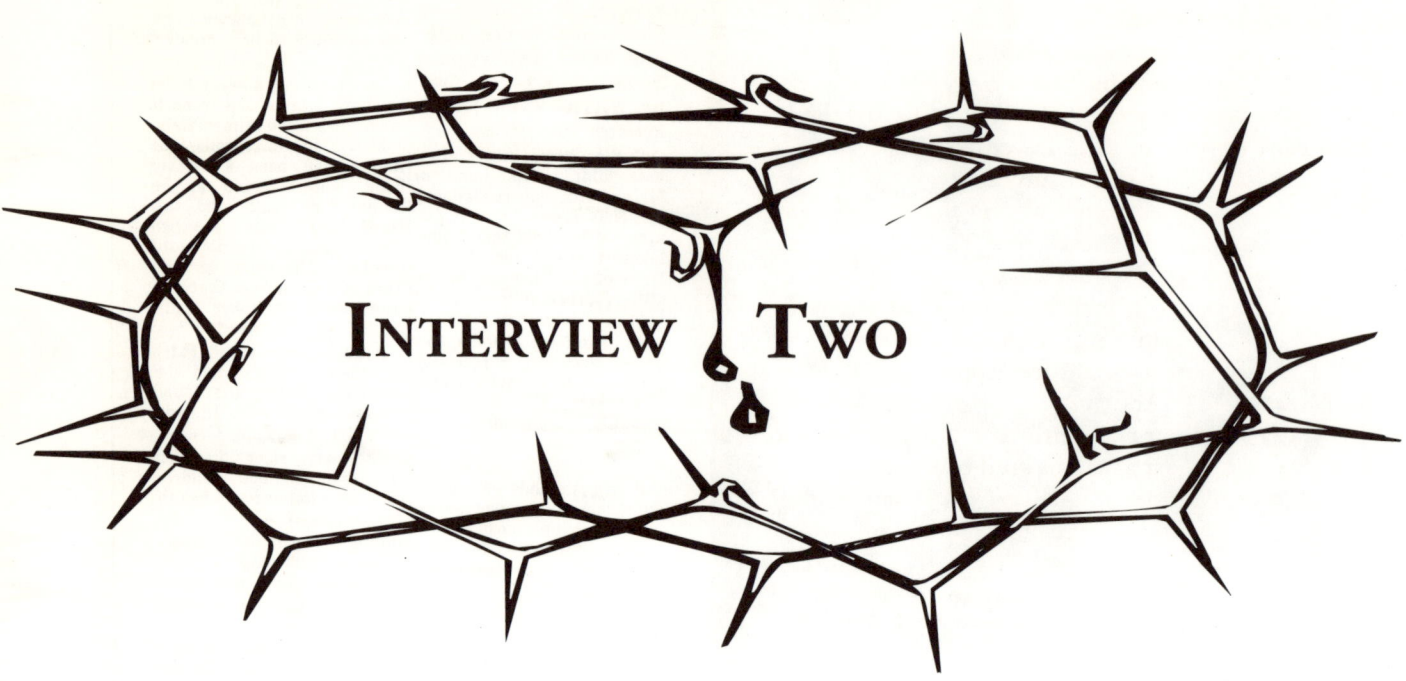

Interview Two

♦ **V: Tell us again how you met Sheree Rose?**
♦ BF: I was living in Long Beach working at the Chelsea bookstore. Every week I'd drive to L.A. to *Beyond Baroque* for poetry readings and the Wednesday night workshops—it was about an hour's drive. Dennis Cooper, Amy Gerstler and Jack Skelley from *Beyond Baroque* hosted a party at the Pacific Palisades home of Alexandra Garrett, a woman who worked at *Beyond Baroque* for many years. I went to it dressed as a character from *Dawn of the Dead*: I wore a bloodstained shirt, had a knife in my back, a severed hand in my mouth, and was painted white with black makeup—it was always real easy for me to look *dead*. I answered the door several times; I did the whole act with my mouth dripping blood . . .

Then this woman dressed like Jayne Mansfield rang the bell: a buxom blonde dressed in a shiny blouse, accompanied by friends. She asked the hostess who I was: "Oh, that's *Bob Flanagan!*" Then the hostess dragged Sheree into a back room and showed her my book, *The Kid Is The Man*—the only book I had out at the time. Sheree had been dating Jack Skelley who was my friend—we were starting a band together called *Planet of Toys* (a novelty band; we played for several years). She had dated Jack a couple times, but then they'd just become friends. I asked Jack who she was and he gave me her phone number. At the time I was dating somebody else, but I was on the lookout for a more serious relationship.

On our first date Sheree and I went to *Beyond Baroque* for a poetry reading. Afterwards we went back to her house and I brought up the subject of SM—I was always looking for ways to bring up the subject! This was in 1980, and Sheree was heavily into the punk scene. She had traveled around with X before they got really big, and was going to concerts where kids would cut their initials into their arms with pieces of glass. So I steered the conversation toward piercing, and showed her this ring in my penis—the first piercing I'd done to myself—and she'd never seen anything like that before. I told her the whole story behind that, and that I was really into SM. On our very first date—we'd only known each other for a few hours—I said that my fantasy was to be a woman's full-time slave night and day, and do everything she said, and only have sex when and how she dictated, and clean her house and take care of things and just be her servant. She thought that was a good idea. That was literally the beginning of our whole relationship.

♦ **AJ: Had she been involved in the SM scene before?**
♦ BF: Never; she didn't know a thing about it. She was in the middle of exploring the singles scene, making up for lost time after a 14-year somewhat traditional marriage and two kids. She found that she hated the singles scene and the bars and the way men treated women. She became a feminist. She wasn't a lesbian or bisexual (yet) but at that point she was searching for something different. When she met me, there was a whole new frontier to explore: a totally different relationship between men and women that she never dreamed of before. For me, driving to her house and not even knowing what she looked

like (we'd had costumes on when we met!) there was this feeling that "this was the person who was going to be *the one* for me." I was at her house practically every day after that.

♦ **AJ:** *Going back a little, tell us how you defined your first "social" encounters in SM parlors—*
♦ **BF:** In an SM parlor, you have a contractual relationship for an hour: "I'm yours and you can do this to me, but you can't do that to me." I even wrote a statement that basically said, "You can do anything you want to me for this hour as long as there isn't any permanent damage." I think that usually the mistresses just do the same thing to you anyway, no matter *what* you tell them! If it's really great for an hour, you're disappointed when the time's up, and if it didn't meet your expectations (which it almost never does) then you feel ripped off. So it's *always* disappointing! And unless you're independently wealthy and have other relationships at other places, and you just go in there for a certain kind of fulfillment and it's not a big deal to spend $100 an hour, then it's okay. But if you're saving up for three months (which is what I had to do; that was all the money I had and sometimes I couldn't even afford to eat for a couple of days) it was really a sacrifice to go there and then come home disappointed.

♦ **AJ:** *What would usually happen?*
♦ **BF:** Typically they would tie you up (bondage) and try to talk mean to you. I was never much into the verbal aspect because it wasn't real; it was all an act. Sometimes there would be some pretty heavy whipping scenes which, if I were in the right frame of mind, would be really great, because then it was like an endurance test—it didn't matter if it were phony, because I still had to endure it. I'd come home with some bruises, and that would be nice—that would be *fun*. I'd have something to think about for a few weeks; I'd fantasize and recreate it in my head to be "perfect" . . . use that as a jumping-off point. But I really wanted this to be real with a real person, without paying for it . . . as part of a *relationship*.

Even as a kid I fantasized about *SM farms*. Women would have these farms, and sometimes I'd be the only person there or one of many, but I'd be the special one—the top slave. This fantasy of a society of women who were dominant and men who were submissive—I hadn't read any books about it, but by the time I'd met Sheree I'd read the *Story of O* five years earlier, and that was a good role model—I just reversed all the roles!

♦ **V:** *Can you fill in more details on that farm fantasy—I just think of barnyard animals—*
♦ **BF:** It's more like being a work-horse doing chores—silly stuff. Now there are ads in the papers about "SM Farms"—exactly what I fantasized about. Somebody somewhere has a ranch with all these slaves on it, and I don't know exactly what they do there, but . . .

♦ **AJ:** *So on your first date with Sheree, you're talking about the fantasy—*
♦ **BF:** But we didn't do anything. I showed her my penis ring, and we may have done some mutual masturbation—

Early performance by the folk-punk bongo trio, *Planet of Toys*. With poet Jack Skelley and artist Rick Lawndale we crooned such undanceable ditties as "Product of My Environment," "I Killed the Puppet," and "Fun to be Dead." 1981, *Beyond Baroque*, Los Angeles.

> **Made of plastic, made of wood**
> **Some of us are no damned good**
> **Some will fly and some will float**
> **Some will get stuck in your throat**

***Planet of Toys*, 1981, Bob Flanagan & Jack Skelley**

I think we both were very excited. At the time I was teaching poetry in Yucaipa, about 90 minutes east of L.A., on a government-funded arts-in-the-schools program. I was poet-in-residence at a junior high school, and the principal wanted me to live there but I refused—talk about being on a farm, there was nothing there! After a few days of driving back and forth I acquiesced and got a motel room, but I refused to live there because every night in L.A. there was something for me to do. Then I met Sheree, and I would stay at her house, get up at four in the morning (usually we'd be partying 'til midnight or 2 A.M.) and sometimes I'd have two hours of sleep, and then, bleary-eyed, drive for an hour-and-a-half and teach for eight hours and then have to attend these "development" meetings, where everyone got together to develop new programs—it was horrendous. I'd been paid $15,000 in advance for the whole year, so I had to keep on doing this job. (This

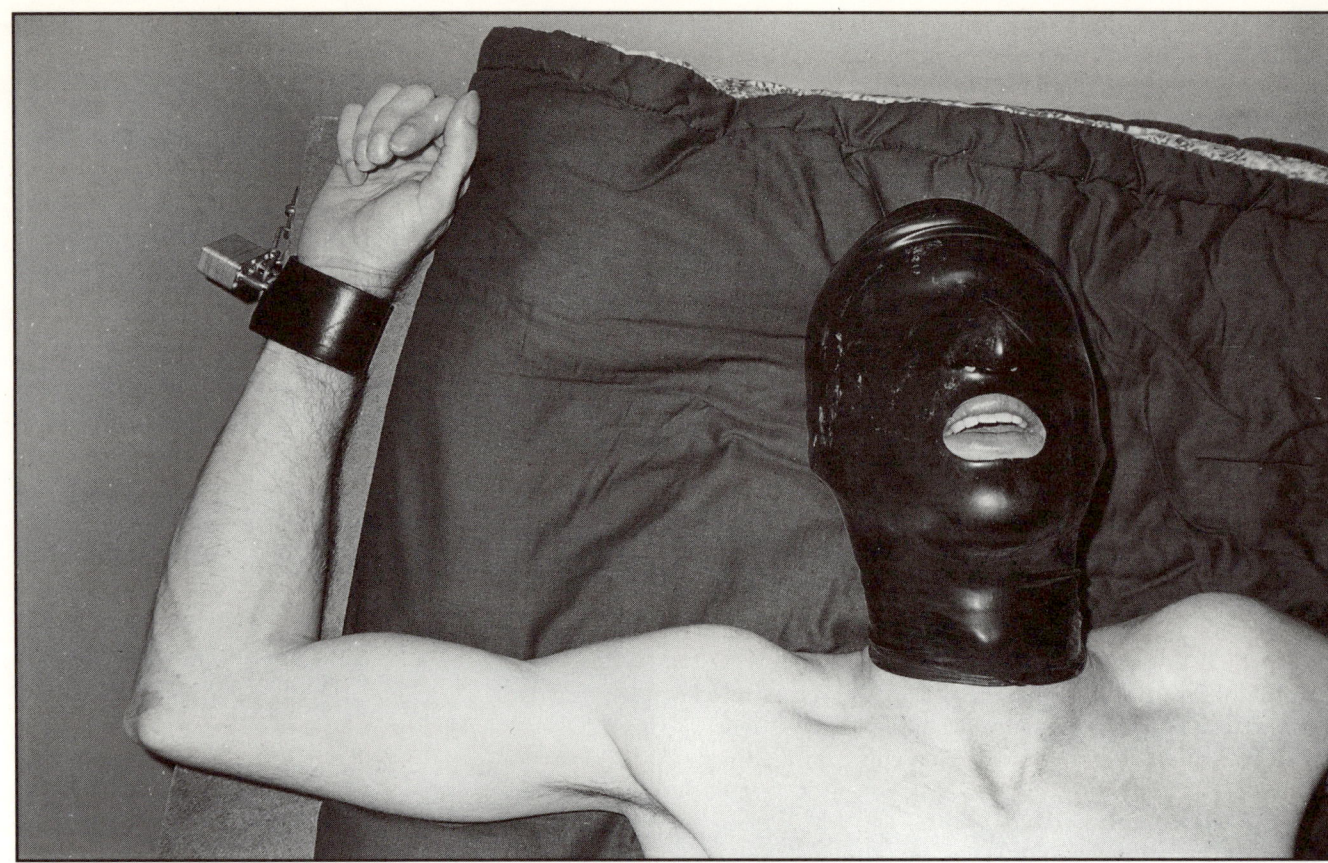

"Sheree put the latex hood over my face so I was in total darkness, everything covered but my mouth which she put to good use licking her cunt and ass and kissing her great mouth. Finally she untied my twisted-up penis and put me inside her. I was motionless and in complete darkness. She moved up and down on me like crazy. She put the cord of my bathrobe around my neck and choked me as hard as she could and we came." —Journal entry, June 2, 1982

was the only real paycheck I ever got for poetry . . . for this teaching job.)

Naturally, when you can *least* afford the time, somebody comes into your life who's really great! For the first nine months everything Sheree and I did was incredibly hot and exciting—I didn't want anything else to intrude. We met in October; by December I'd gotten really sick (103-degree fevers) and this was the first time Sheree had ever seen it and it scared her a lot; she hadn't been around "the illness" before (or any illness). Nobody in her family had ever been sick, so meeting me was a real challenge. The first few years were really terrifying for her.

I didn't tell Sheree how to be a mistress: "You should do this" or "You should do that." I'd explain technical things to her, but the attitude she took on was absolutely perfect—exactly what I'd wanted and was looking for. When I had to sleep in Yucaipa, she'd say, "Don't sleep in a bed unless you're with me" so I'd have to sleep on the floor. We'd talk on the phone and run up horrendous phone bills; she'd control my diet: "Don't eat this" or "Don't eat that." This control by phone was bizarre and exactly what I wanted in a relationship . . . where somebody else had full control.

♦ *AJ: What exactly is the turn-on?*

♦ BF: The restrictions. What really gets me going is lots of restrictions: having to operate in a confined space, either psychologically or physically, and enduring that. There's a sexual component but there's also an almost-spiritual high, a spiritual feeling you get from surviving this confinement. That's why contracts are exciting: "You'll do this and that (but not that)." I've done things like that totally alone, by myself, where I'll define a space. I'd make up a numerical list of things to do, put the numbers in a can, and pull out a number that might say: "Sleep on the floor tonight" or "Stay outside in the back yard all night long naked"—I'd have to do what that number commanded. In a way that was like playing with fate: since fate had dealt me a strange blow which I had to deal with, I countered with an artificial system to checkmate that. I was making a mockery out of something serious that had happened to me, just by making up all these silly rules. And this mirrored the rules I had no choice but to follow: I can't breathe well or do a lot of things because of the *body* I was given. So what I do is a mirror image of that restriction . . . which makes fun of it all.

Also, I am ultimately (this is what every masochist hates to hear, or admit) in full control: I wanted Sheree to be my mistress and make the rules for me. In reality, what usually happens is: the mistress gets bored with making all the rules—they get tired of doing that, and the slave/submissive is disappointed. Periodically this happens with us. I would love to have constant rules all the time, and have to live my life within a weird maze of restrictions.

The same thing happens with different kinds of bondage: if you're into blindfolds or leather hoods or force-feeding, you're altering the senses. You're cutting off one sense (or part of the body) and then the rest of the body takes over. If you're all tied up, then your brain starts over-reacting and working harder. I think the same thing happens with other psychological types of restrictions which just cause different parts of your psyche to work harder. That's why people get a thrill.

♦ **V: How did your relationship build?**
♦ **BF:** I was keeping a journal before we met; then for three or four months all my writing went out the window. I was too busy getting involved with what we did to *write* about it. Sheree came to my parents' house for Thanksgiving and that was fun. Then she came for Christmas (my parents really play up that holiday) and it was like, "Wow, Bob's really happy; he found a girlfriend." My parents are really good about this: if my brother brings a boyfriend home or if I bring Sheree home, they get presents too. So while the family was doing these Christmas things, Sheree and I would go into a bedroom and she'd tie me up with ribbons at my parents' house (which was a whole other thrill) and it was very exciting.

♦ **V: What did you do the first night?**
♦ **BF:** She may have masturbated me that first night—that was just to get to *know* each other . . . very light, casual. Sheree was very experimental and open—as a matter of fact, about nine months later when things got difficult, she had some identity crises about what this all meant. The way she compartmentalized it was: it was all just an experiment. Suddenly she felt really bad doing it, for awhile she felt like it just wasn't *her*. But she does this with everything; she goes through these phases of self-doubt where she looks at everything she's been doing and says, "That's not *me;* that's not what *I* want to be doing." And she was totally influenced by me; she'd never had thoughts like these in her life, except that as a kid, people had always accused her of being "bossy" (which is real sexist; any time a woman takes charge or makes her needs known, she's called "bossy"). So here was a way she could take that label, use it in a sexual context and have more fun with it.

Periodically Sheree has had (especially in the early days) a lot of doubts. In a lot of ways she thought of what we were doing as an experiment—she just wanted to try all these new things. And she was great! The kind of attitude changes that happened, aside from all the sexual or bondage things—well, as an example: within the first month she wanted her daughter's room painted. I said, "*I'll* do it for you!" and I did. Here I was, absolutely serving her, cleaning up her daughter's room and then painting it. When I'd started coming over, Sheree had been living with her two kids and the house had been really disorganized. Not long after I met her, I was home alone with the kids (they were ten and twelve at the time) and one night I just totally revamped and cleaned up *everything:* kitchen, living room, and got the kids involved. Sheree came home to find her messy home almost sparkling . . .

After that, that was my job. I cleaned the house, did the chores, did the laundry, drove the kids back and forth to school, plus I drove to Yucaipa and taught for eight hours a day. I think of this now, when I can barely walk up the stairs! That's been the hardest part for me to deal with: how my health has deteriorated so much. I really *liked* being a houseboy—I'd give up all the art and everything else just to do that. That's my favorite occupation.

♦ **AJ: When you were doing those chores, how would you feel?**
♦ **BF:** The first few days I'd have a hard-on the whole time. If the kids weren't around I'd be naked. Sometimes Sheree would put a little apron on me—she got a kick out of that. At the time she still worked for her father's carpet business, so when she came home everything would be spotless. I know where that came from in me: both my parents had to work two jobs. Since I was the oldest I was in charge of keeping the house clean. It was exciting for me to please them. It was like giving them a gift— they had to work so hard, so it was always great if they came home and found the house in order, all cleaned up. A lot

My 33rd birthday, holding a cake and a gift from Sheree: Lowly Worm, which for some reason reminded her of me. Los Angeles, 1985

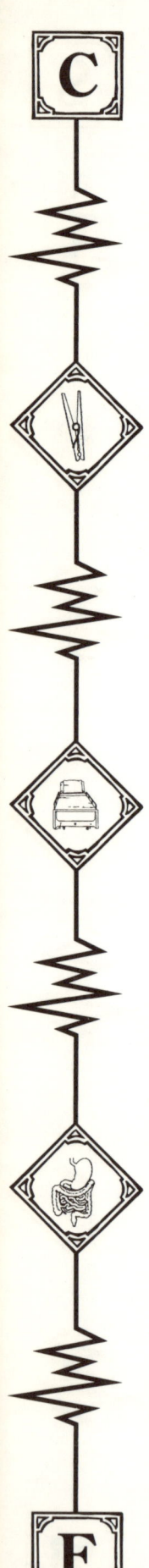

of the slave/servant stuff with Sheree flashes back to that memory of pleasing my parents, especially my mother. I just added the extra spice of sexuality and submission.

♦ **AJ: I'm interested in the evolution of your long-term committed relationship, which is so unusual—**
♦ **BF:** I've been trying to recall how it evolved, too, because it seemed to me that it just happened instantaneously: suddenly we were just doing all these *things*. I already had a certain amount of SM equipment—nothing spectacular, just some belts and restraints. By December Sheree was tying my wrists behind my back and burning my nipples with a hot needle, or she would heat up a pin and drop it on me. I suspended myself by the wrists while she jacked me off a couple times. I showed her a lot of things she'd never seen before and got her wheels spinning. The main thing she brought to it was this *attitude* which was totally and naturally dominant, and you can't pay for that—if you go to the House of Dominance you get all the equipment and people who know how to use the equipment, but . . .

♦ **V: She had two kids, so perhaps she'd gotten some experience from disciplining them—**
♦ **BF:** Her kids weren't very disciplined; she didn't use it with them, and they certainly never listened to her if she tried! Dominance has to involve somebody who gets a real thrill out of somebody else doing anything they say. Sheree liked that a lot; she'd get this little smirk on her face.

♦ **AJ: Is she getting a sexual charge out of this?**
♦ **BF:** I'm not sure if it was always sexual, but there was some sort of thrill about being able to order any man around. There's a certain revenge aspect. She had been in this very traditional marriage for fourteen years; in some respects her husband had bossed her around and there were always arguments if she didn't do what he said. And in the singles scene men always thought they were in control, and could *use* women. Sheree was pretty fed up with all that, and by the time she met me and could express this other side, she went full force: "*I* tell you what to do. We won't have sex unless I say, and *how* I say." She'd always hated housework, so she was real excited about that aspect of our relationship—even if she had fantasized about the sex, she might never have thought of *that*. I think her attitude excited *me,* and the things I showed her and did excited *her,* so it was really mutual, back and forth. And we kept escalating to different activities including golden showers—that happened really fast. I don't know if I suggested this or how the subject came up, but we just did it. Bondage in her bed, not being able to touch her—all these different dominant-submissive type activities started happening.

♦ **AJ: Go back to your second and third nights together—**
♦ **BF:** On one of those early dates I took her to a party at the Chateau—that was early on, because I know I was really embarrassed about some of the things that were happening there.

♦ **V: Why?**
♦ **BF:** At those parties there's lots of male dominance of

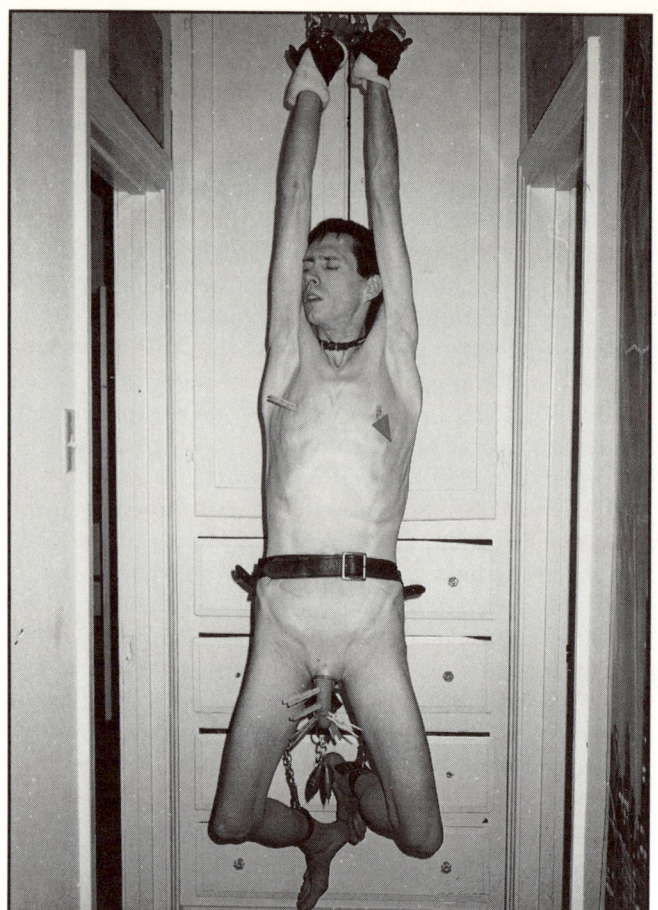

Hung out to dry (and cry). Long Beach, 1983

women, which is very uncomfortable to be around when you're with somebody who's even a *mild* feminist (and Sheree was more than a mild feminist at the time). I had to keep explaining things; I couldn't even say this was consensual because a lot of the dominance was happening to women who worked there and you could tell that it *wasn't* consensual; it was *because* they worked there. So there were some uncomfortable moments, but Sheree liked the atmosphere, liked some of the people, and there was some great equipment to admire. There were both good and bad aspects to a party like that.

At that time the Chateau was a big converted apartment complex. There were a couple of common waiting areas where you could watch videos, each with a big closet with all kinds of whips, paddles, chains, cattle prods, horse saddles—everything. Each apartment had been transformed into a different type of dungeon with its own name and "feel" to it. There was a TV (transvestite, cross-dressing) room with lots of mirrors and costumes; it was painted pink with a very frilly decor. Another dungeon was painted black, with heavy stocks and suspension devices.

If you were going there to be submissive to somebody, you'd sit and interview somebody for ten minutes and tell them what you were into: "I'd like to be whipped, but

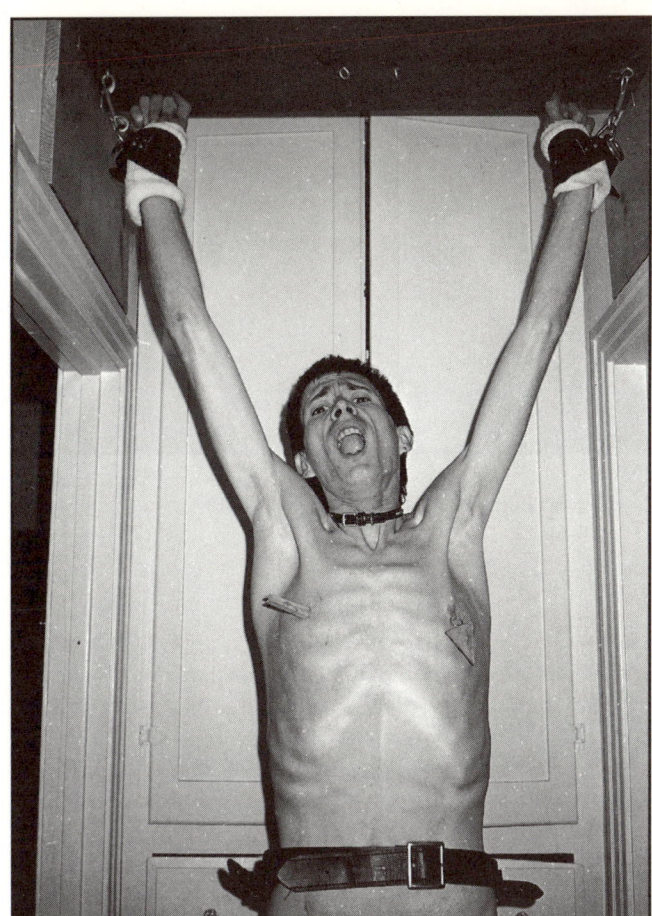

I don't want any marks" or "I'd like to be your foot slave, but I don't want any pain" or "I want *lots* of pain"—you just tell them your boundaries and they pick out the equipment. You'd go into the room and get naked and they'd come in and do a one- or two-hour session with you. Once a month, to make more money and to advertise the place, they'd have parties which were open to the public, and charge $30 or $60. Women were usually admitted free, because women tended not to go unless they were with a guy.

♦ **V: What would happen?**
♦ BF: They'd do demonstrations with some whipping. Usually it was pretty light stuff, but it depended on the people involved. To an outsider watching, a scene could be pretty disturbing, especially if the person being whipped was really into being hurt, or even reacted like he were being hurt. It all depended on the expertise of the person doing the whipping: sometimes it wasn't done very well. If you're new to this, sometimes it's hard to watch. I was always a little embarrassed whenever I brought someone new along.

♦ **AJ: What do you mean by "sometimes it wasn't done very well"?**
♦ BF: There's a lot of technique involved, because there are a lot of places you don't want to whip, like the kidneys. And you don't want the whip to accidentally "wrap around" somebody's body. Sometimes, instead of hitting straight onto the back, the whip would come around the front so you'd get this full force like a faster-than-the-speed-of-sound *whack* that breaks the skin and is very painful. There are certain levels of pain that will take you *out* of a scene. If the pain is too heavy, or if it escalates too quickly, it'll psychologically destroy whatever illusion you're working up to, or whatever feelings are being increased.

♦ **AJ: Explain the pain aspect—**
♦ BF: *Context is everything.* Even people who are into SM are not turned on by getting their hand slammed in a car door. And some people into SM like a mild form of stimulation . . . it's all levels of stimulation—that's all pain is. Some people just like a little mild butt-warming with a hand, and maybe a little bit of whipping so they turn a bit red, but they don't want any sharp, hard or difficult pain; they certainly don't want any marks. Then there are extreme people who are really into being bullwhipped; some people are into heavy flogging with a cat-o'-nine tails until they bleed. There are these extremes and everything in between, and even people who like it extreme (which I've liked at times) don't like it extreme *all* the time. There are times when you just want it to be lighter, and there are times when (if you're in a relationship like I had with Sheree) it didn't matter what *I* liked; it was what *she* liked at the time. That's a different plane entirely.

You have to get on a wavelength with a person, plus you have to get on a wavelength with your own body. And you build up the pain threshold, you don't just immediately get together with somebody and start flailing away at them (unless you've agreed to a pre-arranged punishment type of scenario—some people want to do that, too). Everything I say you *don't* do, some people do! [laughs] But in general most people want a scene to be an erotic, sensual experience, not a *brutal* experience. So even if you're going to end up whipping somebody until they bleed, you start off gently, and there are different types of whips that don't hurt so much—they're made of very soft leather. They have fat braids or tails so they don't hurt very much. But the thinner whips sting and have a much more severe effect. So you can work your way up . . . you can spend hours getting heavier and heavier, then lighten up, then go heavy, then lighten up. Going back to "wrapping around": that's something that comes up unexpectedly and gives an unexpected shock. You're doing something light and all of a sudden one of the tails of the whip wraps around your thigh or some area that's really sensitive and ruins the build-up that's taking place in your body and your head.

♦ **AJ: What *is taking place in your body and head?***
♦ BF: Usually people describe the state you achieve as a "runner's high," where your brain releases endorphins (a natural pain-reliever which is like heroin) to combat the pain. Runners feel that "high" if they run for a long time. Likewise, people in SM describe the same type of thing—

the experience becomes a high, and if you add a sexual component you have a *double high*. There are people who are just "sensation junkies"—that's what they crave. And this *is* an intense sensation.

♦ **V: Aren't your eyes closed most of the time, to aid the fantasy component?**

♦ **BF:** Sometimes your eyes are closed, sometimes you're blindfolded—it really depends on the scene and what you want. In many ways what Sheree and I did were extended fantasy or endurance tests where I wanted to take anything she wanted to do to me, anytime . . . be able to withstand anything and go through it.

Sometimes the whipping feels awful and I can't wait for it to stop, but afterwards the fact that I went through it and that she wanted to do it produces a real rush of sexuality and closeness; a feeling of almost being protected; a bonding between the two of us that you never get with any other kind of relationship—never. It's the knowledge that we both went through this thing together. But a lot of times it doesn't work like that; sometimes a whipping is really annoying and you just can't stand it. It really depends on your frame of mind at the time.

♦ **V: Do the scenes always end in physical closeness?**

♦ **BF:** Of course it depends on the relationship! A lot of scenes I witnessed were demonstrations for a party—sometimes they're just that. But when they work really well, there's usually a bond between the two people—they hug each other afterwards. Ideally, both are going through something emotional: the top is releasing something that's really important (they wouldn't be doing it unless they got some sexual charge out of being in that position) and the bottom is getting their needs met completely, so there are two people working absolutely together to get their needs met. It doesn't always work well, but when it does there's a real chemistry that kind of explodes between them.

♦ **V: What do you think of the idea that people who like bondage may have been tied up and molested at a very early age?**

♦ **BF:** I've heard that from people into SM, and I've also heard that from people who are completely turned off to SM *because* they were abused as children. People process information and experiences differently; someone who's imprinted with nylons and bras when they're a kid may want to dress up in those after they grow up. People have all sorts of strange imprinting—I think the bondage aspect of *my* situation (being a prisoner to other forces) was sexualized so I could survive it. In order to not be terrified by it, I sexualized it.

In extreme cases, people create other personalities. People who are really abused and who can't escape, "escape" by becoming multiple personalities—it's common for multiple personalities to have abuse in their backgrounds. Maybe role-playing as a slave is just a milder, healthier form of having multiple personalities to escape difficulty. Saying this, I hear a million voices in my head of people who *swear* that nothing happened in their childhood; they just, in their adult life, heard about this and

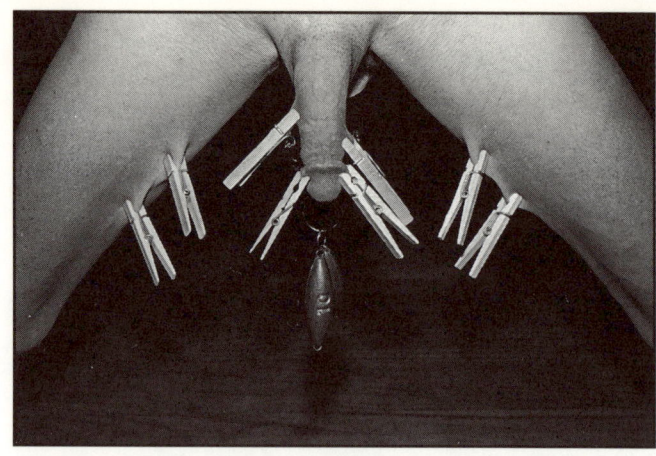

Clothespins and weights. Los Angeles, 1983

got involved, like Sheree—she heard about this scene and it "clicked" in a certain part of her. She can't rationalize or explain it by any kind of imprinting. For me it's much deeper.

I've met lots of people in the SM scene who've had asthma, polio, and other illnesses and who were bedridden as children. They don't *all* become submissive; I know someone who was plagued by horrible asthma and had to stay home from school—very similar to my situation, except that now he's a well-known top and in his fantasies takes the dominant role. The submissive part of me is in utter contrast to the kind of person I am otherwise: I have a pretty strong ego and very strong ideas about what I want to do with my work. To jump ahead to Sheree and me doing SM art, or art that talks about our SM relationship—it's almost ridiculous to watch us then, because I'm kind of a tyrant to work with. When we're making videos, I'm worse than Francis Ford Coppola: "No, no, it can't go that way!" Yet we're doing shows that portray me as being totally submissive.

Sometimes this personality split and the combination of people I am is too much for me to take. Doing art, I work instinctively. I just know I want a particular "thing," yet I'm not always able to articulate why to Sheree or anybody else. I get frustrated if somebody else works at a different speed, so it's really hard for me to work with other people—especially someone I'm close to. I'm much more inclined to say, "NO, dammit!" In a way, our SM lifestyle pretty much dried up when we started doing art together! Our personalities really clashed, and that's something we have to work out. We're pretty much in agreement most of the time, but things always go wrong. Alone, I can just curse myself and that's okay, but when there's somebody else to hang it on, then I just immediately go, "Goddamit!" and then later say, "Sorry, I didn't mean it."

♦ **V: When you met Sheree, did you start reading more about SM?**

♦ **BF:** I probably read *less* after I met Sheree—all that stuff in adult bookstores mostly seemed like *crap* after I

met her. Sheree was more enamored with stores like the Pleasure Chest than I was (the Pleasure Chest, on Santa Monica Blvd, is *the* store for SM equipment, and some of it sells for exorbitant prices). For a long time that was the only place to go; now we've made friends with people who make good-quality equipment; now you can pick and choose. But back then it was *the* place to go; the punks used to go there for their clothes.

I showed Sheree *Fetish Times*—I still have three or four boxes of all the publications I bought in those days. Before we met, we'd both seen *In the Realm of the Senses,* which was really influential—we learned a lot from that movie, and we both had fantasized about it a lot. Choking became one of our favorite pastimes: strangulation during sex.

♦ **AJ: *Before we get into that, you didn't finish the story about when you first brought Sheree to the Chateau—***
♦ **BF:** Oh yeah! We felt some awkwardness because some people seemed overly abusive to the people working there. Maybe it was my own fears. In the early days you're always afraid: "Oh no, I've gone too far. I've showed her too much and she's just going to think it's all awful and horrible, and never want to talk to me again." There are things that happen at parties, and if you're an outsider it looks a lot worse than it really is. Sometimes a whipping scene, to someone who doesn't know the participants or how people react in that situation, seems a lot more brutal than it is, because people will scream and cry and beg for the other person to stop. Yet when it's all over they go [breathless], "Thank you!"—they loved it! And they laugh and joke and have wine afterwards; it's part of the scene to scream and yell and shout and say "No!" That's why in the SM scene there's always "safe words."

♦ **V: *What do you mean?***
♦ **BF:** SM is the only area where "no" doesn't mean no. In every other place, no means no. But you have to have some word that means no, so you say—the typical boring substitute would be "red" which means "Stop. This is past my limits. I swallowed a hairball and I'm going to choke" . . . Whenever psychologically or physically you're out of the scene, you say something like "red" to mean "stop." Or you can say "yellow" which means "my hand's asleep." So the top stops what they're doing and checks out what's going on. Rules like these are really good if you meet somebody at a bar or a party and you start playing for an hour or two; you have to have these kinds of systems to communicate. But if you know someone the way Sheree and I know each other, we don't have that—I know how far she'll go and she knows how much I'm able to take, so there's no communication loss that way. I can scream and yell and—usually if she stops, I'm disappointed afterwards. That's a typical submissive behavior: you beg for it to stop, and then when it's over, it's never enough!

♦ **AJ: *So you were at the Chateau—***
♦ **BF:** I was worried that Sheree would get the wrong idea by this limited view of the scene, and that she might be turned off to the whole idea of SM in general. This was a professional party (as opposed to parties for people *in* the scene); basically, it was a Chateau open house with people showing off their mistresses, and guys hanging around and finally paying for it later that night with a woman. There was a lot of male chauvinism and sexism and uncomfortable feelings. Now things have changed somewhat. There are a lot more private clubs now that have parties—that's one big difference.

At the Chateau Sheree was uncomfortable, although not as uncomfortable as I thought she would be. We didn't do anything at this party, we just watched and talked about it afterwards. Basically I was showing her what it looked like.

♦ **AJ: *What was her reaction?***
♦ **BF:** I think she was turned on by a lot of it. She was turned off by some of the sexism, like: "That guy is a real pig; don't pay any attention to him," but, "Over there, that couple's really into it; let's see what they do!" So she came away with more positive feelings toward it.

I wish I could remember the first time we actually did something; it seems like we've *always* been doing things. I know she must have whipped or spanked me not long after we met, but I can't remember what the occasion was. Typically, after these parties we'd go home and do our

Book of collaborative poems published by Cold Calm Press in 1990. Cover art by L.A. artist Jim Shaw.

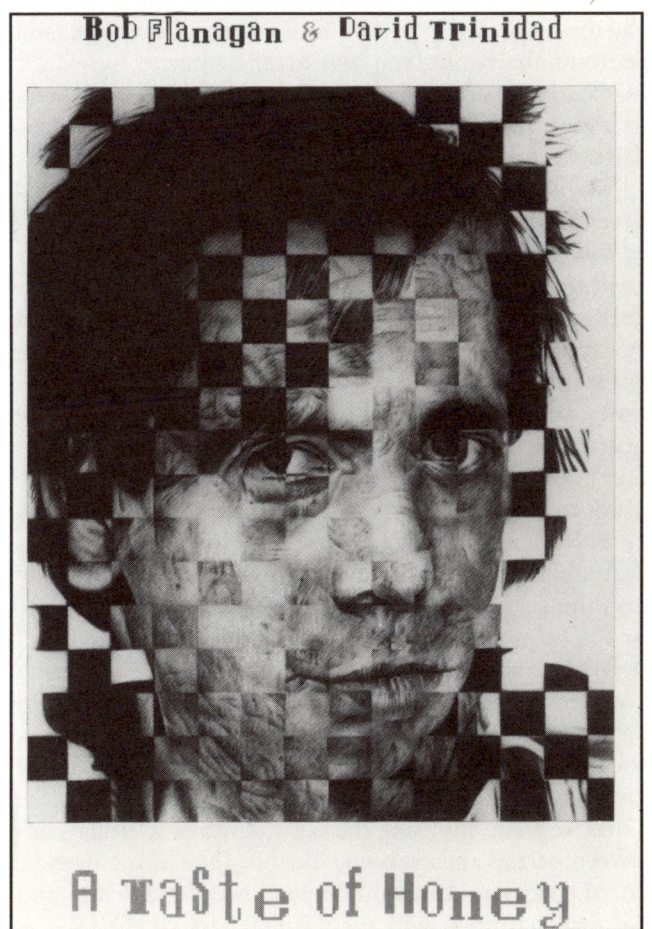

own experiments with things she saw at the party. My journal got pretty fuzzy after we met, and I was commuting between Long Beach, Westwood and Yucaipa—that's why I have a hard time remembering this period of my life. Plus, I was in some nirvana-land, getting everything I ever imagined happening to me . . .

♦ **V: Maybe you'll remember if you can recall the equipment you used?**

♦ **BF:** I don't remember which whips or equipment I had when we met, but we definitely expanded our supply. Several years ago our equipment got stolen, so we had to start over again from scratch. As usual we were going from one party to another; we were at a performance in Downtown L.A. and had two bags in the back of the car and the car was broken into and both bags were stolen—some of our favorite toys. I wonder what the thieves thought of these handcuffs and whips . . .

One time some people broke into our house and stole a VCR which had some raw footage of a piercing video Sheree was working on, of a woman getting her clit pierced (luckily Sheree had copied it). I wonder what the people who stole it thought of *that* . . .

Sheree came up with something I'd never fantasized about: the idea of infantilism—treating me like a baby and having me drink out of a baby bottle. I think it was exciting because *she* brought it up. That's something you rarely see in most SM magazines, because it's embarrassing to admit to people; that's a real sub-group of a sub-group: *baby-men*. There are magazines dedicated to that, but usually they're tucked away in a little corner of the store, and the most bizarre ones you have to send away for. When she worked professionally, Sheree met a couple of baby-men. In a way, that's one of the more "natural" longings to understand: why someone would want to be a baby . . .

We played around with that, as well as other things I'd never fantasized about, because Sheree wanted to try *everything!* So we asked at the Pleasure Chest, "Do you have anything to do with infantilism?" and the clerk misunderstood: "No no, we don't do any of that!" He thought we were referring to kiddie porn, which is *not* what infantilism is: it's grown men dressed up as babies (sometimes women too, but not usually. If women are in the magazines they're usually portraying the mother, and if they're dressed as babies it's just play-acting). It's mostly overweight men who tend to look very pudgy, like Baby Hueys. There are private newsletters advertising giant diapers and big pacifiers. Anyway, infantilism wasn't really my "thing," but still it was fun to experiment with it.

♦ **V: Did you ever do cross-dressing?**

♦ **BF:** Sheree and I met on Halloween, and the following year we went to a Halloween party and she had me dressed up in a blue dress—she liked leading me around by a collar dressed as a woman with wigs and make-up. People loved it; it was an SM Halloween party so we fit right in. Then we went out using the same costume to other Halloween parties and everyone liked it. One of my friends, poet David Trinidad, would have a couple of drinks and fall madly in love with me. "Bob," he'd say. "You look beautiful in that blue dress!" And then he'd kiss me.

I was of the frame of mind that I would do anything Sheree thought of. I even told her that if she wanted to not ever tie me up again, that's okay too. What I really liked about Sheree was this dominant attitude. It's hard to maintain, though, on a 24-hour basis. After twelve years it comes and goes. But that's what I really like—even to this day. I wish we could get more of that going, because now, physically, I can't do a lot. But to submit to that attitude is the greatest—that's what turns me on the most.

♦ **AJ: How did you establish a commitment?**

♦ **BF:** I gave Sheree Leopold von Sacher-Masoch's book, *Venus in Furs,* to read (checked it out from the Cal State Long Beach library) so she could really see the psychology behind the whole thing of being a slave to somebody; to me this was a great role model. From reading that, Sheree got the idea of making a slave contract. That's when we started to cement our relationship—when we put it on paper. Plus, she was afraid of commitment anyway, so this relaxed her: she only had to do this for six months, and if neither one of us liked it, we didn't have to renew the contract. Our first contract was just a verbal one, but by Christmas we had a contract that I would be her slave for three months . . . later we expanded that. That was based on *Venus in Furs*—we wouldn't have thought of it otherwise.

It's a bit hard to separate what I knew at the time, what I read about, and how all of this evolved, because it's all meshed together. We went to the Pleasure Chest hundreds of times, we went to "tack" stores to buy riding crops and hardware stores to buy rope—nylon rope is good but it frays if you don't burn the ends—

♦ **V: Soft, thick cotton rope is good, but it's hard to find. That's what they use in Japanese bondage books—**

♦ **BF:** Yeah, in those Japanese SM books they really spend a lot of time devising intricate patterns—it's really an art: all those knots and designs . . . With our contracts, I could have committed forever, but Sheree wanted to know that in three months we wouldn't have to do this ever again if it bothered her. *I* wanted to know that it was going to last at least three months, and wasn't going to stop during that period of time. The contracts were just copies of Sacher-Masoch's: I would be Sheree's slave and do anything she said. I would be in charge of cleaning the house, and I couldn't masturbate or have any kind of sex unless she said so. My body belonged to her completely, to do with whatever she wanted. I wasn't allowed to be with anybody else, but *she* could be with whoever she wanted to be with. There was no penalty of death, of course—this was a totally non-binding, non-legal agreement specifying in concrete terms what our boundaries would be. And I still haven't been with anybody but her for twelve years.

♦ **AJ: So you don't do scenes with other people?**

♦ **BF:** In the early days I may have done scenes if she did them with other people, but I haven't been with anybody else sexually. A couple of times we split up for brief periods and I tried to have scenes with other people, but I

Sheree and I bare it all for a Mike Kelley print, a version of which was later used for the Sonic Youth CD, *Dirty*.

to find somebody that you mesh with that well. There's a lot more people who just like playing scenes for a night, or for a party or maybe a weekend, but I like the idea of it extending over a lifetime . . .

♦ **AJ: You also loved her—**
♦ BF: Yes. We talk about this a lot. I love her much more as my dominant, because that's how we met. It wasn't like it was something else first, then after a year I said, "By the way, I'm also into this . . ." First it was, "I'm into this," then it was, "By the way, I love you!" From the very instant we met, without even knowing what we each really *looked* like—

♦ **V: That's right; when you were attracted to each other you were both disguised as dead people—**
♦ BF: Yes. I think I've talked to Sheree every day since we met (even if she's out of town, or I've been away at the hospital). I don't think a day has gone by that we haven't talked to each other, and it's not just to call and talk about being whipped; we talk about movies or what's happening with her. We're really wrapped up in each other's lives, and now it's in ways that have nothing to do with SM. Nevertheless, for me everything is better when that SM is working, because *that's* the ultimate closeness with somebody, and because that's been with me all my life. The problem is: it hasn't been with *Sheree* all of her life. So, it's not necessarily the ultimate closeness for *her*: to be my mistress. This is a difference we have to deal with, because while it's my very core, it's something that was added to her life afterwards—she can take it or leave it. But it's always that way: there's always one partner who's more into it than another.

was disappointed so much—I thought, "Sheree and I had the best!" I felt I could never take it far enough with anyone else. After Sheree, scenes with other people seemed so superficial; I can't go backward to that. I'd have to be with somebody I'm really wrapped up with emotionally, as I am with Sheree. First of all, it's just not that common

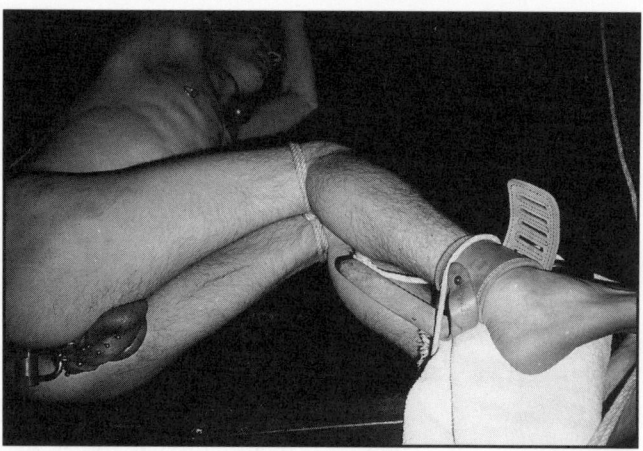

I can't tell up or down in this photo, probably the same way I felt the night it was taken. An SM party where I am just about to have the soles of my feet whipped for some earlier indiscretion. Los Angeles, 1984

♦ **V: Plus the bonding is based on a shared stigma—**
♦ **BF:** Yes. I *want* to give something up and be a part of somebody else; Sheree (like a lot of people) maybe doesn't want to give something up of herself. I'm not just talking about SM—with bonding in general, to be with somebody means giving up a part of yourself. And I think the sicker I get, the harder it is for her . . . there's an urge to push me away, because she knows that I'm going to be taken away anyway, and that's difficult to face.

A lot of couples, when one person has a life-threatening illness, often split up for just that reason: it's too hard to face. I had no choice but to have this fate, but she can control her own destiny by saying, "Enough is enough! I want to end this relationship." And she has established certain distances, because it's just too hard to deal with the illness and what might happen.

♦ **AJ: Do you talk about this?**
♦ **BF:** These days we talk about it a *lot*—more than anything else.

♦ **AJ: Well, most people live very superficially—**
♦ **BF:** This has been a very transformative time for me, because I'm turning forty and everything has flipped upside-down and sideways for me.

♦ **V: . . . Did you ever have any problems with Sheree's kids?**
♦ **BF:** There were stormy moments when I moved into the house with Sheree. I thought they were spoiled Westwood brats, and they saw me as an intrusion on their lives—which I was. But now her son shows his friends *Modern Primitives* and says, "That's my *mom!*" His friends are all into tattoos and they go, "Your mom is *Sheree Rose?!*" They have an entirely different relationship with their parents than I ever had with mine. I could never communicate with my parents in the negative way they do with theirs; there's lots of fighting. They were undisciplined, and Sheree always felt inadequate as a mother—she kept second-guessing herself and they would use that to their advantage.

I came in as this outsider authoritarian figure who knew the "right" way to do everything. Once I was taking the trash out, doing my slave duty, while Sheree and her kids were just screaming about something. This was early in the relationship when I could have jumped ship. I told myself, "This is crazy. I don't need this in my life. Why am I doing this? Why am I here?" Then I made a decision; I said to myself, "I'm never going to get from anybody else what I'm getting with Sheree. Okay, this is what I have to bear."

The daughter and the father still live in the house which Sheree and her ex-husband own together, and the son lives up north. As far as our SM lifestyle was concerned, the kids loved it—they didn't know the sexuality of it (not openly anyway; maybe they perceived it) but early on they would say, "Mom, I need to go to the store," and Sheree would say, "Bob, drive the kids to the store." I cleaned up their rooms, I cooked dinner and cleaned up afterwards, I drove the kids to school—

♦ **AJ: You had this middle-class existence—**
♦ **BF:** Very much so. The neighbors hated us for a lot of reasons: for three or four years I had a band going, and we'd have rehearsals every Sunday. Also, we'd have parties that would last for three or four days (like one Labor Day weekend when people showed up in waves). The house had a lot of rooms, and after a party was over there'd still be people in a back room you'd forgotten about. One neighbor across the street called the police every time we did anything, just to harass us.

One time we had a Janus society [SM social club] meeting with several guys dressed as women serving other people, and Sheree's kids didn't bat an eye—they were 13 or 14 then. I think they came away from their upbringing with much more tolerance for other people's strangeness. They're very conservative themselves; very normal and straight, but very tolerant, too, because they've seen a side of people not normally seen, and they're not judgmental about it. Now they know Sheree's work and they've gone to her shows; they've seen her photographs. And their friends see us in print before they do. Sheree went with her kids to buy the Sonic Youth album, *Dirty*, which has our pictures on the artwork, and when her kids saw 'em they just went, "Oh, *mom . . .*" (I don't want to see *my* mom's butt sitting on a bunny in a photograph, that's for sure. It's very odd.)

♦ **AJ: Can you recall any more events with Sheree?**
♦ **BF:** There were so many. One year she had a surprise birthday party for me, with all our SM friends. I was blindfolded and taken into the back of the house. She had commissioned one of her friends to make a big wrought iron cage—you couldn't stand up in it; it was about four feet long and three feet high. This was the beginning of Lent (in March) which we used to observe. That's one Catholic holdover I really liked: giving something up, or having to endure something for forty days and forty nights. This cage was set up in Sheree's bedroom, and for forty

days and nights I slept in it; instead of sleeping in the bed, she'd lock me in. Also (and this was weird, even for most of our SM friends) for forty days and nights I ate nothing but oatmeal. We'd go out to a restaurant with friends and instead of eating real food, I'd have to open a little packet of instant oatmeal and eat that.

♦ **AJ: Did you take vitamins?**
♦ **BF:** Yeah, lots of supplements. I could drink anything, but I could eat only oatmeal.

♦ **AJ: Did it hurt to sleep in the cage?**
♦ **BF:** Sometimes I felt cramped in the morning; sometimes I didn't sleep very well. After awhile I got used to it. But it was really a turn-on—I loved it!

♦ **V: Why did you eat only oatmeal?**
♦ **BF:** When we were kids in New York, we were very poor. One time all we had to eat was oatmeal, so that's what we ate for breakfast, lunch and dinner. I told Sheree this story and she said, "Oh, great—*that's* what I'll have you do!" I got a parking ticket, and as punishment (and to save money and pay for the fine) Sheree ordered me to eat nothing but oatmeal for several weeks. I loved those oatmeal fasts—that's as close as I could get to real fasting, because I have to eat a minimum of 4000 calories a day just to maintain the 135 pounds that I am. It's a lot of work. But oatmeal is very nutritious, and I can put milk and sugar in it . . . plus I have protein shakes in between. Also, oatmeal is very cleansing—it's a good regimen to undergo. So I just loved it; I loved the challenge, and it didn't end until we went to Las Vegas for a weekend, where I got to eat a buffet meal. Even when we've been apart, I've done that to myself: "From this time to that time I'll only eat oatmeal." Recently I thought, "Maybe I won't eat anything but oatmeal until my show, because I'm 'way over budget." But it's hard to maintain that by yourself; sometimes I can be self-disciplined and do it, but it's much more exciting if another person is controlling it.

Anyway, this "oatmeal discipline" freaked out even our heavy SM friends. We'd go to their house and they'd be making dinner for us and Sheree would say, "Oh, Bob can't eat that—he has to eat oatmeal." So she'd set a dish of oatmeal down and I'd have to eat it off the floor. For some people that was a bit far-fetched, but that's the kind of thing that really gets me off! It's embarrassing, but that's the fun part of it. With SM friends I didn't care, but we also did it in front of "straight" friends. They knew our situation, but still it was somewhat unusual.

When I first started working at *Beyond Baroque* I was on the oatmeal diet. At first people thought it was strange that I never had lunch. I'd go to a 7-11 store, get a cup of hot water and add instant oatmeal and eat it in my car, secretly. It was like an anorexic eating disorder: *oatmealia*.

♦ **AJ: What does the embarrassment feel like?**
♦ **BF:** It's a rush. SM has its humiliation built into it, and I don't like the kind of humiliation where somebody's yelling and calling you names artificially. But humiliation that comes out of maintaining your lifestyle is putting your money where your mouth is: you *claim* to have this relationship, so be consistent and act submissive even in front of friends. . . .

On the evening of our tenth anniversary Sheree planned an elaborate night out at one of our favorite restaurants. She had me dress up in the original costume I wore on the night we met (my *Dawn of the Dead* makeup and bloody shirt, which I still had), and she dressed up as Jayne Mansfield again with her blonde wig and big tits. It was Halloween, so it wasn't so unusual to be out at a nice restaurant dressed like this.

The waiter came over and took our order for drinks and appetizers. We ordered, and Sheree got this great asparagus dish, but all I got was a bowl of oatmeal. "Oh, I *see*," I thought. "Isn't that cute—now let's get on to the real food." The waiter was looking at me funny. Also, he never talked to me directly; it had been pre-arranged that he'd only talk to Sheree—he wouldn't even acknowledge that I was there. Then Sheree asked me what I would like, and I said, "Filet mignon," but when the dish arrived it was oatmeal! It turned out that Sheree had talked to the owner, who was a friend of ours, and worked all this out in advance. Through at least four courses plus dessert, every dish that arrived was oatmeal—I was sick of it, but I loved it! And from that point on from Hallow-

Jim Ward demonstrates his butterfly board technique at a Society of Janus play piercing program. Los Angeles, 1984

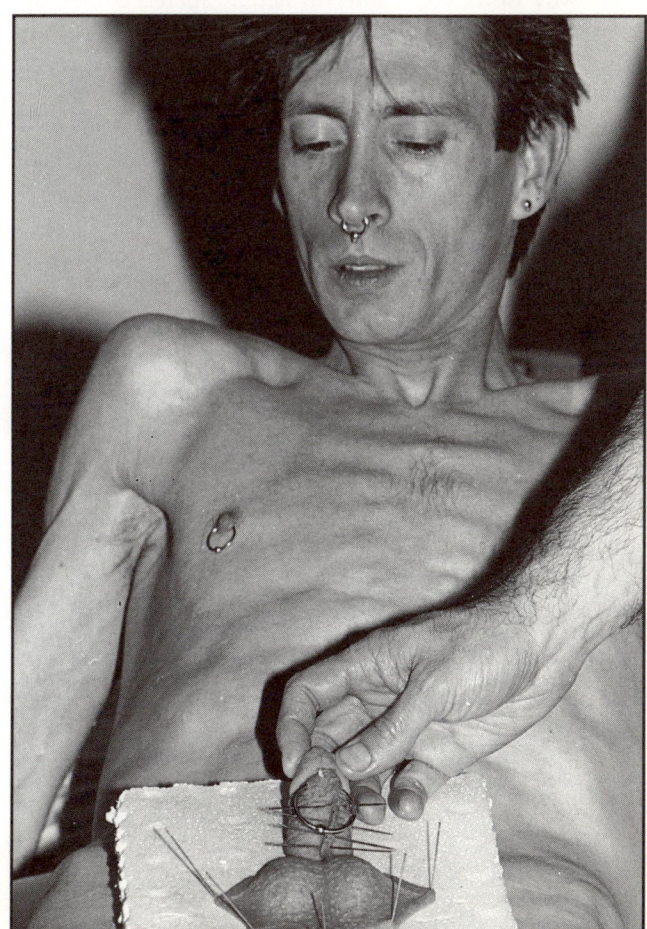

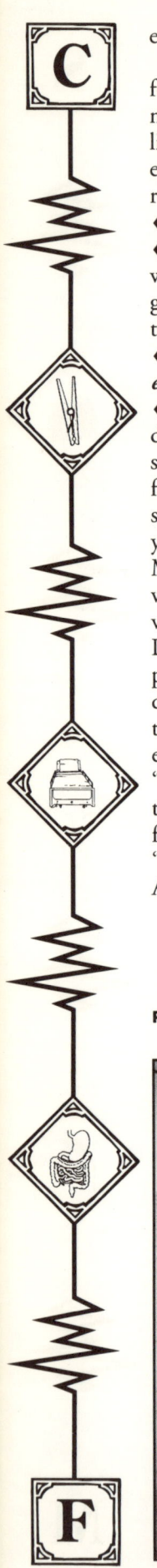

een to Thanksgiving, all I was allowed to eat was oatmeal.

About a year later we found out from a waiter we befriended that some of the waitresses on the staff were almost crying, they were so upset at seeing me humiliated like this in public. It upset them! I thought they were enjoying it, or at most thought we were just weird. But it really upset them that Sheree was doing this to me.

♦ **AJ: *Was this a major turn-on for you?***
♦ BF: Yeah. Actually, at that point it was just funny; when we *first* did it, it was more of a major turn-on. It's always good when rules are established, and having to do this through Thanksgiving was a turn-on, certainly.

♦ **AJ: *Afterward, did you go home and do something erotic?***
♦ BF: At this point we'd been together for ten years, so I don't remember! A few weeks earlier I'd given Sheree a surprise anniversary party. We were supposed to go to a friend's house for dinner, and when we got there, about sixty of our friends (most of whom we'd known for ten years) were there. They read pieces dedicated to us, and Mike Kelley read his piece titled "One Hundred Reasons" which is a list of different spanking paddles that he'd invented funny names for, like The Bonecrusher, Mommy's Little Helper, Daddy's Little Helper, and the Waker-Upper . . . all names for punishment paddles. But what I didn't know was: Mike had secretly arranged with Sheree to bring this big fraternity paddle. I'm sitting in the audience waiting for him to begin his reading, and he says, "Bob, why don't you come up here?" Sheree comes up too; she pulls my pants down and in front of all of our friends she has me over her knee, and while Mike reads "One Hundred Reasons" she whacks me a hundred times! Actually, that became a collaboration; later we made a video, with Mike reading and Sheree spanking me a hundred times. You can see my ass getting darker and darker and more bruised.

♦ **AJ: *How did that feel?***
♦ BF: It was hard to take, because whenever I do a performance I prepare in advance. This time I had to *immediately* get into the "mood." I kept thinking, "Oh no, don't make me do this; I don't want to do this." But I couldn't disappoint all the people there. And the whole audience was like Howdy Doody's peanut gallery counting, "One, two, three, four . . ." along with Mike Kelley. I think that some people were uncomfortable with this, and others got into it and enjoyed it. By the end, I was really glad I did it; it was a memorable way to mark the evening—literally, since a pretty heavy paddle was used, whacking away until I was black-and-blue. It was fun and I really enjoyed it.

Again, this was embarrassing at first. It was like jumping into an ice-cold swimming pool, but I had nowhere else to go. I would have looked like a bigger idiot saying "No," so I just did it. Every part of me was going, "No, I don't want to do this," but then you just say, "Do it, because you'll look like a worse fool *not* doing it." And once you throw yourself into it, a certain "high" comes out of enduring it. When you're first counting, number one hurts pretty bad, but by the time you get to fifty you think, "Now I'm half over," and you're committed to enduring the whole process. And there's no place to go; there's no way to get away; you just have to surrender. And any time you surrender, there's a free, floating feeling—*if* you don't get panicky. At home I might panic (if I didn't have an audience) but in front of an audience I'm not going to panic, because there was too much at stake to panic in

Preparing myself for 24 hour bondage under Sheree's house. The "feeding" tube in my mouth leads up to a hole drilled in the bedroom

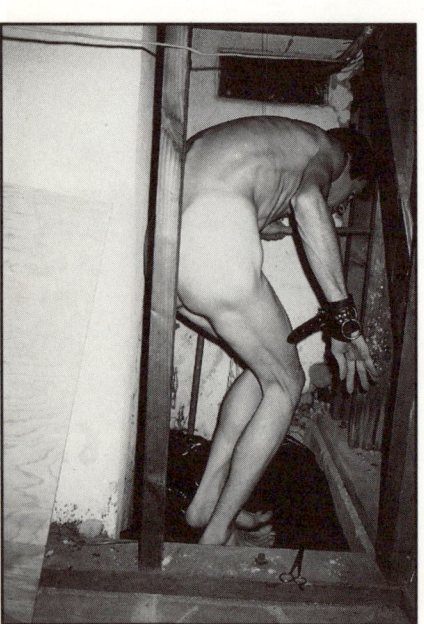
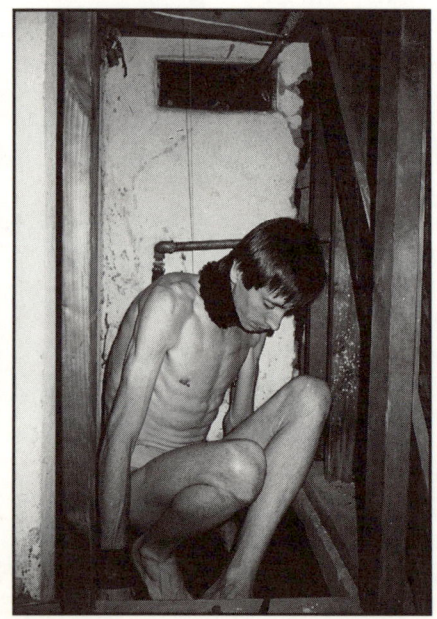
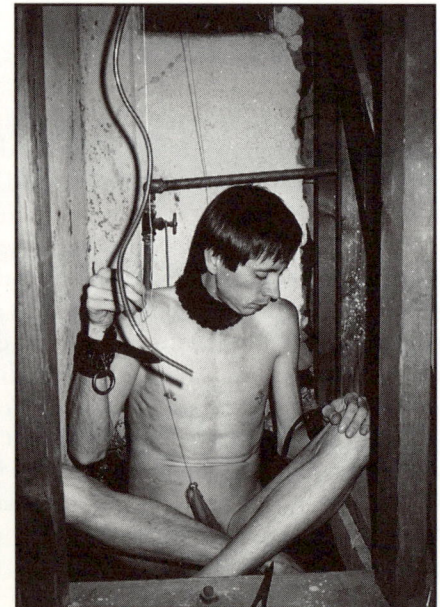

front of my friends.

♦ **AJ: How do you describe the surrendering?**

♦ BF: It's like a floating sensation of *freedom*. It still hurts, but you know that fighting it is going to feel worse, and I think, "This is what I've always wanted: to be under somebody else's control." Ultimately I got what I wanted; if I'd fought it I wouldn't have gotten what I wanted. So it was very fulfilling to have an impromptu situation like that. Plus, it was a friend's idea—it wasn't even our idea. It was based on our reputation, so I had to live up to that reputation.

♦ **AJ: Is it also a liberation to demonstrate that to other people?**

♦ BF: Oh, yes. Some people might feel embarrassed or think, "Poor Bob," but I'm living out my fantasies; I'm getting what I want. There's also a cockiness to it: showing how much I can *take*. Years before I met Sheree I went to an SM party and somebody asked for a volunteer and I volunteered—first time I had the guts. They put me in stocks and caned me and spanked me and it was pretty intense—it went on for awhile. Afterwards, there were guys sitting around naked drinking beer, and one of them said [bass voice], "Well, he's got more balls than I do!" So there's a certain cockiness to this—right, I *do* have more balls than you!

♦ **AJ: It takes courage to do something so revelatory of yourself and your deepest desires. Most people keep all that hidden—**

♦ BF: There's a certain pride in the fact that you have the guts to live out your fantasies. In this situation I didn't plan it, I just had to think fast and cooperate . . . go along with the program. That turned out to be a fun evening and also turned into a great collaboration with Mike. Based on this, Sheree is working on a photo book showing 100 asses in different stages of bruising . . . like the Yoko Ono of the '90s! [In the '60s, Yoko Ono photographed a hundred people's buttocks as an art project]

♦ **V: Most people think of SM just in terms of leather-and-chrome, not oatmeal—**

♦ BF: Not everyone's willing to go this far with it. There are different ways of controlling people, and SM still involves chrome, leather, and piercing. One of the ideas Sheree and I both loved was the idea of male chastity. She loved the idea of being fully in control of my penis—not just fucking, but even masturbating; she wanted to be fully in charge of it. I could be told not to masturbate or have sex and I certainly wouldn't have, but the idea of being in some kind of bondage all the time was exciting to me. The Pleasure Chest sells these little cock cages with straps and padlocks, but they hurt like hell, and with me they always slipped off—that genital tissue is so elusive and malleable that you can squeeze out of almost anything. So they were a ripoff; they'd charge $40-$60 for something that would always come off. I kept looking for different ways to lock up the penis; I remodeled jockstraps with cups on them, but nothing really worked.

Then we started getting heavily into piercing. I had my nipples pierced, a Prince Albert (through the urethra), and an ampallang, which goes horizontally through the head of the penis. Plus, I have a guiche, which is a pierce behind the balls, between the legs. I got the idea to take the guiche and the Prince Albert and lock them together with a big padlock, so if I got an erection I couldn't do anything about it. Sheree had the key, naturally. Sometimes I'd go for two weeks or more with no sex, no erections—except for what I call my morning *alarm cock* [bad

floor, through which Sheree can provide me with water, protein shakes, or whatever fluid concoction she desires. Los Angeles, 1983

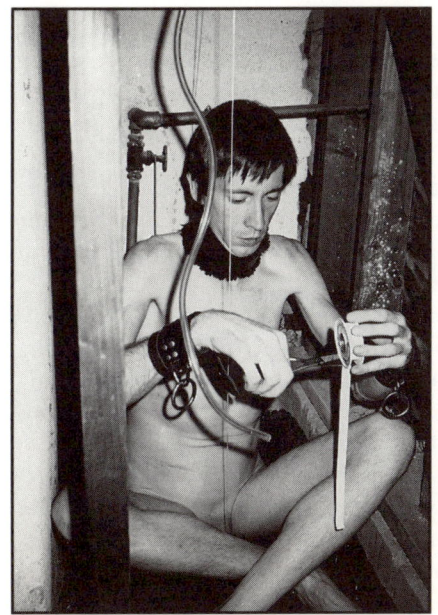
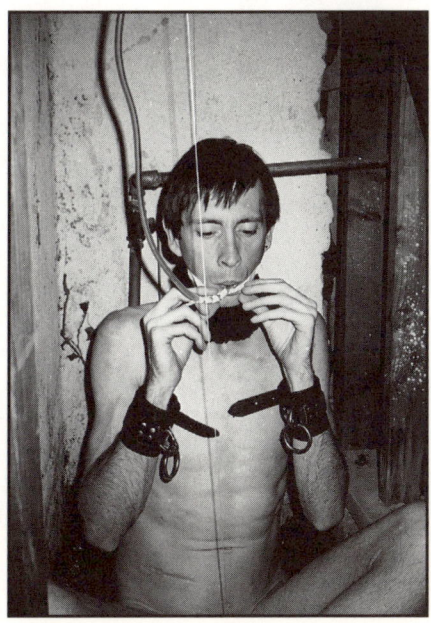
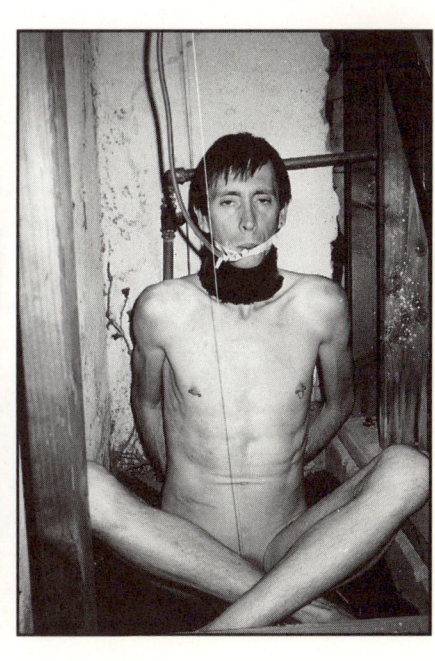

pun], which woke me up at 5 AM, hurting like hell. Again, just as with the oatmeal, Sheree had control over this part of my body, and that was the real turn-on; I loved that.

Unfortunately, even though the rings were large gauge, the Prince Albert pierce started getting thinner and thinner from being pulled on the padlock too much. My urethra was stretched out much longer than previously, so I took out the Prince Albert because I didn't want to have a slit there. The ampallang still remained, although even that was beginning to migrate a little, due to being pulled along with the other ring. That tissue is like butter, and things just kinda slide through. I'd like to have plastic surgery to make that tissue tougher, so I can go back to doing that again. Nowadays anything's possible.

Another thing we really loved was choking during sex . . . .

♦ *AJ: How did that come about?*
♦ BF: I think we saw *In the Realm of the Senses* again. This is something Sheree initiated, because I don't remember ever fantasizing about this. It always seemed like a dangerous thing to do, and I don't remember ever thinking about trying it. However, around 1982, during most of the times we fucked she would wrap this soft, velvety bathrobe cord around my neck and choke me while she was on top. The orgasm was absolutely incredible. She would squeeze it, then let the air back, then squeeze it again—it was very controlled yet very risky at the same time. I wouldn't recommend this to *anybody* unless they know what they're doing (not that *we* knew what we were doing; we were just lucky). I already knew that hanging by the neck was not a good thing to do; it's impossible to control. But the tension that built up during this choking went directly to the genitals. Sheree could stop and start and stop and start, and it was a race as to whether I would pass out or cum—whatever came first.

♦ *AJ: How does it feel?*
♦ BF: Instantaneously erotic; I can't explain it any other way. I don't want to explain it too well because that'll make people want to try it, and I don't think people should—I don't advocate it. Some part of the brain that makes orgasms more intense is affected. No matter what the situation was, whenever Sheree choked me I would instantaneously get hard—it was automatic. So that was a really good cure for any kind of distraction—especially if she were on top of me looking down at me. Sometimes she'd have this great look on her face, like she was really into what she was doing, showing a fierce intensity of control. After all, if she didn't want to, she didn't have to stop!

♦ *AJ: There's an incredible amount of trust between you—*
♦ BF: Exactly. I wouldn't do that with anybody else, ever. And when the actual orgasm comes, there's so much stress and tension built up that there's just an *explosion*. And Sheree could feel it, too.

♦ *AJ: Did you use a gag?*
♦ BF: No, just a steady pressure under the adam's apple. The windpipe gets somewhat constricted, but what mainly gets constricted is the blood flow to the brain. I'm usually breathing during all this (it's harder to breathe), but it's the constriction of blood-flow that's doing all the work. You get light-headed; it's like half-fainting and cuming at the same time—it's a really blissful experience. That's why people die when they do it alone, because there's a feeling of ecstasy and the part of the brain that stops getting blood is the rational part that says, "It's time to stop doing this now." Meanwhile, another part of the brain is saying, "This is so pleasurable—*don't* stop!" That's why people pass out and die hanging there. This should only be done with another person who is not under the influence of anything whatsoever.

♦ *AJ: Does this relate to your illness?*
♦ BF: I think it's ironic that I get turned on by being deprived of air, because I have so much trouble breathing anyway. It would be even more ironic if I died that way. But I think that's just a coincidence.

♦ *AJ: So choking was never a childhood fantasy?*
♦ BF: No; certainly as a kid I never thought of it. But there's a lot of things that became erotic after I met Sheree, like enemas. She got a job working in a place where they did enemas, and came home with this giant enema bag

Sprawled out on the bathroom floor imbibing an after-dinner wine enema. Los Angeles, 1983

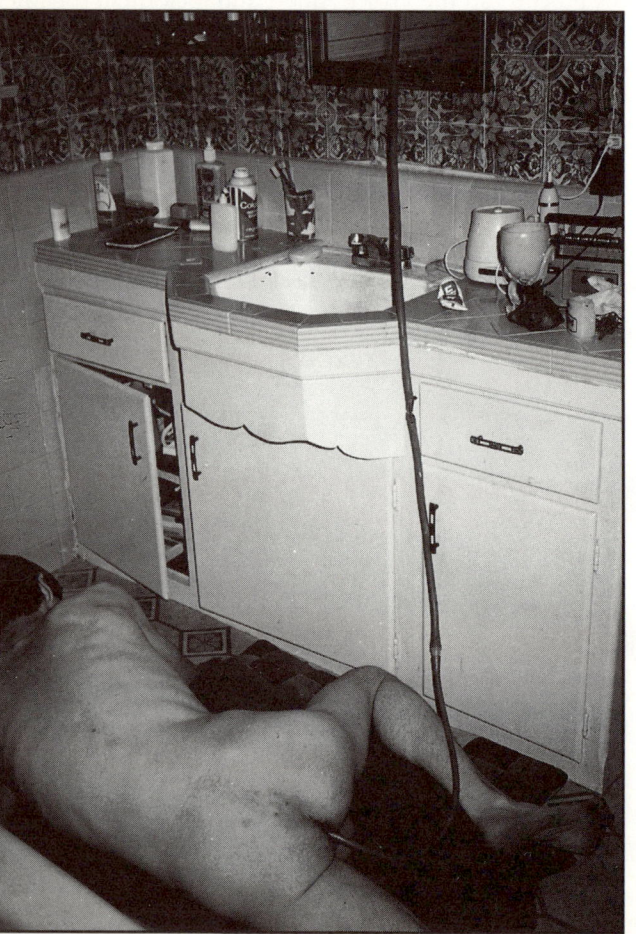

which I'd never seen before. And she put wine in it: one cup of really cheap port wine to two cups of water, and it's an immediate high—within ten minutes I'd be literally singing. The room would be spinning around and I'd be lying on the bathroom floor singing and humming and being goofy and drunk. Yet the bad effects of drinking, like getting sick to your stomach, weren't there; I was just drunk. Usually this wore off pretty quickly; it didn't last as long as a whole night of drinking. It's pretty amazing, though, and now and then I'll give myself one. I don't really count this as SM because it's too much fun. It's erotic having somebody else do it to you, but—!

I used to love all-night bondage being tied up outside in our back yard. This goes back to being a kid and hiding naked outside at night. A couple of times Sheree tied me to a post with my hands behind my back, and I stood all night long from midnight to sunrise. Then she went to sleep in the house and I had to occupy myself. The first half hour is a real turn-on, but then reality sets in: being very tired and not being able to sit down, having to endure this standing position. The perfect time to do this is during the summer when you have cold nights and then it gets warm in the morning. I love the feeling of the sun coming up; I think, "God, I made it; I didn't think I was going to get through this." During the night there's nothing I can do about it; Sheree's in bed and I can't scream because all the neighbors would wake up and see me standing there naked. As much as I might hate it during the hours in between, there's literally nothing I can do but accept the fate that I'm stuck to this post.

I love *endurance bondage* like this. Even before I met Sheree, I set up elaborate systems where I had to be tied up for a period of time and not get free until something happened. One time I froze some keys in ice, locked myself up with padlocks, and couldn't get out until the ice melted four or five hours later.

♦ **AJ: When you were tied standing to the post, could you fall asleep?**
♦ **BF:** I'd nod off and then wake myself up because I'd start to fall. This was sleep deprivation combined with restriction. I would literally count the seconds, minutes and hours just to pass the time, and almost go into a hypnotic state just from doing that. Personally, I never had an out-of-body experience doing those types of things, but I probably got close. I had moments which seemed blissful where it felt like I was floating, but I think I'm just too "Westernized"—I stay in my body. And because of my health, there aren't many envelopes of time where I can actually *do* this very often.

During these endurance tests it can get difficult. I get afraid that the house will burn down; I start thinking of everything that could go wrong. I liked when Sheree had to go out for a few hours and I was tied up inside the house, but this was very dangerous . . . although I liked it *because* of the danger—if there were ever a fire, it would be goodbye! But how often is there ever a fire? Not very often. There's also the fear of earthquakes; it seems like there's more now than before. But if that's where I am

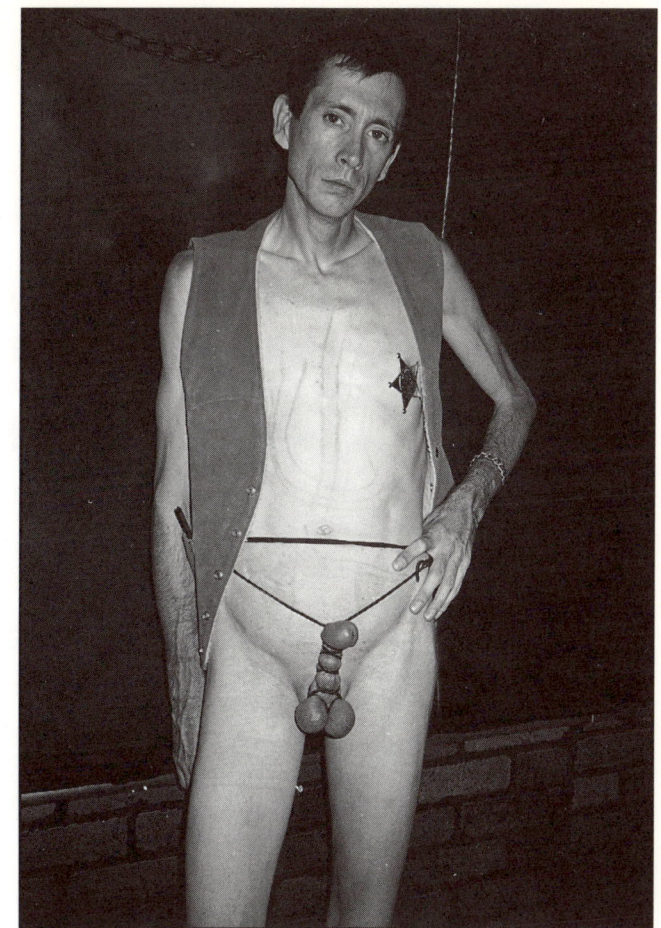

"Don't try and understand 'em, just tie and rope and brand 'em." Los Angeles, 1983

when the earthquake hits, then that's fate! However, Sheree won't do this anymore; she can't concentrate on what she's doing if I'm home tied up—she's always thinking of what might go wrong. But if I'm in a metal cage when the earthquake strikes, that's probably the perfect place to be—better than under a desk.

One time Sheree tied me to a bench outside, overnight. It's sheltered by trees but there's still an area of sky overhead. A police helicopter approached overhead—they weren't looking for *me,* but if they'd spotted this naked guy tied to a bench—! I started yelling for Sheree (I knew she was awake) and she came out and got me. There's another problem with being tied up outside: spiders. Once I was outside and I started feeling spiders dropping from a tree overhead, all night long. I could feel them bite me, but I couldn't do anything! That was *real* endurance. The next morning I had welts everywhere. Luckily I wasn't allergic to them. [shudders]
♦ **V: Luckily, they weren't brown recluse spiders—**
♦ **BF:** I just heard on the news about a woman who's almost dead from a brown recluse spider bite, somewhere in L.A. I've always liked outdoors stuff—actually, that's as outdoorsy as I get.

Parachute and 10 lb. weight on balls. Los Angeles, 1988

It's not for gliding gently down to earth, although it does send me soaring, this simple piece of black leather snapped gingerly around the balls, and attached to its dangling chain: 20 pounds or more. The feeling in my gut is not that different from falling, or a good punch in the stomach, except that this gets me hard—a stubby little hard-on, distorted from all the weight pulling at my manhood. If I weren't already sterile from bad genes I might be concerned about "hurting myself," as my mother used to say. But I'm in seventh heaven, stroking my stump of a penis as this excruciating pendulum swings back and forth between my legs, my feet pressed deeply into the carpet, but I feel weightless, head in the clouds, as high as a kite on a drug called PAIN.

♦ **AJ:** *You went to the Catholic church; didn't you get taught about the lives of the saints?*
♦ **BF:** I don't remember that, but I certainly heard about the Stations of the Cross and Jesus whipping the money-changers out of the temple—that was memorable. What I liked best was: all the different rules you had to follow. As a kid, Lent was a big thing to me; I loved the idea of giving things up. Sacrifice was a big theme that I liked and carried with me.

♦ **AJ:** *Was it a turn-on?*
♦ **BF:** Not back then, although maybe now it is. I was intrigued by (and perhaps identified with) the idea of being a martyr, especially since I was sick a lot. Saints always had something they were burdened with, and I remember thinking, "I'm suffering—maybe *I'm* a potential saint!" Suffering, sacrifice, and pain are themes of the Catholic religion; I remember going to church and kneeling for hours, enduring the horrible torture of just having to be there. It seemed like it was always hot—about 200 degrees—so that was endurance, too. As far as I know, I never related this to anything sexual.

♦ **AJ:** *Can you show us your journals?*
♦ **BF:** Yes. This one was done when I was about ten years old.

♦ **V:** *[looking at journal] This newspaper article about you says, "Bobby has a vivid imagination, as reflected by the monster models he constructed." [see page 15]*
♦ **BF:** I had all those Aurora monster model kits, and I started out making a Frankenstein. Eventually I built this board about three feet long that had three different landscapes: a graveyard, a laboratory, and a city. And all the models were interacting.

♦ **AJ:** *Nowhere is there mention of the name of your illness. Whenever people are around illness or death, it's always, "Let's not talk about it." Your art is about subjects that people are really frightened about—*
♦ **BF:** Right.

♦ **V:** *This article says you wanted to become a motion picture writer-producer-director, and that you had your friends act out parts according to your direction—*
♦ **BF:** We made a couple little movies. Yes, I think what the illness and SM have in common is: they're both subjects people are afraid to look at. I have one piece which is all about coughing, and I've read it several times and people have a hard time sitting through it—it's relentless.

♦ **AJ:** *Maybe you* **are** *a saint, illuminating subjects that make humans very uncomfortable. [laughs] Also, saints did very similar masochistic acts.*
♦ **BF:** [laughs, searching through old journal] Here's from when I was going to the Chateau, just before I met Sheree. April '79: "I got a nervous and flustered feeling. Tonight I'm going to the Chateau. I've made an appointment for two hours of bondage in 'the cell' and an hour's worth of dominance. Went back and forth as usual whether or not I should go—do I want to spend that much money? Do I want to go to the Chateau or do I want to see Mistress Mickey?" [a private mistress who advertises in the paper]. "I'm going to the Chateau. It's more expensive and they don't have the ambience some of the other dungeons have, but the people there are really into what they're doing" [good actresses]. "Besides, I want to be in one of their shows someday" [the parties they have]. "This time maybe I can get some pictures taken with my polaroid. I'm nervous, though; I feel feverish and weak. Tim" [my brother] "was supposed to come over this afternoon. If he doesn't come soon I'm going to tie myself up until I have to leave tonight. I want to prepare myself. I want to get a lot and take a lot. I want to get hard while I'm there"—usually I don't get erections there because it's too scary—

♦ **AJ:** *What do you mean?*
♦ **BF:** Well, you don't know this person, really. I went so infrequently and was such a stranger every time I went to these places that—

♦ **AJ:** *It's interesting that you need a real relationship—*
♦ **BF:** Oh yeah! The Chateau is all about money . . . quick in-and-out, and there's no time to build a relationship. People who have lots of money and can go on a weekly basis do establish a rapport with a person, so they can feel comfortable—that's different. A lot of times there's nothing sexual at the time; it's sexual later. At the time it's just the actual sensations.

♦ **AJ:** *Don't they have a rule: no intercourse?*
♦ **BF:** Usually there's no intercourse, although they may vibrate you with a vibrator or something to get you off. [continues reading] "I want to jack off while she's beating me. I hope she's good. Mistress Laura" [the one I had last time] "is out sick tonight. I don't know what the other ones are like; maybe they're better . . . No sign of Tim. I walked to the store and bought some film for my polaroid. I'm saving my piss in a bottle to be used later on" [probably to drink. I almost never did this; I thought I was going to do something with it later on but I never got up the nerve that particular time. I never drank anybody's pee or even my own but I always thought I would try to. But it was just too scary and intense for me to think about doing. It was a fantasy at the time; it wasn't something I was ready to live out or do—until I met Sheree; *then* it was different. Now it's a silly thing and it's easy to do, but at that time it was scary and an extra step I didn't want to take.]

[continuing] "I'm saving my piss in a bottle to use later on. I'm doing this thing to the hilt. Maybe it's being in control of myself that excites me, forcing myself to do things I don't want to do or go places I'm afraid of, like the Chateau. I don't want to drink piss—my own piss, anyway. I pissed into a wine glass earlier but I couldn't bring myself to drink it. Before the night's out I will. I'm going to piss into my food, too. I have all sorts of things planned for myself tonight. I want a sign to show my mistress I am sincere; I'm going to pierce my penis again and leave the pins in for her to see. I'm going to take pictures of everything and send them" [this is crazy] "to the *Dominant and SM Express.*" [It's like *Fetish Times* except that you could tell there were real people involved. A lot of times the "letters" are just written by people in an office somewhere, but *SM Express* was edited by a real

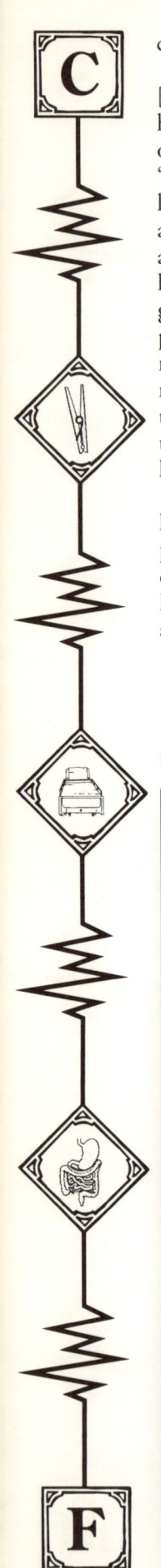

couple in New York.]

"Maybe I can find somebody I can go to regularly" [this was always the quest: to find someone you could have a relationship with]. "I want to be a slave to someone" [a year before I met Sheree, I'm talking about this.] "I can go to Val" [a woman I was seeing at the time] "for love and affection, and I can find a dominant to hurt me and make me serve. That could be a beautiful balance, and I could find it. I'm going to try the complete list letting my mistress know what I want" [that's pretty arrogant—that's not very submissive! But that's what I was paying for.] "I'm going to try the complete list, letting my mistress know what I want. Tim called; he was busy moving; we'll get together some other time. I finished typing my preferences for tonight's session; I'm going to transcribe it here because I think it is interesting and very honest."

[this is a list I wrote for the dominant to read beforehand] "I like stringent bondage, so that I can't move any part of my body. I like ropes, leather and chains. I especially like being in full suspension hung by the wrists. I like to be whipped and paddled, not only on my ass but also on my thighs and back as well." [A lot of times you go to these places and they just whip your ass; it's safer and people want to keep the marks hidden anyway, so you have to push them and let them know you want to be whipped in other places. A lot of times they *still* didn't, even if you told them to.] "I like a lot of marks and bruises to look back on, at the end of the session. If I bleed a little, too, that would be good. I can take a lot of whipping if you start out light and work up to it. I can take a lot of pain as long as I know none of it will be permanently damaging. You can put alligator clips on my nipples and attach weights; you can even pierce my nipples—I've pierced them many times myself with straight pins. I would love to have someone pierce them" [I'd been doing it myself, so I'm fantasizing having somebody else do it] "again, if there were no fear of infection. Someday I would like to have permanent nipple rings. I like cock-and-ball torture too as long as nothing is permanently damaging. I am not much into verbal abuse but I do want to be under your power. I will do anything you ask. I like the feeling of being punished by someone who understands and cares. Someday I would like to try golden showers, permanent nipple and cock piercing, and being whipped and abused in front of an audience." [everything on my wish list came true!]

"None of this is meant to restrict you in any way, only to show you where I was coming from. You have full reign with me; I have very few limits and I love testing the limits, so do what you want with me. One final thing I should tell you" [this is so silly: the fears you have when you go to these places]: "I don't usually get a hard-on during a session; that usually comes later. But I would sure like to. It might help if during the last part of the session" [if I went to a *real* mistress with this, I'd be creamed!] "when the whipping is the hardest, I were tied-up facing a wall or something so I could rub myself against it and possibly cum. It would be nice if I could, but as I said, I'm usually too afraid and excited to get an erection during a session."

♦ **AJ: You must know some "real" mistresses now—**
♦ **BF:** Oh yeah, I've met several. I never went to them because I met 'em all after I met Sheree . . . [here the journal continues; this is not the list anymore] "Now to start my hours of self-abuse before I leave for the Chateau. I'm going to keep a complete record. First I put the rice into the refrigerator to get cold" [this is for force-feeding myself]. "I have to eat dinner, don't I?" [the rationalizing tone here is sometimes pretty funny] "Wait 'til you see the dinner I have planned for myself. Right now I have to close the blinds so no one can see. I have to pee again into the bottle. I have to shit, too, but that goes into the toilet—at *this* stage of the game, anyway. Load the camera. I want a shot with alligator clips on my nipples and weights attached. That didn't work; timer fucked up and went off too soon. Try again. *Bing*—picture of my face. Not bad. Now I want my balls attached to the weights on the ceiling." [I had a parachute ball-stretcher attached to this pulley on the ceiling, and pulled that up and took a picture of it.]

Los Angeles, 1986

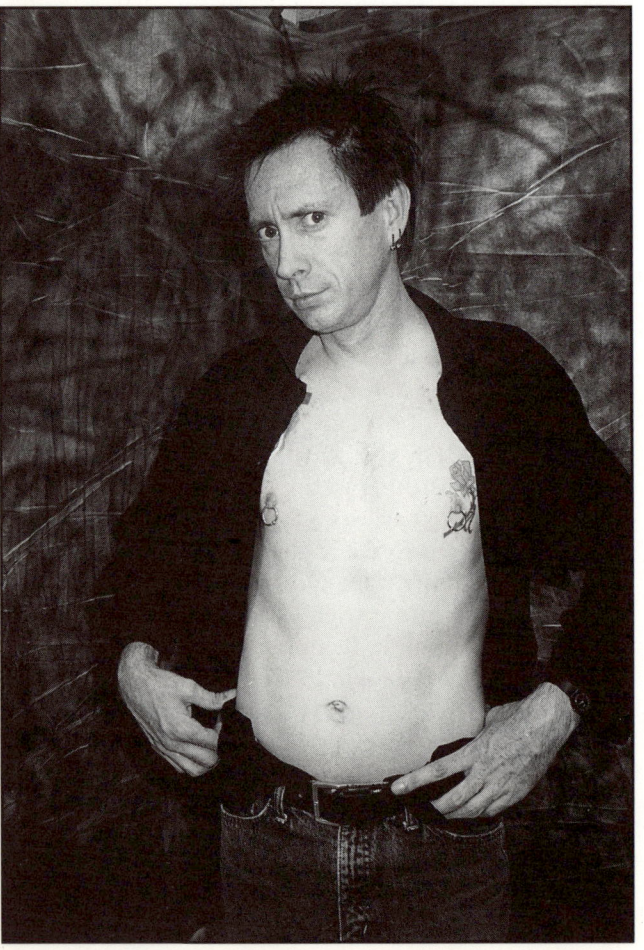

48

"Okay. Now I want to pierce my cock: two pins in the head. Have to sterilize the pins. I've done this before; that time it was eight pins all around the head of my penis. This time just two for show. It's a hard thing to do but what a feeling when it's through! What a sense of control over my own body, and it gives me a hard-on the way it looks. I want a permanent ring there—but then there'd be nothing to look forward to! The water's boiling now [this is my "sophisticated" way of sterilizing my needles: boiling water, which doesn't do a thing. The burning with a match works except that it puts all this carbon on the needle—I have a couple permanent carbon tattoos I accidentally gave myself, because all this carbon built up on the needles. You can use a disinfectant solution like Cetylcide—that's one they use at the Gauntlet. Flame is probably the best way to kill everything off short of an autoclave—*that's* the best, but not everybody has an autoclave.] "The water's boiling now. I need a rubber eraser to place on the opposite side of the skin so the pin will have something to brace itself against.

"I have everything I need: pins soaking in alcohol, cotton balls, paper towels, the eraser and my cock. I'm scared, nervous. I get a pain in the bottom of my foot all the way up my leg" [for some reason, when I pierce my penis my feet hurt. The soles of my feet get this cramped feeling—always happens. Maybe it's an acupuncture point; there's a nerve network there.] "One in—christ it hurts! It doesn't hurt so much once it's in." [these are just regular straight pins, not piercing needles, so they're not very sharp] "I'm going to go with one pin. I think it looks better that way: one pin in the head of my penis. Say cheese—smile! The pin doesn't show very well. I tried, but the pin's there to show my mistress. Now it's dinner time. 7 PM. Kate" [a writer friend] "just called and said I sounded distant—if she *only* knew! Dinner: cold rice, cold vegetables, and now I'm pissing into the plate. Just enough piss to make a nice sauce. The rest gets saved for later. I have to be tied up to eat, my hands tied behind me."

[I had to invent all kinds of different ways to tie my hands behind me; I got like Houdini. When I was a kid, Houdini was a real role model. I did magic tricks anyway, so my parents always saw me tied up on the floor—but it was okay because I was just pretending to be Houdini, trying to get out of my bonds: "Ooh, he's going to get out of that; isn't that cute?" I got really used to tying myself up. I can tie myself up in front with my teeth, and then pass my legs through my arms—I'm pretty skinny, so I can end up with my wrists behind me. I'm a minimal contortionist.]

"I have to get on my knees and eat off the floor. I have to eat the whole thing. I have to clean my plate." [at 7:30, a half hour later] "I ate *some* of it. I ate a lot. I hated doing it, and I loved hating to do it. There was too much food and I couldn't make myself eat all of it. As punishment for not eating all of my food, I will have to drink a wine glass full of piss." [this is the problem: when you're trying to dominate yourself, you just can't follow the rules and make up new rules; you pretty much just drive yourself

The *Fuck Journal* was published by Hanuman press in 1987.

totally crazy.]

♦ **AJ: It's great that you're making these commentaries while you're reading this journal—**
♦ **BF:** I can't remember what my state of mind was until I read this. "I've always chickened out after the first bitter taste, but not this time. This time I drink all of it. Besides, I need something to take my stomach pills with." [I have to take these enzyme pills, so I force myself to take them with the piss in a wine glass. However . . .] "Every sip makes me retch. I'll vomit if I try more. I got the pills down, though. There's just so far I can go being my own master! I need someone else now to push me past my limits. I need to surrender to someone else." [And that's what I was looking for, the whole time.] "Eight o'clock. I'm dressed and ready. I'll leave in around a half an hour. This is the hardest time: just waiting. No, the hardest time is walking through the door. I'll have some wine now and wait. 8:25: I'm leaving—shaking hands, fast heartbeat." [I get all worked up; that's part of the fun, I guess.]

[Now it skips to 2 AM] "That's it: I'm tired, I can't go into it all, but it was a good session. As usual I want more;

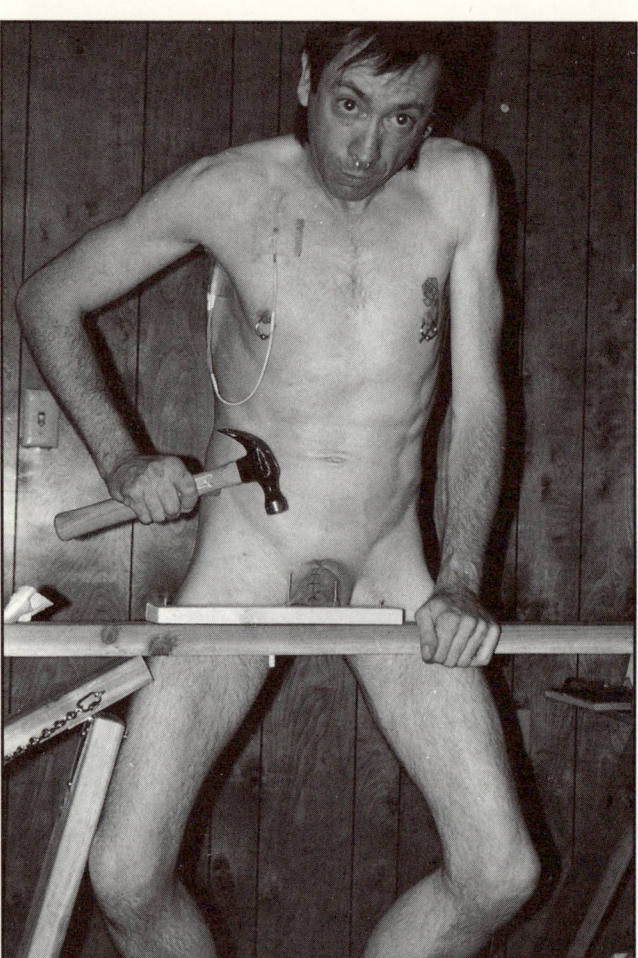

"If I had a hammer I'd hammer in the morning; I'd hammer in the evening all over this land."

The startled look on my face is due to the fact that just a second before this was taken, instead of hitting the nail on the head, I missed and almost hit my dick on the head, something I've done before and prefer not to do again, not even for a Threshold program meeting on "Auto-erotic SM," Los Angeles, 1989

don't know if I'm through tonight or not. Could jack off and sleep or I could tie myself up all night." [That was a long entry. The day afterwards I continued writing:] "I still have some of the nervousness and excitement in me. It wasn't a perfect session but it was exciting. She stuck a pin in my dick and I bled all over the place." [I know how much it can bleed, but I think it got to her. She got freaked out, too; I don't think she expected all that blood. This was before AIDS. Now that's a pretty risky thing to do. All she did was poke me with a needle; I don't think she put it all the way through, but I think she tried to put it through and—blood just spurts out of there; out of the head anyway. That's it.]

It's funny to read this and see what I was doing. In this same journal, later on, I actually nailed my dick to a board and it bled all over the place. Want to go to that part?
♦ **AJ: Yeah!**
♦ **BF:** This is August 18, 1979: "It figures I'd be writing here now when I haven't been writing for so long. What I have to tell now are more masochistic tales. Not to say other things haven't happened worth writing about; camp was the best this year that it ever has been. I'll be going there forever, it seems" [this was 1979, and I'm still going to the cystic fibrosis camp] "writing good poems before camp, good times with Jack and Laurie, too—a lot of things happening and some should be written about but I haven't felt like it. Now I feel like it. Now I'm in a *strong*, self-abusive mood and I feel like writing about it.

"The journal is on my mind, I guess, because last night this asshole named Jerry G. found the journal lying around and started reading it while I was turning the lights out at *Beyond Baroque* and shutting the windows." [this really happened, and it pissed me off.] "My journal is sitting on a desk, and he picks it up and says, 'Hey—someone's got *quite* a diary!' I look over and he's reading my journal and what part is he reading, drooling over? The pages having to do with Mistress Mickey and the Chateau—that's what. 'Hey—put that down!' I tell him. He keeps reading. 'Put it DOWN!'

"Then he starts talking about Mickey and how he saw her at the Venice town council meeting." [I guess he knows her. This guy Jerry G. has since popped up in the weirdest places. When I was doing the Janus hotline for people who call to find out about the club, I recognized his voice on the answering machine and purposely never called him back, because I knew what a jerk he was. But when I left the hotline he has since joined the club, so I see him at these parties now. He lived in Venice and came to *Beyond Baroque* all the time. He was very politically active so he went to town council meetings, and he's also into SM so he wound up going to some of the same mistresses I used to go to. He didn't know me; he didn't know what I was into; he was not a personal friend or anybody—he just picked up my journal and started reading it. And not only just reading it, but announcing to the room that "Somebody has *quite* a journal!" At that time I was not very open about all this except to a few individuals.]

[to continue:] "Then he starts talking about Mickey and how he saw her at the Venice town council meeting. I change the subject quickly and hustle everybody out of there quick. As I think about it now, it doesn't really matter who knows and who'll believe what [this guy] says anyway, but it took me off-guard—that was a shitty thing for him to do. And coincidentally enough, I've been in quite a mood again since camp. It started when I remembered that Mistress Laura said there'd be a party in September, and that there was a chance she might pierce my nipples. Anyway, I'm into it now: sleeping tied up on a bare mattress with no blankets, sheets or pillows, submerging myself into a tub of ice-cold water" [I'd put a tube in my mouth and let the water fill up way past my head so I'd just be totally submerged in ice-cold water; that was a *real* turn on—]

♦ *AJ: Wait! When did you start doing that?*
♦ BF: The first time is described in this journal here. It just came to me; I thought of something to do: water torture. I've only done it that one time when I had a really deep bathtub which enabled me to lie down on the bottom with the water going 'way above my head. First I had to stop floating. The feeling of ice-cold water slowly creeping up over different parts of your body, getting higher and higher, then steeling yourself to allow the water to rise higher and higher above your face, forcing you to breathe through a tube . . .

♦ *AJ: How long did you stay immersed?*
♦ BF: Not very long—just long enough for the water to fill up the tub: maybe five or ten minutes.

♦ *AJ: That's actually dangerous. You could die if your body temperature plummets too low—you go into hypothermia.*
♦ BF: Actually, I didn't use ice cubes or anything—just cold water out of the faucet. Also I wasn't in there very long. The *really* scary thing I did was with Becky, my first girlfriend: a totally insane, scary idea I came up with. We were into golden showers then. I loved those ceramic soap dishes that were built into the wall—then you'd have something to chain yourself to. So she would chain me by the neck and I'd be in the bathtub all night long. That's probably when I first started getting into pee; I'd have to pee, so I'd just be peeing all over myself while I was tied up in the bathtub by the neck, with my hands tied behind my back so I couldn't move. Usually I would just say, "Becky, would you do this? And this?" Like a lot of people, after a while she'd get tired of me asking her to do things, and get frustrated (although she would do them anyway).

This one time I wanted her to tie me up by the neck in the bathtub so I couldn't get out, then turn the hot water on with the plug in. For some reason, the consequences—what might happen—didn't occur to me (I hadn't read enough articles about people who've been scalded to death to realize that this was seriously dangerous). And to top it all off, I knew that I'd probably be screaming for her to turn the water off, and I didn't want her to give in to my pleading, so I told her to go downstairs and listen to a record or something so she wouldn't hear me. This was like, *out there* early on—I almost ended my SM career before it started!

Becky did it. She started the hot water, the plug was in, and it was getting hotter and hotter, getting up to my feet, ankles, and finally I'm realizing: "This is *serious*." Then I'm screaming for her to come get me. Luckily she either heard me or instinctively got it in her head to come up. I said, "This isn't working," and she figured I was right and let me out. But that was close . . . I could have been seriously burned. It started coming up my ass crack—ugh! [shudders] But I survived it, and it's a real turn-on to think about, still.

I have one other "severe" story to tell. Janus L.A. was a club for SM people from all different walks of life—now it's called Threshold. Basically it's a social support group for people into SM; they have parties and demonstrate safe techniques. It's been going on since the early '80s. Sheree and I had been doing SM for about a year together, and then she started to feel we were the only people in the world doing this. She didn't believe me when I told her there were others out there. Even though we'd been to a couple of professional parties, she claimed that people who lived it as a lifestyle were so unusual . . . it didn't exist anywhere else but with us. And she was getting uncomfortable with that. I said, "No no, it's out there," but she felt lonely and isolated, because at this time there were no support groups that we knew about.

So we put an ad in the *L.A. Free Press* to meet other couples into SM. A woman and a man answered our ad—they were the only couple who called us back. Lots of single guys called wanting to meet Sheree, but we wanted a couple. We didn't necessarily want to *do* anything with them; we wanted somebody to talk to. So we met this couple (she was a professional, but was actually into it in

Sewn up and nailed to a two-by-four. Threshold program on "Auto-erotic SM." Los Angeles, 1989

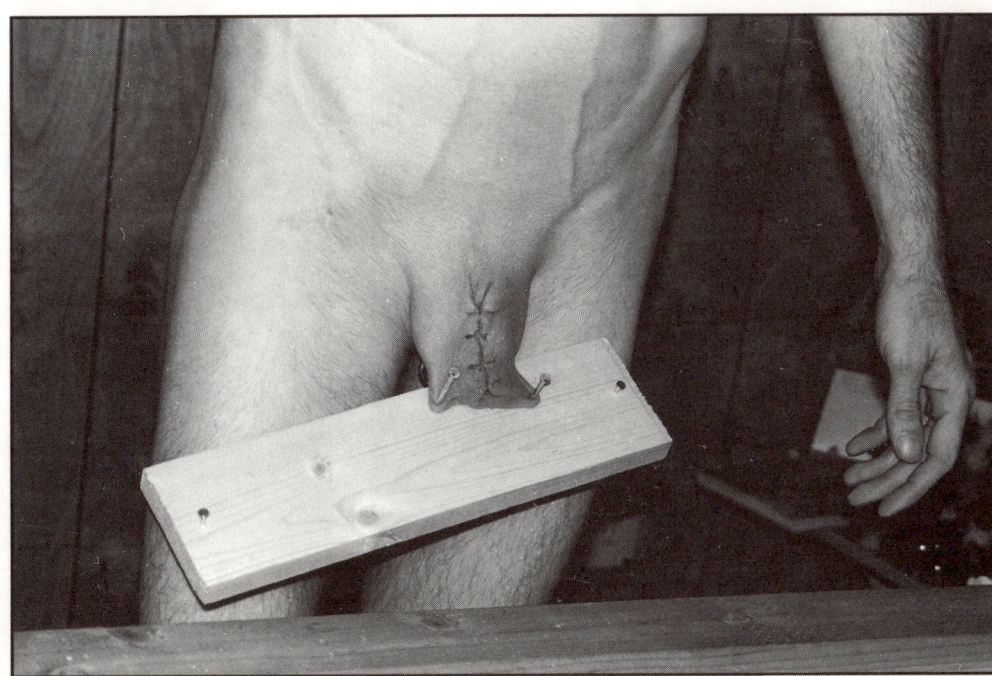

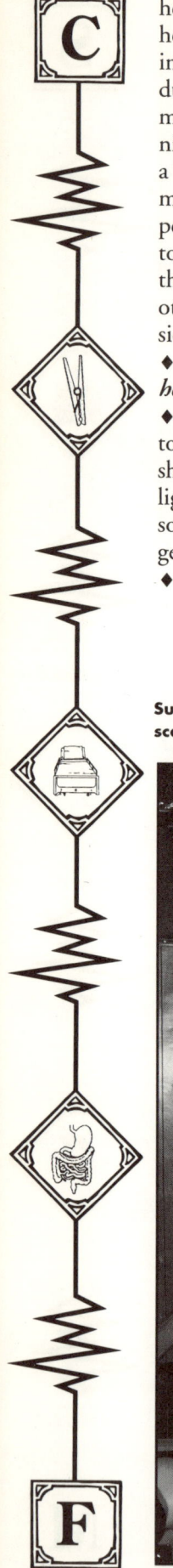

her own life). They were very nice: Mistress Victoria and her husband who was submissive to her. We started seeing each other socially; we'd go out to dinner. She had a dungeon in Whittier (where Nixon was born) and she made a living off it; that was what she did. She was really nice and very attractive, too, and through her we went to a bondage SM party where we met a lot of future Janus members. It was at a professional house, but filled with people who were really into it as a lifestyle. This was a totally different atmosphere than the Chateau. Most of the mistresses present had worked there, but there were other patrons who you could see had a relationship outside of the Chateau.

♦ **AJ:** *Did you do anything with Mistress Victoria and her husband?*

♦ **BF:** After we got to know them, we played a little bit together. She and Sheree did a few things together, and she did things to me. We played with each other very lightly, but nothing heavy—it was more just to talk and socialize and share things with, and to go to parties together.

♦ **AJ:** *How did you and the other submissive get along?*

♦ **BF:** Basically we just waited on the other two. I think he may have been naked and I got naked, but we didn't do anything together ourselves. Sexually there was more between the two women; there was nothing between us two men. That's when Sheree first got into bisexuality in an SM context. I think the guy was a little older than I was. We saw each other quite a bit and then it just sort of dropped off. She came over for lunch a few times when she was free, and we went to San Francisco together—that's when we first met the Janus people in San Francisco, and that's how we got into Janus later on. But at this party, it was the first time I'd ever been in public with Sheree in an SM context. And it was good for Sheree to be around Mistress Victoria, who had been doing this professionally for years—she knew a *lot*.

This was the first time Sheree had a girlfriend who was doing the same things she was doing, and she really felt good about that. It was the opening night for this bondage place called Ball and Chains on Santa Monica Blvd, and the two of them tied me to a big bondage table in one of the dungeons. I'm tied up on my back, spread-eagled on this table, and it's a funny table. It can move all

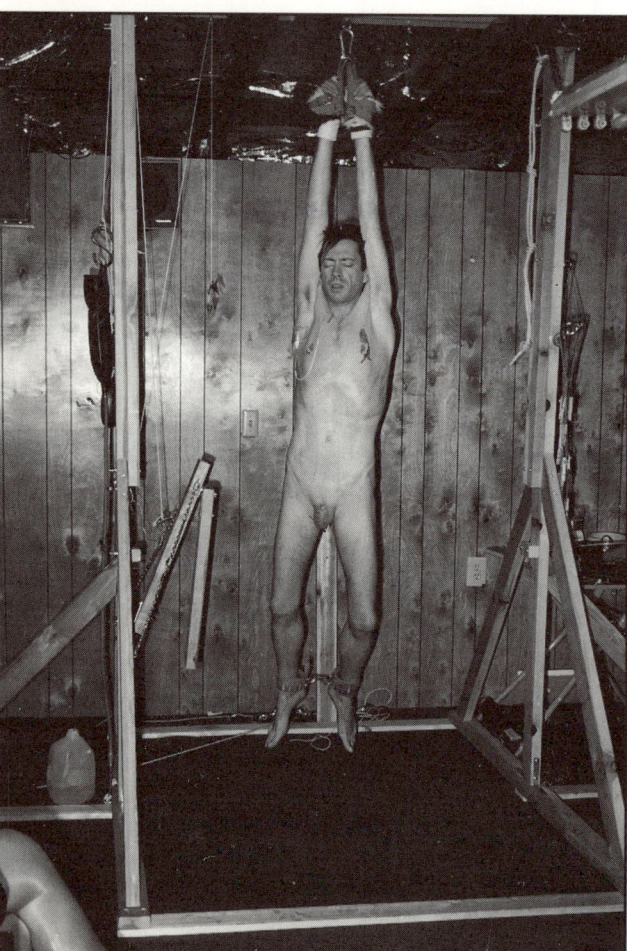

Suspended from, what Jesse Helms calls my "auto-erotic scaffold." Threshold program. Los Angeles, 1989

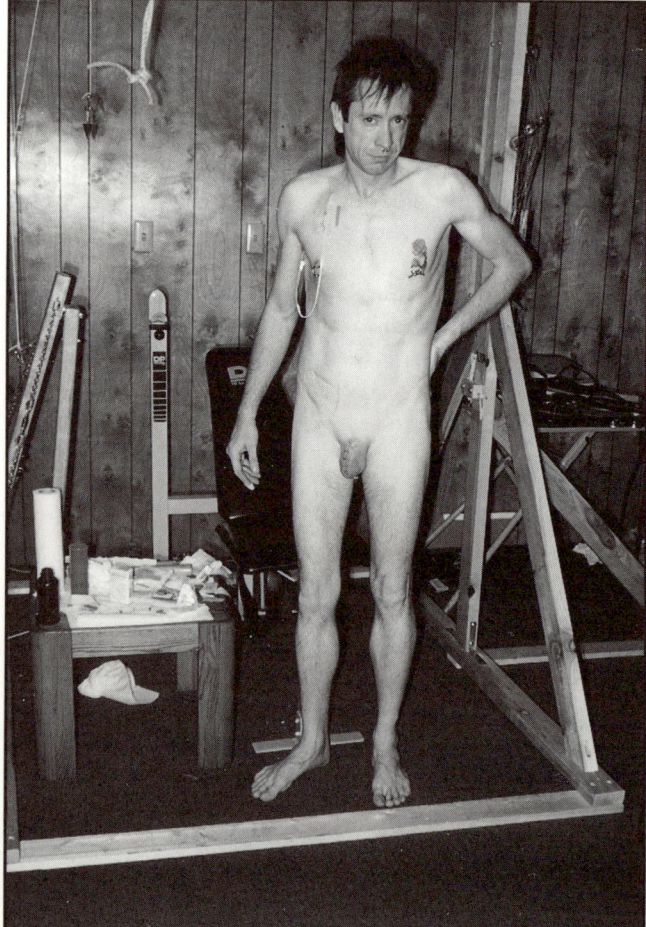

I keep the audience and my penis in stitches at a Threshold program on "Auto-erotic SM." Los Angeles, 1989

the way over so you're upside down, then all the way over so you're right-side up; it can turn 360 degrees. I was tilted up with my feet higher than my head, and both of them were whipping me on the thighs with riding crops, back and forth—which is pretty intense. While that was happening, this professional mistress who works there came up to me and asked, "Are you into chains?" (I'm tied up; my arms are spread-eagled.) I said, "Yeah!" although I shouldn't have said anything; what did I know at the time? She took this cat-o'-nine-tails made of dog-collar chains and went "Whack! Whack!" as hard as she could. I started screaming—I scream a lot anyway, and Sheree and Victoria didn't know what was going on—it was above them.

For months afterward I had these black scabs caused by the chains—it looked like a truck drove over me. I'm boney; I was thinner then than I am now, so there was no meat on my chest at all, and that's where she was whipping me. To get back to the story: everybody was hushed; there were lots of spectators around (that's what people do at these parties: watch other people get whipped). And usually nobody ever gets very heavy; it gets *somewhat* heavy and has a certain level of intensity to it that people accept . . . but this was *'way* over people's limits; they couldn't believe it! People who have become friends of mine since then said, "I remember you that first night, and I thought you were really *something,* taking it." I said, "I didn't have any choice!" So I started to gain a reputation, that's for sure! I still don't know if it was *respect,* but it was certainly the beginning of my reputation as somebody who is really *out there!* [laughs] Sheree took photos of me, and it looked like a tractor drove over me.

♦ *AJ: So this was really* **uncool?**
♦ BF: Yeah; it was totally uncool and the owner knew it. I think the woman was on drugs (a lot of people took quaaludes in those days, and the owner offered me a couple quaaludes to shut me up; he was really afraid this might ruin his opening night). To tell the truth, once it was over I felt incredibly excited, and I loved telling the story. I would think about it afterwards and go, "Hmm . . ." Sheree was totally embarrassed; naturally she felt responsible. Here's her slave, and he gets attacked like this. But it happened so fast that nobody expected it; it was *so* uncool that who would think it would ever happen? And I've never seen that level of disrespect since—and I've been to a *lot* of parties. Nobody's ever gone up to somebody else's slave while the mistress is working on him and started whacking away . . .

♦ *AJ: What happened to that woman?*
♦ BF: Most of those women don't work at those places for very long. The owner made all kinds of excuses for her and I think she may have gone home early, I don't know exactly what happened to her. It certainly changed the entire evening! After that, people just sort of sat around talking more than doing anything. It was pretty weird. And this was our first public party! Luckily, Sheree was with this friend whom we were able to talk with afterwards, because if this had been Sheree's first experience, I

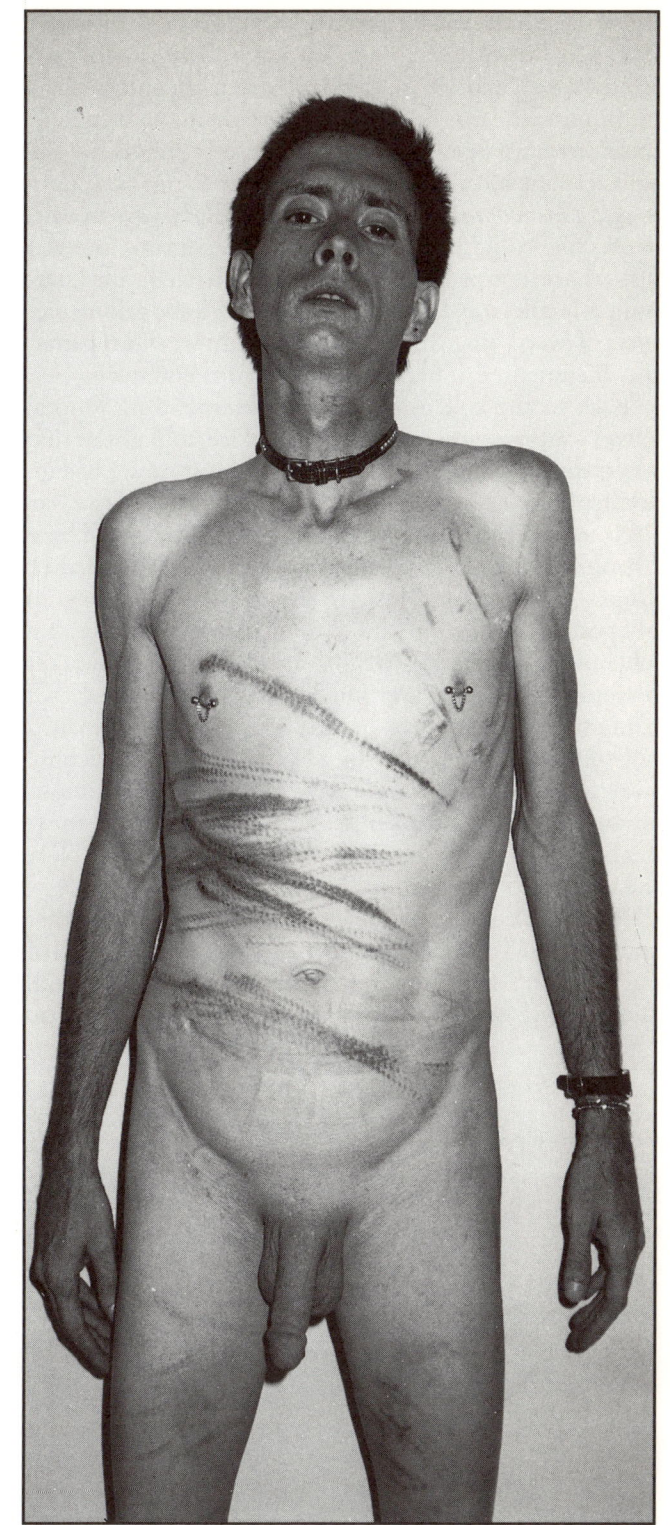

The aftermath (or should I say afterglow) of the first SM party where Sheree and I actually played together in public. Los Angeles, 1982

I get the shit beat out of me at this club called Ball and Chains. I'm tied up in front of a room full of people as she [Sheree] and Victoria whip me on the thighs with riding crops. Someone named Erica asks me if I like chains. When I say yes she takes out this dog chain and beats me across the chest with it. At home, alone with my Mistress, we fuck and the pain disappears as I cum inside her. —*Fuck Journal,* **August 13, 1982**

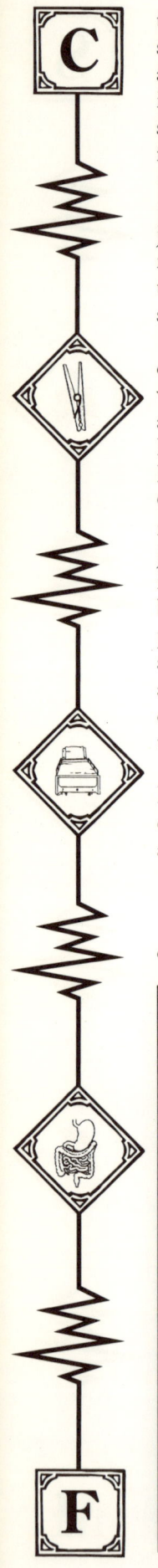

think she would have stopped a lot of things. Even today she's a little sensitive about that event, but now it's just another great experience that I survived. She internalized it, thinking she should have done something to stop it, or shouldn't have been in that position to begin with—she feels responsible and inadequate about it, but . . .

♦ **AJ: This woman could have done real damage to you?**
♦ BF: She could have cracked or broken a rib—she was just whacking on bone with a chain. It bled. The sternum is fragile, too. One thing—Sheree started taking pictures of everything we did, so every event we did together she documented. That's our little semi-tragic story.

Back to the cold water [finds corresponding journal entry] "Submerging myself in a tub of ice-cold water; that was great: peaceful and hypnotic. And just now I had an accident. I nailed the head of my cock to a board the way I saw in a magazine the other day, and got so excited by it I had to try it. I'll try to drive the nail in a little further. Oops—I missed, and just [I thought] tapped the tip of my poor cock. It didn't hurt; the nail was handling that job, but shit—it started swelling up immediately. I thought it would *never* stop, and imagined it bursting and that being the end of me and my sex life the way I know it. I pulled the nail out as quickly as I could, using an alcohol swab to stop the bleeding. The penis bleeds an enormous amount: just one little pinprick and it looks like a murder had taken place; imagine what a nail hole is like! Now there's a big black knot on the end of my dick!

"All I can do is hope it goes away. I'm amazingly calm. I've had accidents before and they always seem to turn out all right. After extracting the nail, stopping the blood, and putting ice on my throbbing knot, I tied myself up on my stomach, wrists attached to ankles—don't ask how, it's too complicated. I got excited and jacked off and when I looked down—shit, the whole towel and mattress were soaked with blood. There were some spatters of blood far away from the towel, even, which made me think for a second—more than a second—that I'd really fucked myself up and was cuming blood. I stayed calm, though, and methodically cleaned everything up just like Tony Perkins, my blood swirling down the sink like Janet Leigh's. After that I pissed in the sink—thank god it came out yellow and not red, like I was afraid it might. I'm still not through. I'm going to try and keep this mood going for two weeks when I plan on seeing Mistress Laura again. And two weeks after that maybe she'll put a nice pair of rings through my nipples. I'm excited again just thinking about it, but I have to slow down now. I've got to stretch this out for a long time. I'm going to make it a lifestyle, not just a mood."

In 1979 I was trying to go to school; in two months my sister would die; I was under a lot of stress, and this was a release of all that stress. Plus I think I was coming to a whole epiphany with all this . . . working up to a frenzy with it.

♦ **V: How did your sister's death affect you?**
♦ BF: We expected it; it was amazing she lived as long as she did. She was much younger than I, so we weren't *that* close, but we were very connected in that we had the same disease. I always knew that her fate might be mine. There was a lot of guilt involved, because every time she got sick I kept hoping she would die because she was *so* sick. It just seemed like there was no future for her at all; she couldn't do anything but stay home all day. Even if she'd *try* to do things, it seemed so pathetic—for her own sake we wished that she would stop fighting it, but she fought really hard to stay alive. So some guilt about all that was relieved when she finally did die around Christmas time.

♦ ***AJ: If you really know you're going to die, perhaps you can feel free to do your heart's desires and live your life more fully without compromise. You can go right to the heart of what you really want to do with your life—***
♦ BF: I think about that a lot. If you don't have long to live, you want to pack as much in as you can and get as much sensation in your life as you can. I see a lot of teenage boys and guys in their early

Getting my nipple pierced at the Gauntlet. Los Angeles, 1983

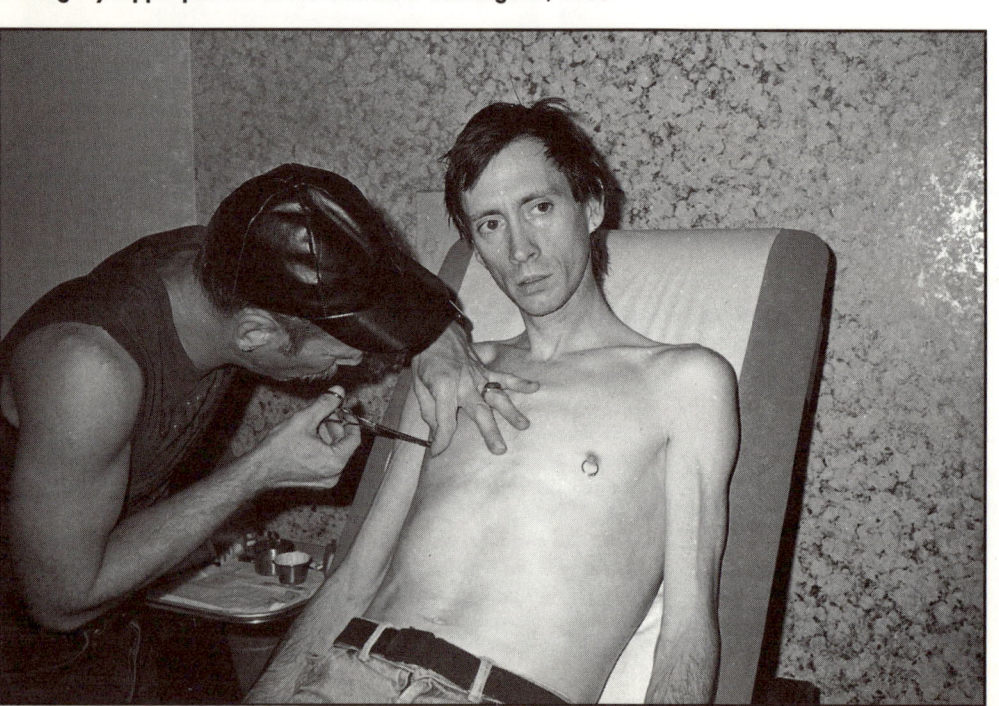

twenties with CF, and they're not necessarily into SM (they wouldn't talk about it if they were) but they are kids who like really fast cars. I know several who have smashed up car after car—they drive like maniacs. One who recently died was heavily into drugs—he didn't die from drugs, but . . . these kids are *wild*. And I think this is the way *I* chose to be wild. I didn't have any connections with the people who did drugs (in many ways I was kind of conservative) but perhaps this is my wild streak, my side that is comparable to these guys who have almost death wishes, as far as driving and drinking and whatever else they do.

♦ **AJ:** *In facing death, one can unleash a creativity that's beyond "Oh, I have a short time to live, so I have to cram in all these crazy experiences."*

♦ **BF:** There are shamanistic cultures that believe in "little deaths." You can experience these little deaths along the way, and they prepare you for the "big death," or they release a lot of tensions linked to death. That's what a lot of SM activity is: these little, planned-out scenarios that are like dying: "I'm underwater and I could drown!" But it's only for five or ten minutes; it's only experiential and then it's over and you walk around and live out your day, *relieved*. A lot of times after these SM experiences I'll be totally at peace; I'll feel great. And I won't have to think about it anymore; it's just something I did and got worked up to do. Especially in the early days, these feelings would build and build until I'd have to do it, but once I'd had enough sensation and gone far enough, there was an immediate release afterwards, and I felt peaceful, calm and sharp—like I could do anything.

♦ **AJ:** *But you're a rarity; you're quite "well-adjusted." In the "normal" world, a lot of people never achieve these kind of releases and find peace—*

♦ **BF:** There's a lot of judgmental negativity going on; maybe a lot of people do think of doing things like this but immediately dismiss them as "crazy."

♦ **AJ:** *Even in the SM community, you're rare—*

♦ **BF:** But I've met a lot of people who have had similar experiences, thoughts and feelings since childhood. A lot of people don't talk about this; what's rare is finding people who *talk*. There are people who have experiences but stay mum. I've known several women who have done lots of things since childhood.

♦ **AJ:** *You have a clarity, honesty and transparency in your whole life—*

♦ **BF:** I think going into the arts gave me a way to express all this. I learned that my writing was best when I wrote about things that I knew—which was this subject, so a lot of my pieces just fell together. There are probably people who don't write and aren't artistic who do this stuff, but have no way to communicate or demonstrate it to other people.

♦ **AJ:** *It's very important to have that channel—*

♦ **BF:** Yes . . . It was always my fantasy that when I got sick enough to the point where I wasn't going to make it, I would do the ultimate acts: I would hang myself by the neck, castrate myself—things I'd always fantasized about but couldn't do because they were too risky or final. I had

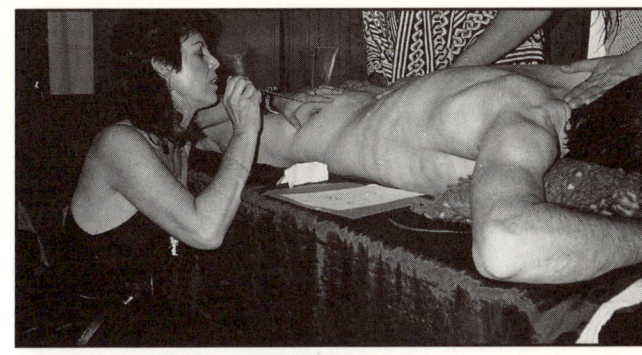

A kiss from the Mistress, after she brands me with her initials, under the tutelage of Fakir Musafar at a Janus program meeting. Los Angeles.

this idea that I would go into the desert with this scaffold I'd built for my shows, set it up and do the ultimate—anything I wanted to do to my body, because I didn't have to worry about surviving it; the point was *not* to. It's a great fantasy, but there are several things wrong. First of all, that could only happen at a point where I absolutely couldn't go on anymore, and then I'd probably be too sick or weak to do anything except lie in bed. And I couldn't get anyone to help me, because I don't want anyone else to bear that responsibility. Plus, as long as my parents were alive, I couldn't do that to them: have that be the last thing they remember about me. But it's still a hot fantasy!

It's a turn-on to think that I could do absolutely anything to myself, and it's also a total control thing. I've had two good friends in the SM world who have shot themselves. They were both incredibly controlling . . . submissive, but very controlling. And one had gotten old—he wasn't feeble, but he started feeling ineffectual in lots of ways. One day he went to his carport and put a shotgun in his mouth and blew his head off. A week later this other friend, a transsexual who just didn't feel she fit in anywhere (as a man she had been a Marine and was still very much into guns; she had a huge gun collection. She was Sheree's submissive for awhile, and the two of them used to go out into the desert and shoot at rocks, just target practice) killed herself, out of desperation and because her hormones had gotten so completely out of whack. She used *two* guns, one on either side of her head, just to make sure nothing went wrong. Very efficient!

♦ *AJ: Was this a typical suicide, where life isn't working and the person is desperate?*
♦ BF: I don't know. With the first guy, everything in his life was planned out, and he had planned this suicide for months. His family didn't know about his lifestyle, yet he had been involved in the scene for well over twenty years. He led a very meticulous and orderly life; he was the kind of guy who had tools, and every tool had its outline painted on the pegboard so you knew where everything went. And he died the same way he had lived: fully in control.
♦ *AJ: What would have happened if he had disclosed his life?*
♦ BF: I don't think he cared what people thought, but if he had told other people about this part of his life, he might have lost control over it. Whereas I like surrendering . . . *losing* a certain amount of control—but *I* determine the surrender and who I surrender to. Because I'm fully aware how out-of-control my life is: some days I wake up and can't breathe at all. Then I have to adjust, and do something different than what I had planned to do.

People always say, "Oh yes, the masochist is always in control," and they always say that in a *pejorative* way. But I don't think it's that bad to want to be in control of your life; it's when you control *other* people's lives that you get in trouble. But to want to control your life, or have control with adaptability—this almost goes back to that AA prayer: "Give me the strength to change what I can, and accept that which I can't change—and learn to know the difference." That's a good prayer for lots of reasons, and without knowing it, that's the way I've always lived.

That's why a good SM relationship is one where the dominant is in control of what he or she wants to do, and the bottom is in control of what he or she wants to do. The great part is when they're both getting what they want; when they've controlled their lives to the point where they're both in the position to get it. I always hate people who do scenes and then complain: "So-and-so's always asking me to do *this!*" I think, "Then why are you a dominant? You're there to *do* it!"
♦ *AJ: I sometimes hear people say that being dominant is the hardest job—*
♦ BF: The fact that people look at it as a *job* is what's wrong! To me, there are so many things in my life that are hard to do, so I can't understand people complaining about things in life that give *pleasure*. Sometimes life is work!
♦ *V: Back to the beginning of your relationship with Sheree—*
♦ BF: I met Sheree in October 1980. In November 1980 I wrote in my journal: "November 28. In bed at mom and dad's." [this was probably written during Thanksgiving] "The start of a new journal. I haven't written much in the old one lately. It was almost finished anyway. Maybe these new pages will inspire me into doing something. Maybe my new life will inspire me. It seems like there *is* a new life going on: Sheree—Mistress Sheree. I think about her all the time. I've told the whole family about her; I try to work her into every conversation. She lives in

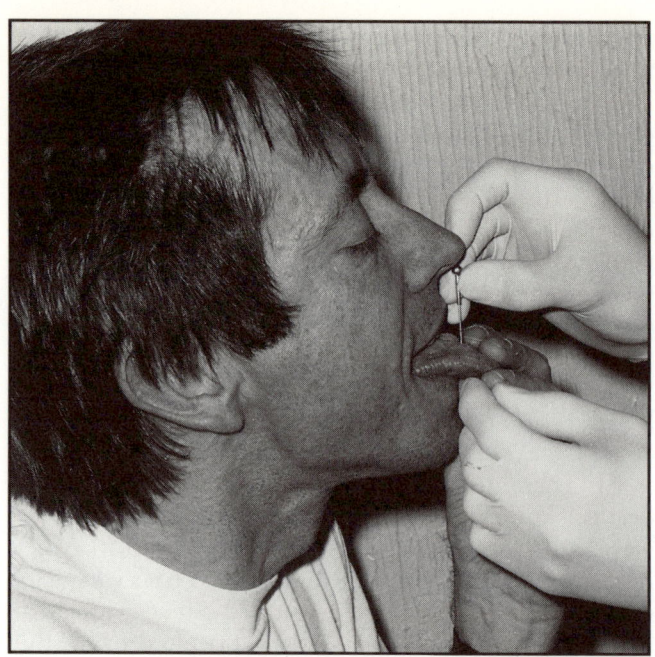

New tongue jewelry. Los Angeles, 1990

Westwood, she has two kids, she has a crazy streak, but I can't tell her the best part: I am totally submissive to her. She is the kind of woman I have fantasized about all my life. But this is no fantasy, this is no game, it's the real thing.

"I'm giving myself to her completely. I want to do whatever she wants me to do. This is crazy; I've only been with her these past two weekends—that's all it's been—and I know already that I'm in love with her. How do I know? Well, I think about her all the time. I want to call her—I should say I *need* to call her; 'want' is a controlling word" [She came up with the idea that I could never use the word "want" around her] "and I'm trying to eliminate all my controlling nature. I need her. Even after only two weeks, I know I would feel a great loss if I could not be with her. I don't know how to explain all this or even where to start, but it's important that this relationship be recorded. This is a different kind of relationship.

"Again, just thinking about her: I want to jack off." [*that's* very romantic!] "I am wearing her black panties and the head of my penis is sticking out from the top of them. I can feel it getting thicker. I am playing with the ring I have inserted through the foreskin. It's *Sheree's* ring now, and Sheree's penis. She said tonight that she might like to see me tattooed. Maybe she'd have me tattooed on my penis." [that came true; last year I got a tattoo around my penis and balls] "I'm not writing very well right now; this is too much to tell and to think about. I can only do it in bits and pieces. Right now I want to stop writing and masturbate and sleep and possibly dream about her. Sunday seems so far away." [that's when I'd see her again]
♦ *AJ: Did Sheree ever see these journals?*

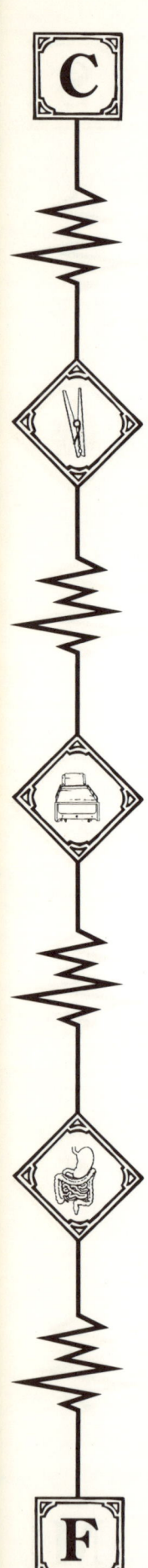

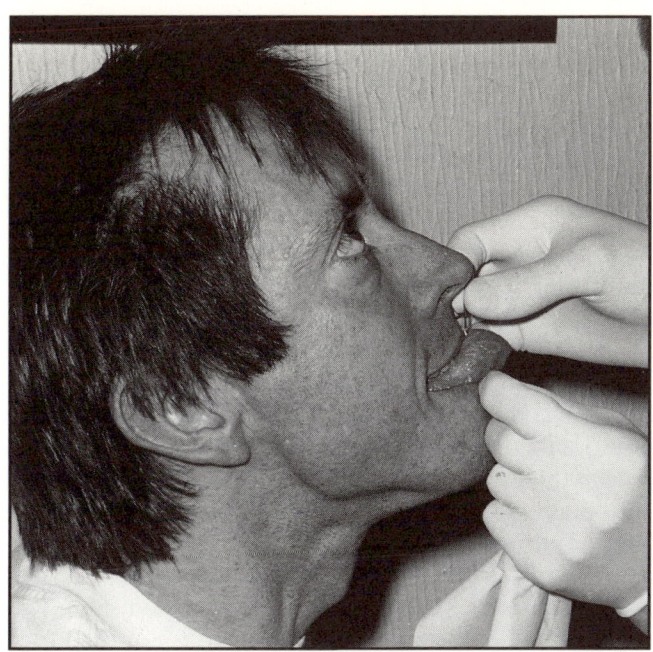

♦ BF: Oh yes. After awhile I'd write journals solely for her to read. The *Fuck Journal* [a book published by Hanuman Press] was her idea. It records a whole year of fucking and SM—just little paragraphs every time we fucked in 1982. She wanted a record of every time we fucked, and it was all done in this little literary engagement calendar book which has drawings of different authors. In between are all these scrawlings about us fucking.

[looks through journal, reads] "In bed at mom's. Can't sleep. Anxious about going home. I'm actually excited as if I were going on a big trip. I'm going home. Sheree will be there, and I will not be able to spend enough time with her before I have to go to Yucaipa on Tuesday. How much time is enough? Right now, the way I feel, no time is enough."

[Flipping through journal] Now I'm back in Yucaipa teaching kids again—the journal gets real boring . . . Now I'm drunk . . . Here's the night John Lennon got shot. We were at her brother's place in Malibu and she was tying me up and we did some things. Then we got in a car and heard all these John Lennon songs on the radio and were wondering, "Why are they playing all these John Lennon songs all night long?" Finally we found out he got shot.

We'd have spurts where Sheree would just not want to do SM anymore. I'd be angry and we wouldn't do it for a long period of time, then we'd do it again. So the journals go back and forth: "I'm her slave again . . . I'm not her slave . . . I'm her slave again."

[reads from *Fuck Journal*] "Fucking on acid—it lasts forever." [this is one of our three-day parties] "I'm so deep inside her I feel like I'm inside-out. Still flying—I can barely feel my penis but it's hard, and while we're fucking, the sound of an exercise record comes on the radio: 'Up Down/Up Down . . .'"

"She lets me fuck her and sleep in her bed as well. We fuck with me on top and sometimes on our sides, tied up, face down, spread-eagled in bed, blindfolded and whipped, butt vibrator up my ass; turned over, spread-eagled, fucked and whipped some more. We fuck again, slow and steady, me on top, no bondage. We fuck after a terrible day of nothingness, me on top, her hands around my neck choking me into a shaking, quivering cum. Tim's birthday.

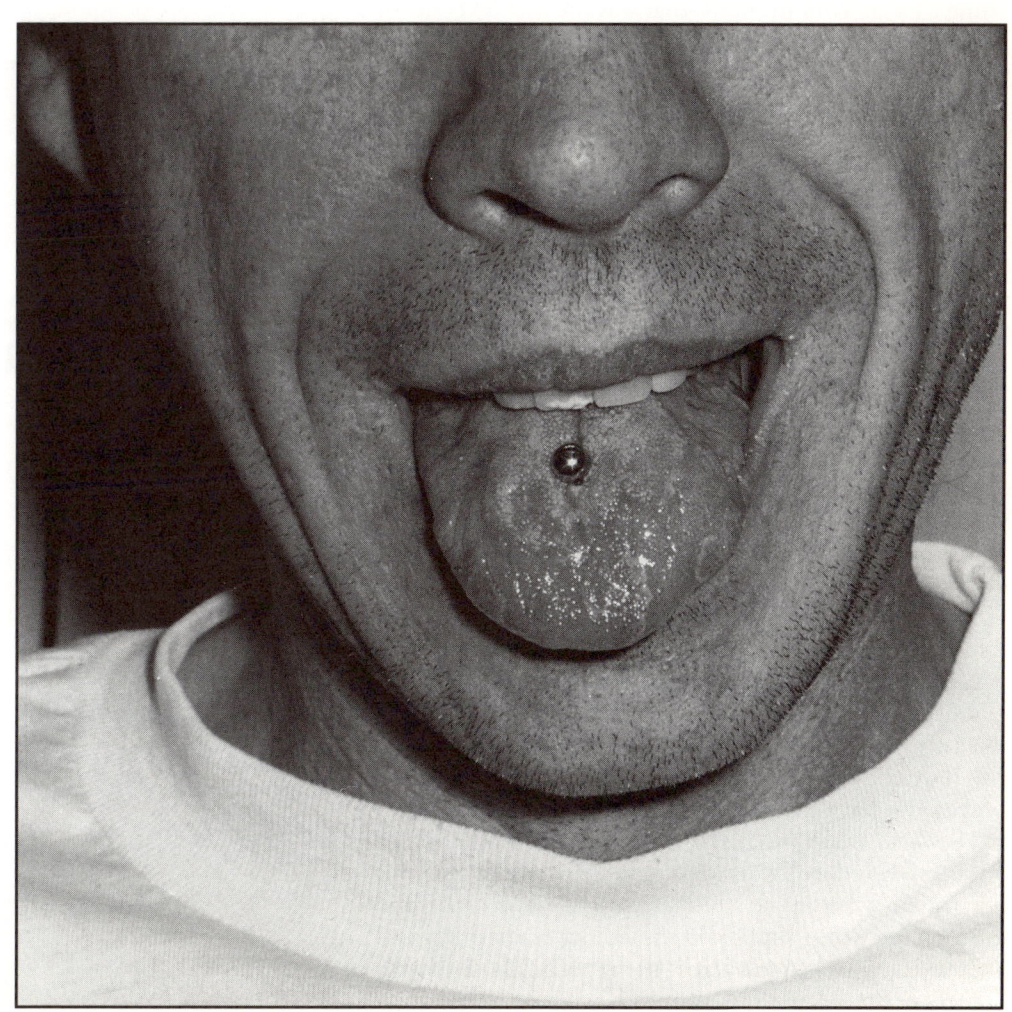

Drinks and presents. I show off my pierced nipples and later lick her nipples and eat her under the covers until we fuck and she chokes me. We cum."

♦ *AJ: Maybe you can describe one of those three-day parties—*
♦ BF: They weren't SM parties; basically poets might be visiting *Beyond Baroque* and we'd have them over. One was a New Years' Eve party that just stretched out; another was when a gay couple who were friends of ours got married.

♦ *AJ: These weren't sex parties—*
♦ BF: Although . . . after a couple glasses of wine I usually had my clothes off! Somebody once sent me a postcard that said, "I never went to one of Bob Flanagan's parties, because I heard that he would take his clothes off and be naked and run around with his piercings showing, and I didn't want to see that."

♦ *AJ: So your friends got used to seeing you naked—*
♦ BF: That's probably why they hung around: waiting for something weird to happen. It didn't, usually.

♦ *AJ: Can you describe a typical scene?*
♦ BF: We never had a "typical scene." We tended not to repeat a lot of things. With us, a typical scene had a lot more to do with attitude—with me being submissive and doing work around the house, running Sheree's errands—really boring! Most of the SM stuff we did was just me doing a lot of work for her—that was the *real* SM part of it! She would tell me, "Do this!" and the more direct she was, the more exciting it was.

♦ *AJ: In an authoritarian tone of voice?*
♦ BF: Sometimes. We'd get into arguments; it was hard for me to stay submissive if I disagreed with something she said about art or philosophy, because I'm also very opinionated. Our relation got tangled, especially after we started to collaborate artistically. And if she got stoned she made no sense to me at all. Then it was hard for me to stay submissive.

One time we were with Jim Ward and some friends of his in a car looking for a restaurant. Of all days, it was Mother's Day—the worst day to be looking for a restaurant. This happened a lot when Sheree and I went out to eat: *total disaster.* Either the restaurant would be closed or you couldn't get in. Then somebody else would suggest another restaurant, and . . . basically, you'd spend hours driving to restaurants you couldn't get into. Even when I'm a slave, one thing that remains with me is: I can get testy and annoyed. Then I talk in a whining tone of voice, which drives Sheree (as my top) crazy. I've told Sheree, "Punish me. Hit me if I do that. This is what it's all about; this isn't just SM for playtime. If I'm really shitty to you, you have the right to whack me and do *whatever it takes,* because we have this contract."

However, when we tried to work that punishment into our lifestyle it didn't work that well. Here we are out with our friends who are all familiar with the SM scene and the piercing world, and I said something really shitty and Sheree just whacked me across the mouth. Those friends of Jim's never talked to us again! They felt so uncomfortable being exposed to that: "Whew!" Jim Ward still talked to us; he takes a lot of things in his stride, but the other people in the car were very put off. Whereas I was excited by it; I thought, "Oh, great!" I felt embarrassed and put in my place—this had effectively shut my mouth.

♦ *AJ: How did Sheree feel?*
♦ BF: The wrinkle in this whole thing is: that doesn't make Sheree feel any better. It might make *me* feel better, but I think it makes her feel creepy. I think there's a part of her that feels good, but if I'm being shitty, then hitting me doesn't stop her being mad at me. The best way to get back at me is to totally ignore me and turn away from me—*that's* my worst punishment. Hitting me when I'm doing something shitty just turns me on—it's more of a *reward* than a punishment. As for those friends of Jim's, we thought: "To hell with them—they should have known ahead of time what this is about."

♦ *AJ: Did you develop any more punishments?*
♦ BF: Sheree's actually pretty bad about punishing her kids, or me . . . meting out punishment is not her forte. We'd keep a book, and if I did something wrong I'd get ten whacks later when we came home. The problem was:

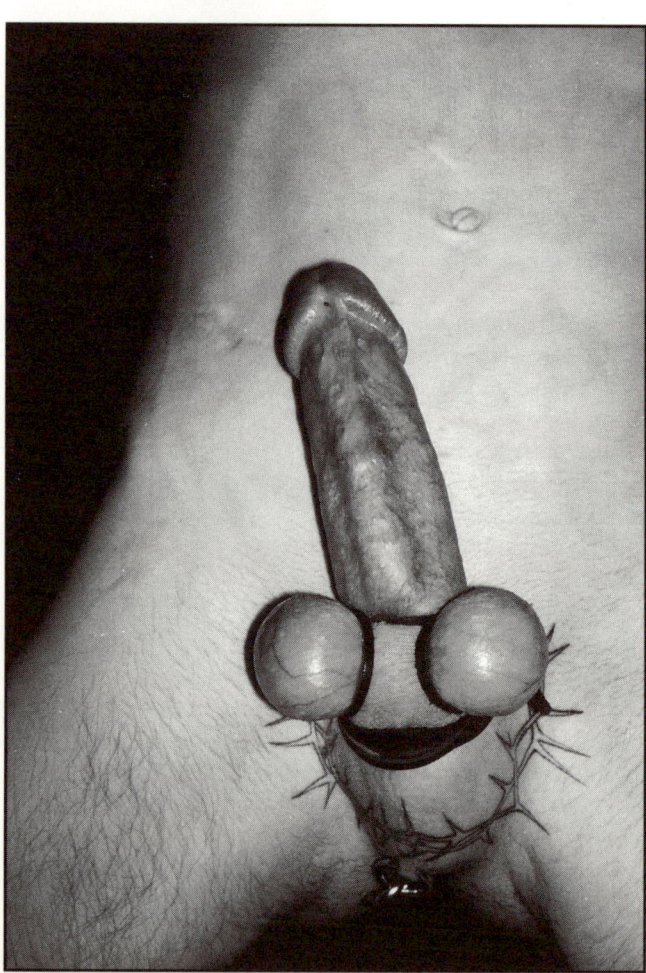

"He is risen." Los Angeles, 1991

she would never feel like doing it, and months would go by before we got around to it—it was like hitting a dog weeks after it peed on the floor. It takes *work* to keep a contract going, and neither of us worked that hard at it. That's probably why most people don't really do this for long.

♦ **AJ:** *What about a relationship like a husband and wife where the husband is the dominant? Isn't that just like status quo society where men dominate women anyway?*
♦ **BF:** The difference is in how the people feel. If the woman's doing something because she really gets turned on by it, that's great. But it's still hard to watch males dominating females, because it fits into such a familiar pattern that's in society already. Even though I know women who love to be whipped, and men who love to whip them, I don't necessarily like to watch their "relationship." Unless the woman's really going through an orgasm and it's obvious she's really enjoying it (and a lot of times you don't know she's enjoying it until afterwards), I don't like to see women being told what to do by men.

The women I know who are into SM are also powerful, dominant women outside of the SM scene. Often they're managers in companies and have a very strong ego and will . . . these are women who are submissive to their husbands, yet dominant in the external world. You can't really make generalizations because everyone is different.
♦ **V:** *How did you meet Jim Ward [who publishes the piercing publication, PFIQ, and owns a chain of piercing studios called The Gauntlet]?*
♦ **BF:** My first piercing jewelry was obtained from a couple in Oklahoma who sold somewhat inferior jewelry through the mail. I probably first heard about the Gauntlet through *Fetish Times* or one of the SM papers. After I met Sheree we went there for the first time. First I got my nipples pierced, then I got the Prince Albert, and then all the other pierces. The first thing Sheree ever videotaped was me getting my Prince Albert, and she got so excited watching the piercing that she pressed the pause button just as the piercing was starting. We went home to watch it and there was nothing there! So I had to take it out, let it heal, go back and have it redone so she could make a videotape. What I have now is actually my *second* Prince Albert. Jim did all my piercings.

There was a year when Sheree's kids went to Paris with their father, and we had the run of the house. The extra room in the back of the house became a perfect slave's quarters. I painted that room grey, turned a table into a bondage table, and put a standing post in the closet so she could tie me up in the closet when she went out for errands. That was fun—I used to lie tied-up and spread-eagled all night . . . simple things like that, nothing elaborate. One time I tape-recorded everything I was saying while tied-up, and it was embarrassing: all these pseudo-spiritual ramblings.
♦ **AJ:** *Did you feel "transcendent"?*
♦ **BF:** Oh yeah! I've heard people describe out-of-body experiences, but I've never gotten that far. Anyway, it's still a great feeling when it's all over, and I keep wanting

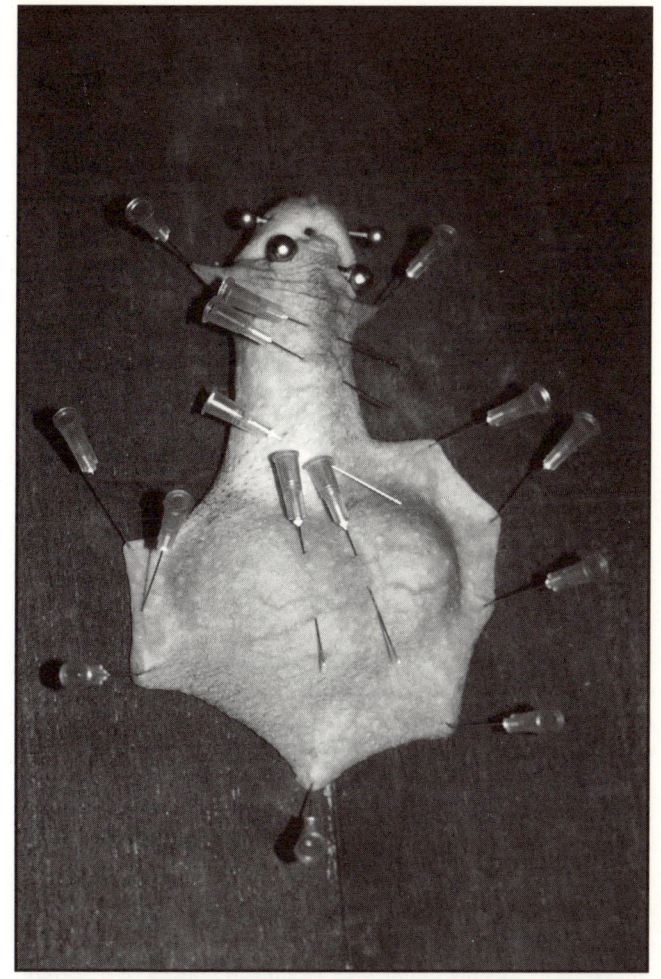

Pain junkies are lucky, and I'm the luckiest. Due to a long history of medical problems, some highly specialized equipment is mine for the asking. Like these needles: sharp, clean, efficient—a vast improvement over the dull straight pins and sewing needles I used to use. But even with these surgically honed hypodermics, it takes pluck and perseverance to pierce your own penis. Human flesh is as tough as nails, and there's a voice in the back of the brain that screams, "What the fuck are you doing?" But I say, "Fuck off," as I play Cupid to my stupid love-sick dick, each fiery pinprick another shot of adrenalin coursing through the veins of my porcupine pal, thick and purple, bobbing in front of me like a festive party balloon just begging to be popped.
—"Needles," from *The Book of Medicine,* Los Angeles 1991

to do it over and over again . . .

Sheree also had different female slaves at different times. But it was too hard to deal with these different personalities; it didn't really work out. They didn't live with us, but one woman came over quite a bit. It was a mess having to deal with her, me, and the kids all whining at the same time—it was too much! And this woman was a little off-kilter, so it was difficult having her around.
♦ **V:** *What are some of your favorite films?*
♦ **BF:** *Pigs Is Pigs* was a very SM cartoon with a lot of bondage and force-feeding. It didn't star Porky Pig, but

a "generic" pig. I saw it when I was very young and remembered it forever ... A lot of the performances Sheree and I do are documented on videos.

♦ **V: Didn't your performances start out as poetry readings?**

♦ BF: Yeah. I just naturally started telling jokes; in the early days I used to read with a half-pint of tequila and get drunker and drunker—that was a Bukowski-esque thing to do: get drunk and tell jokes while reading. If I was nervous, that got me over it. I started making up or improvising poetry, pretending that it was written down, but it was really blank pages I was reading from. Even before that, I thought I wanted to be a stand-up comedian. I also thought I wanted to be a singer, so I started playing the guitar and appearing at hootenanny nights at different places, and I was really terrible!

I was in a band and performed a lot onstage. I never intended to be a performance artist, but a couple things happened. Sheree was documenting all the SM activities we did at home, taking photographs. She started showing them around, and we helped start the L.A. Janus society (now it's called Threshold). Janus is the Roman god of portals or doors; he was represented with two faces, one in front and one behind. Cynthia Slater, who died of AIDS, started the Janus Club in San Francisco and she came up with the name. These organizations not only host parties but also demonstrations (bondage, piercing, etc) and Sheree and I started doing demonstrations together for Janus meetings. We did a number of different events; one night we did a whole evening of SM comedy where I just told jokes and different stories about my life. Once I was branded by Fakir Musafar for a demonstration—that was my first branding, around 1988.

♦ **V: How did you meet Fakir [featured in Re/Search #12: Modern Primitives]?**

♦ BF: In '84 I was working for Jim Ward at the Gauntlet in L.A. as an assistant piercer, plus I did the mail orders. In the early days Fakir would come to Los Angeles periodically and work with Jim—that's how I came to be branded.

♦ **V: What does branding signify to you?**

♦ BF: To me, any kind of mark that's a sign of ownership is exciting, including tattooing, and at this point I wasn't yet tattooed. Piercings are not necessarily permanent, because they can be taken out, so it was always exciting to have something that was going to be a mark on me forever, like Sheree's initials. The idea of branding was frightening—although when it happens it's like an electric jolt that's quickly over. Fakir's theory on branding is: when you burn human flesh, it's not like burning an animal. The burn expands and gets thick, so if you use a traditional hot branding iron, the mark will just become a big blob—all the lettering or lines will expand and blur together. You have to use a very thin line so that when the brand expands, the lines don't merge into each other.

Fakir uses pieces of tin heated up with a butane torch. He shapes the tin with tin snips and pliers and holds the pieces with needlenose pliers—which may not be as accurate as it could be. On me he did two hits to form two letters (with this particular process you can't shape them all at one time). The problem here is that the temperature varies, so one mark may be deeper than another mark ... it may come out a little uneven. My brand looked great for a couple years, but my skin is so pale that when it finally healed, it was barely visible. If I'd had a tan or darker pigmentation, the design would have shown up better: "SR" (for Sheree Rose). It's very faint, but if I get spanked, it gets red and rises up a little bit so you can see it.

♦ **V: Tell us more about the branding—**

♦ BF: It was very ceremonial. There was an audience of about seventy people watching a stage with a table covered by a blanket. Two people were being branded: a woman (who had a top) and myself (obviously, Sheree was my mistress). I was lying on the table, and some close friends were holding my feet and hands down in case I jumped—they didn't strap me down. I could see Fakir heating up the pieces of tin, and there was nothing I could do. That was the worst part: watching the preparations.

Fakir gave a running talk. First he gave a half-hour lecture on how to do branding, how to take care of it healthwise (that's what these programs usually were about: how to do something safely, in case people wanted to do it themselves or have it done). The worst part for me was

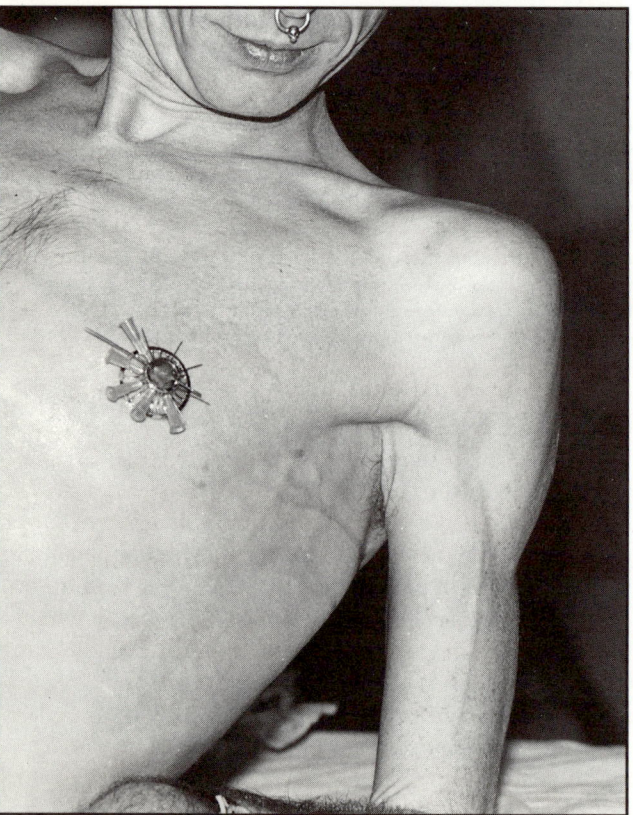

Jim Ward makes my nipple look like a Fiat hubcap at a Society of Janus play piercing program. Los Angeles, 1984

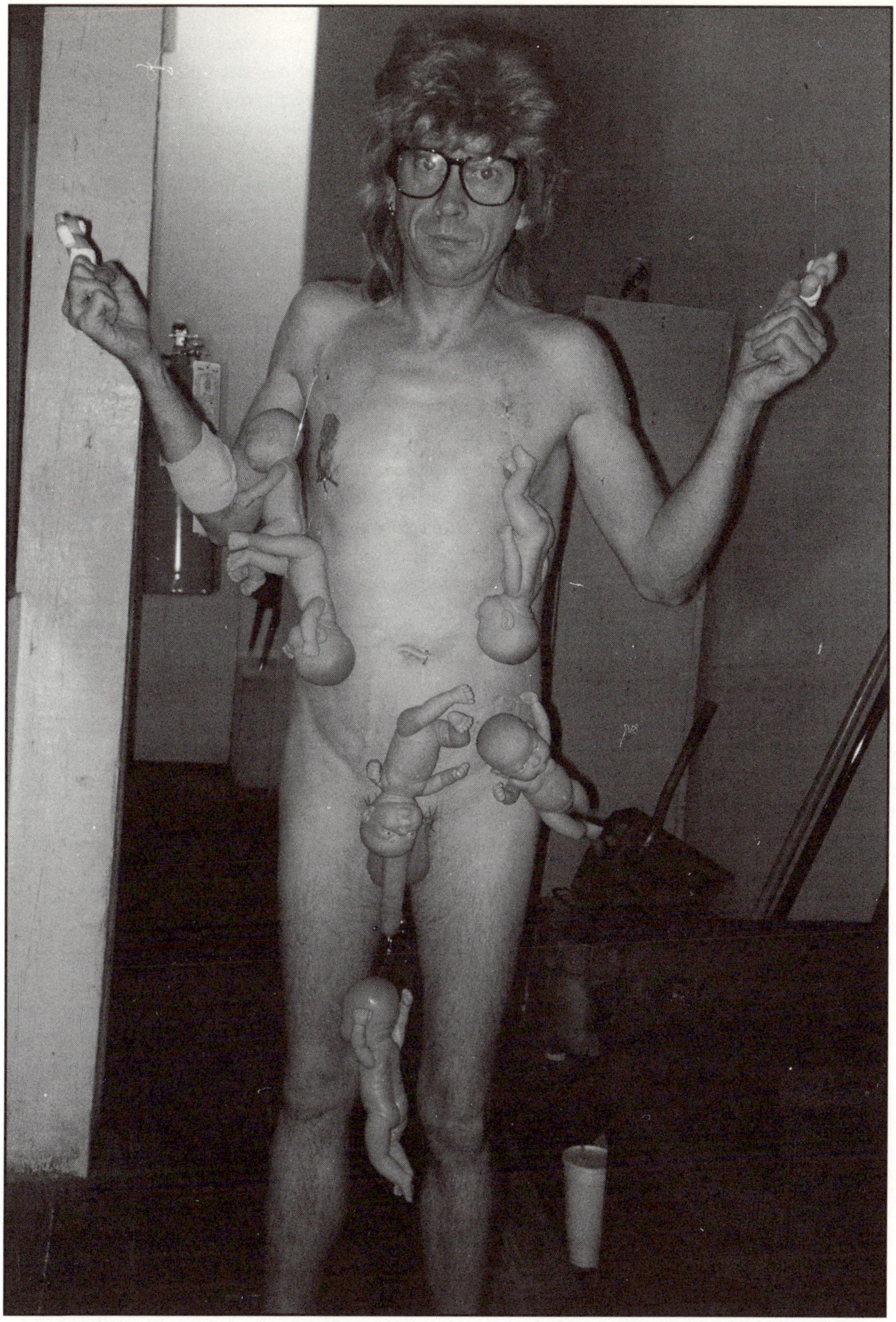

As "Randall Terry" clone, forced to bear children by having them dangle from my flesh with fishhooks. Pro-Choice benefit with Sheree at LACE, Los Angeles, 1992

the beginning. Once Fakir began, it didn't feel as horrible as I expected—it's not like burning your finger on a stove where it continues to hurt. It hurt for a day afterwards, but it wasn't that intense.

♦ **V: *Did you cry out?***
♦ BF: I always scream at anything—screaming is just a way of getting through the experience. I don't know if it hurt as much as I screamed, but—! Then I just left the brand alone; I let the air take care of it. Any kind of oil is bad for a burn; ice is good but you don't want to apply it too much because you *want* it to scar. And if you apply Vitamin E, that might minimize the scarring. Anyway, it formed a great scab which I wished I'd saved. Afterwards, people came up and talked; it was a lot of fun.

The branding felt great; it was a kind of rite of passage, and was more verification that I belonged to Sheree. Maybe that didn't last, but at the time it seemed like a real commitment. The experience itself, with friends around to hold your hand, seemed like a feeling of real closeness. It didn't hurt as much as I'd thought. There were two passes with the iron; one for each letter.

♦ **V: *What other programs did you put on?***
♦ BF: I did an autoerotica program: SM activities for one. It was a culmination of all the things I used to do at home by myself. That's when I first nailed my scrotum to a board in front of an audience (later I did it for non-SM audiences; my shows evolved from things I did at home). Originally I built my scaffold for use at home, just for me, but my private demonstrations for SM clubs became "performance art." At the time I didn't know that a regular "straight" audience would get anything out of it. I didn't want to do just straight SM performances; I wanted to add something that was different, so I brought in things I was writing at the time and incorporated them into the show, and told jokes.

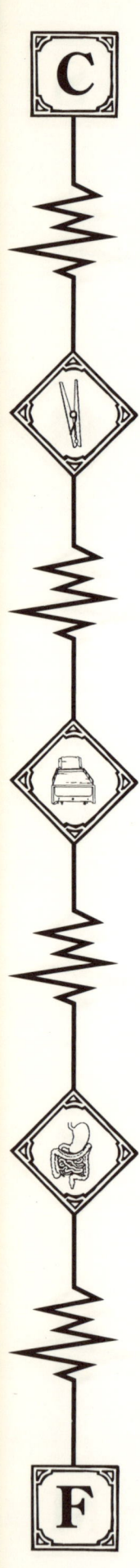

I also put on several showings of movie clips that have influenced me (compiled on a videotape: *Pigs Is Pigs, The Boston Strangler, Mutiny on the Bounty,* etc) and talked about them. I did one show using the scaffold, but suspended seventeen TV monitors from it to represent my body going through different stages of torture: medical, sexual, etc. I also did a show called *Bob Flanagan's Sick* in New York (at Art at the Anchorage), and in L.A. A magazine from London called *Performance* gave me a bad review; the writer compared me (which I thought was great) to "an amateur magician at a children's birthday party; embarrassed *and* embarrassing." But I thought, "That's what I've always wanted to be!"

♦ **V: How did your "Nailed" performance come about?**
♦ **BF:** Brian and Stuart from AMOK Bookstore proposed the show as the finale of a book signing for *Modern Primitives.* We got together and planned it like a circus sideshow of erotic body manipulations . . . to show people doing different strange, dark things to (or with) their bodies. It was a mixture of vaudeville dancing and stripper dancing, comedy, and really dark SM. Sheree had a slave for the evening, and she cut designs into the slave's breasts with a knife—normally, that's something that's done in private, but the woman really enjoyed that and got off on it. To some people this was really shocking to see; a lot of blood was flowing . . .

I had a scaffold in my bedroom; it was a weird contraption with chains and water weights enabling me to suspend myself for indeterminate periods—here again I was the subject of fate. So I set that up in public and as a finale, the audience had to watch me being suspended, and wait for the weights to drop so I could get down. Brian and Stuart provided great lighting and music, including Leonard Nimoy singing "If I Had a Hammer" (plus an Israeli version) when I nailed my scrotum to a board. That's really easy to do, but really hard to watch. I get a *charge* out of doing that in public because the audience—especially the men—are just squirming; it drives 'em crazy.

While onstage I talked about my life and improvised jokes and stories. This was a turning point for Sheree and I, and I think Club Fuck and a lot of other underground clubs in L.A. were inspired by that—

♦ **V: Tell us about these clubs—**
♦ **BF:** They aren't that underground anymore; now they attract a lot of people. Periodically the club organizers take over a bar for their events. There can't be any nudity or genitals showing, but there's lots of pasties and leather clothes and fetish outfits. Basically, these are dance clubs, but throughout the evening people do whipping demonstrations or piercing or hot wax or *something.* I really think our "Nailed" show was the inspiration for a lot of this scene; this was one of the first times that underground dance people saw an SM demonstration. Since then, more and more people have done SM demonstrations in public for a general audience.

♦ **V: What else happened at that "Nailed" show?**
♦ **BF:** It started off with a hot wax candle dance with Angel (Elaine from the Gauntlet) and her friend Debbie. They did this erotic dance that was almost burlesque—really fun; actually, they did *two* dances: one with knives and one with hot wax. They played around with cutting each other and dripping hot wax on each other while they danced. They were squirming all around each other so it was pretty hot and sexual. Elaine had lots of tattoos, including angel wings on her back, and people got off on the bare breasts and nudity—it was exciting. A few people passed out—that happens at almost every show. At the Kitchen in New York, Sheree showed slides while I did a reading, and just *describing* nailing my dick to a board made somebody pass out. I also stuck clothespins all over my body, and somebody passed out just from *that* . . . not because it was bothering him, but because he liked it so much! (We found this out afterwards.)

I never *planned* on doing a performance art career; it just evolved. One thing led to another . . .

♦ **V: Why don't you describe the Southern Exposure show you did for our Modern Primitives month in October, 1989, San Francisco—**
♦ **BF:** Okay. Both the Olio show and the Southern Exposure show were called "Nailed"; Olio was the first. At Southern Exposure I set up the same scaffold onstage and told some of the same stories, except that instead of the dancing girls I played a recording of my poem, "Why." Actually, it's not really a poem; it came about because I asked myself, "Why am I involved in SM?" I started writing down all the reasons: "Because it feels good; because it gives me an erection, because it makes me cum . . ." and this whole list of reasons just flooded out of me in one day; there was very little rewriting.

I played a tape of "Why?" while I did an endurance ritual where I put fifty clothespins on my body attached to chains leading to a container which is filling up with water very slowly. When filled it's heavy enough to pull all the clothespins off my body—which is really painful. They rip off as part of a domino effect; when the first one goes, the rest of them go *z-i-p,* all at once. The clothespins are attached to my nipples, thighs, scrotum and the head of my penis, and even though they're just clothespins, when they yank off it's pretty painful. They're also painful to put on, but then the pain subsides. While putting them on, I have to talk to the audience (this generates some adrenalin flow); after that, it's just a matter of waiting for what's coming. This is kind of dreadful, because I know what's coming, yet I have to wait for it to happen. I didn't want to just do a live sex show for people; I wanted to bring in my work—that's why I played a tape of "Why" while this was going on, and it was very effective.

At Southern Exposure gallery, that was the first time I sewed my scrotum up in public. I had a needle and dental floss and—again, this is something I started doing at home. It was just auto-eroticism: something to turn myself on, because I liked the way it looked and felt to put my penis inside my scrotum and stitch it up and leave it there for a couple hours. A video monitor showed this happening up-close, and I talked and told jokes while doing this—that puts people off-guard. Some people regard this as dark and scary, and they start to feel squeamish, but they'll accept it better if I'm sitting there telling jokes like I'm working on some macrame or needlepoint—well, this *is* a form of needlepoint! Then I did the scaffold/clothespin ritual and read another poem, and that was it.

During each show, Sheree showed her slides of SM-scene people she's been documenting for years. That Southern Exposure show got Jesse Helms' attention—somehow he got hold of a flyer. He actually turned our careers around because once *Jesse Helms* started asking about us, suddenly other people started asking us to do work and were far more interested. We were *nobodies* until he targeted us—I should send him a thank-you letter!

♦ **V: It was intense to watch the sewing-up process—**
♦ BF: It did bleed a little bit.
♦ **V: And it looked strange, almost like a sex inversion—**
♦ BF: Yes, I think it's a castration fantasy. It's weird to look down and see nothing there. I added a little extra something the next time I did that at an SM demonstration for QSM in San Francisco: before I sewed the penis up inside the scrotum, I pushed the penis head into the shaft of the penis and sewed the loose skin around it so it looked like it was totally cut off! Then I sewed the rest up together.
♦ **V: You don't have a foreskin—**
♦ BF: No—I'd be doing all kinds of things if I did.
♦ **V: Do you wish you did?**
♦ BF: I probably would have cut it off myself by now—who *knows* what I would have done? I would do a lot of bizarre things to it; that's for sure.
♦ **V: I've seen a book just on foreskin play—**
♦ BF: I've heard about that.
♦ **V: What does the idea of castration mean to you?**
♦ BF: It's the ultimate point of no return. It's a fantasy I don't understand. It's an erotic possibility to think about, perhaps because it's so extreme. At that point all the attention is focused on the genitals. It's fun to fantasize about extremes that aren't necessarily going to happen. Sheree used to talk about castrating me—then I would just be her slave with no possibility of sex at all (which is a fun fantasy) but it's impractical. I used to type up the personal ads for the Gauntlet's magazine, *PFIQ*, and this was a very common fantasy. I've read a couple articles about the pathology of this . . . about men who in alcoholic fits or frenzies of depression have cut off their genitals—that always fascinates me.
♦ **V: The Skoptsi's [late 19th century Russian sect] formed an entire cult around castration, but then they died out—**
♦ BF: Castration is the ultimate extreme of everything I do or fantasize about. It's the ultimate way to go.
♦ **V: Do you think it's a powerlessness-enhancing fantasy?**
♦ BF: I think so. If you're submissive to someone who does this to you, then you're not worth anything except to them. They really do have power over you; the symbolism is so strong. However, it's no fun for them if they like to

Society of Janus "Cowpersons and Indians" party. Los Angeles, 1983

fuck! So it's a self-defeating act. Maybe that's why it's one of those things that persists in the realm of fantasy.
♦ **V: It's part of your whole exploration of gender boundaries—**
♦ BF: —Gender *demolition*!
♦ **V: Does Sheree ever take a male role?**
♦ BF: No, but some of our female friends have gone fully over to cross-dressing as men. Actually, Sheree is sort of a *femme top* in a lot of ways, which I like.
♦ **V: Does she use a dildo on you in a "male" way?**
♦ BF: Oh yeah! That's a new thing. We started to play around with that in the early days, but stopped. Recently she got a dildo harness and has gotten much more into acts of anal penetration where I'm totally in a passive female-like position with her on top using a dildo, and that's great—I've enjoyed that.
♦ **V: How does that feel?**
♦ BF: Like total surrender. Usually I'm tied up on my back with my legs over my head, and she's on top pumping away. I'm sort of virginal there; we've only been doing this regularly for a couple of months, so it can be pretty rough. But again, it's a *new* thing so it's incredibly exciting. It's a form of bonding, just as if she were a man and I a woman.

Being penetrated is great—I think that's why I like piercing. It's just a great feeling. I think I like being penetrated more than Sheree does, so it's a good switch. Penetration is the newest frontier! ■ ■ ■

BOB FLANAGAN  SUPERMASOCHIST

WHY:

BY BOB FLANAGAN

Because it feels good; because it gives me an erection; because it makes me come; because I'm sick; because there was so much sickness; because I say FUCK THE SICKNESS; because I like the attention; because I was alone a lot; because I was different; because kids beat me up on the way to school; because I was humiliated by nuns; because of Christ and the crucifixion; because of Porky Pig in bondage, force-fed by some sinister creep in a black cape; because of stories about children hung by their wrists, burned on the stove, scalded in tubs; because of "Mutiny on the Bounty"; because of cowboys and Indians; because of Houdini; because of my cousin Cliff; because of the forts we built and the things we did inside them; because of what's inside me; because of my genes; because of my parents; because of doctors and nurses; because they tied me to the crib so I wouldn't hurt myself; because I had time to think; because I had time to hold my penis; because I had awful stomach-aches and holding my penis made it feel better; because I felt like I was going to die; because it makes me feel invincible; because it makes me feel triumphant; because I'm a Catholic; because I still love Lent, and I still love my penis, and in spite of it all I have no guilt; because my parents said BE WHAT YOU WANT TO BE, and this is what I want to be; because I'm nothing but a big baby and I want to stay that way, and I want a mommy forever, even a mean one, especially a mean one; because of all the fairy tale witches, and the wicked step mother, and the step sisters, and how sexy Cinderella was, smudged with soot, doomed to a life of servitude; because of Hansel, locked in the witch's cage until he was fat enough to eat; because of "O" and how desperately I wanted to be her; because of my dreams; because of the games we played; because I've got an active imagination; because my mother

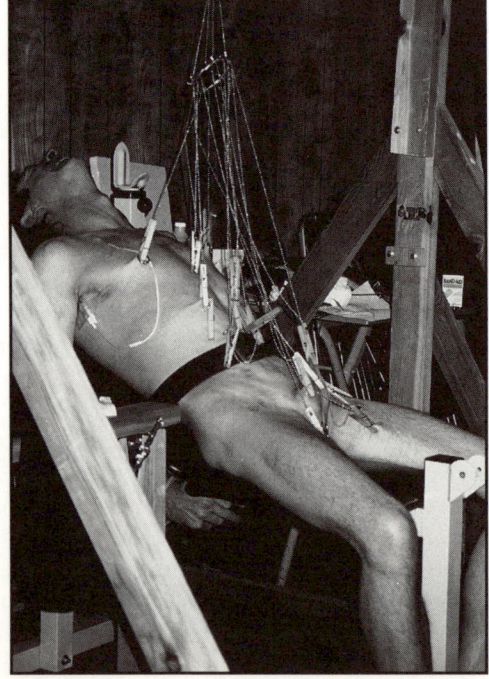

bought me tinker toys; because hardware stores give me hard-ons; because of hammers, nails, clothespins, wood, padlocks, pullies, eyebolts, thumbtacks, staple-guns, sewing needles, wooden spoons, fishing tackle, chains, metal rulers, rubber tubing, spatulas, rope, twine, C-clamps, S-hooks, razor blades, scissors, tweezers, knives, pushpins, two-by-fours, ping-pong paddles, alligator clips, duct tape, broom sticks, barbecue skewers, bungie cords, sawhorses, soldering irons; because of tool sheds; because of garages; because of basements; because of dungeons; because of The Pit and the Pendulum; because of the Tower of London; because of the Inquisition; because of the rack; because of the cross; because of the Addams Family playroom; because of Morticia Addams and her black dress with its octopus legs; because of motherhood; because of Amazons; because of the Goddess; because of the moon; because it's in my nature; because it's against nature; because it's nasty; because it's fun; because it flies in the face of all that's normal (whatever that is); because I'm not normal; because I used to think that I was part of some vast experiment and that there was this implant in my penis that made me do these things and allowed THEM (whoever THEY were) to monitor my activities; because I had to take my clothes off and lie inside this giant plastic bag so the doctors could collect my sweat; because once upon a time I had such a high fever my parents had to strip me naked and wrap me in wet sheets to stop the convulsions; because my parents loved me even more when I was suffering; because I was born into a world of suffering; because surrender is sweet; because I'm attracted to it; because I'm addicted to it; because endorphins in the brain are like a natural kind of heroin; because I learned to take my medicine; because I was a big boy for taking it; because I can take it like a man; because, as somebody once said, HE'S GOT MORE BALLS THAN I DO; because it is an act of courage; because it does take guts; because I'm proud of it; because I can't climb mountains; because I'm terrible at sports; because NO PAIN, NO GAIN; because SPARE THE ROD AND SPOIL THE CHILD; because YOU ALWAYS HURT THE ONE YOU LOVE.

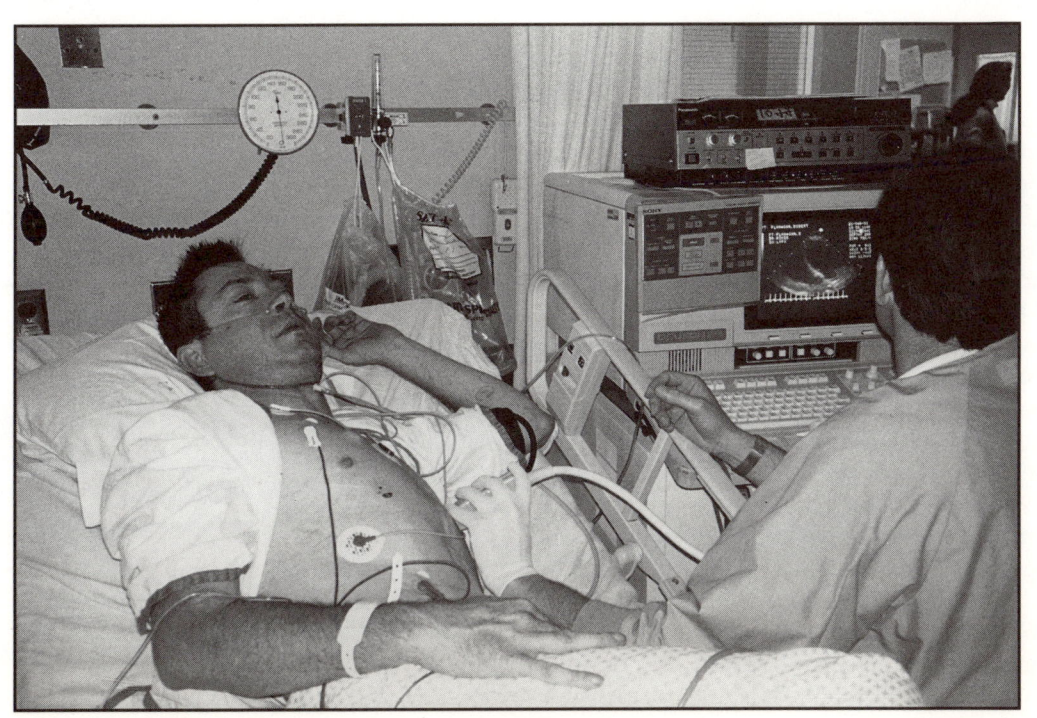

BOB FLANAGAN SUPERMASOCHIST

INTERVIEW THREE

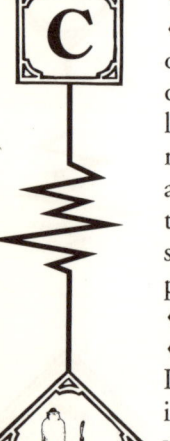

♦ **V: What is your Santa Monica show about?**
♦ BF: It's the culmination of all my work, and it focuses on where Cystic Fibrosis and SM converge. I built a wall of 1,400 kids' alphabet blocks, four feet tall and eight feet long, using the letters C F and S M. I called a block-making company and asked if they could just make C F and S M blocks for me, but they said "No, it'll cost you too much money if we retool." But it took so long to sand off the old letters and paint on new ones, that I probably would have *saved* money having them retool!
♦ **V: Who made the blocks?**
♦ BF: I talked to a lot of block-making companies before I found Uncle Goose, this old mom-and-pop company in Michigan that still makes big, old-fashioned-style blocks with 3-dimensional lettering and classic drawings of chickens, cows, and dogs.

I erased all the drawings of chickens and cows and substituted my own images of whips, dominatrixes, doctors, enema bags, oxygen tanks—my own personal talismans or iconography. Now I'm making a toy chest decorated with the same iconography: there's a big penis on the front, a doctor and a dominatrix, an ass on the back, lungs, intestines—everything that's a part of me is on this box. And inside are a collection of weird kid's toys that have dual meanings and purposes: jump-ropes, plastic handcuffs, boxing gloves and doctor-nurse kits. You weren't supposed to play doctor (that's "bad"), yet we would play master-slave games which are a few steps up from playing doctor, even when I was ten. Still, "playing doctor" was *the* metaphor for playing sex games.

You've seen those "Visible Man and Woman" models which show the intestines and bones—they're anatomically correct. When I was ten I became really sick and almost died—they even brought in a priest to read the last rites! I had to stay in this Catholic hospital for a month. My parents felt so bad for me that every day they went to this toy store that was going out of business and bought me a new toy. The nuns were going crazy, complaining, "Those toys collect dust!" The whole room was filled with puppets, record players and also the Visible Man. Every

The Visible Man and children's play area, from "Visiting Hours." Santa Monica Museum of Art, 1992

time I see one, I think of that time.

I bought a Visible Man, painted the parts and pulled them all out in slow motion for a video; you see the heart and lungs dismantled. I want one of these to be on display in the "waiting room" of my exhibition—but the thing is, the Visible Man doesn't have a penis! Everything else is anatomically correct, and there is the barest suggestion of balls, but nothing else. To remedy this rather crucial deficiency, I bought another model kit, cut off the thumb and drilled a hole in the tip, then attached this to a hole I drilled in the groin area, and the thumb became a penis. I've been doing home-IV drugs using this pump: a plastic bulb with a condom of drugs inside it, and if you release the pressure it drips the antibiotic through the tubing without the necessity for a mechanical pump. I saved all the old ones, figuring I could do something with them someday. Using the brand-new penis and these IV pumps and tubing, I made the Visible Man into a model of myself: spitting up mucus, shitting, and dribbling cum. I filled the pumps up with white hair conditioner for "cum," and green dandruff shampoo for phlegm. And for the ass, I used wood putty mixed with brown wood stain.

I'm also remaking the game called "Operation" which has been around since I was a kid. I remember a lot of games having to do with touching the body. To me these were always subliminally erotic, like "Twister." "Operation" is a board game with an image of a naked person, and you have to take out his heart, etc. I'm making some changes: instead of the red light bulb being in the tip of the nose, it'll be in the tip of the penis. So every time you touch something, this little red bulb in the penis will light up! People will be able to play with these things in the show.

♦ *AJ: Your show is like an SM exploratorium—*
♦ BF: Yes; an SM/medical exploratorium. Because I've been very ill this past year, this show has a lot to do with being sick—that's changed my whole SM lifestyle. Nobody likes to be getting older, *but*. . . So the focus of the show is where my SM came from; where it started. All around the room will be the text of my poem "Why." Visitors will read that and end up at the scaffold of seven

Detail of The "CF/SM" Alphabet Block Wall in "Visiting Hours." Santa Monica Museum of Art, 1992. Photo: David Familian

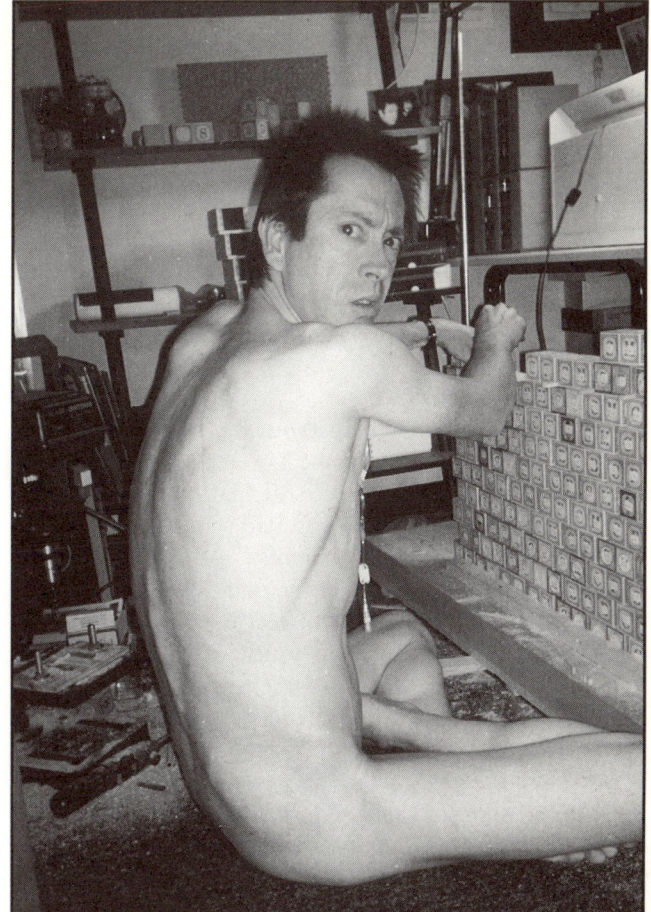

Working in the nude, with a butt full of sawdust, building my alphabet block wall for "Visiting Hours." Los Angeles, 1992

video monitors showing videos (from previous shows) representing parts of my body: the head, chest, two hands, two feet, and the penis. The "face" video shows me getting slapped and force-fed; it's mixed with movie clips of scenes like Jesus on the cross. The "chest" monitor shows me getting my nipples pierced, after which Sheree carves her initials on my chest, and blood just flows. The "penis" monitor shows all kinds of torture, masturbating, and urinating into the screen.

♦ *AJ: Describe that—*
♦ BF: First of all, the scrotum is sewn up so you don't even *see* the penis. Then slowly you see my hands come into view, unstitching the scrotum in about six stitches. One thing leads to another; I pee into the screen (we put a sheet of plexiglass in front of the camera lens, so it looks like I'm peeing into the audience's face), I whack myself in the balls with a brush, and work up to this frenzy where there's one cut after another of me masturbating. After 15 minutes it ends with me nailing the head of my penis to a board. Putting a nail through the scrotum is easy and doesn't bother me, but putting a nail through the penis head—I only did it *once*—that time when I missed the nail, hit the head, and all this blood spurted out. Anyway, I thought, "I can do this for the video" (even though it'd been ten years since I'd last tried it), and it's even tougher

to do that when the video lights are on. So we tried *four* different times, but I couldn't do it. I tried drinking lots of tequila; Sheree set everything up, but I still couldn't do it. Then the day this video was supposed to premiere at LACE [Los Angeles art space], I thought, "This whole video means nothing without this as a finale; it *has* to end with this act." So that morning, finally I got my nerve up. The nail went in a little crooked—you see my hand pull back a little at the last second—but the nail went in. There was a two-by-four board in front of the camera, I laid the head of my penis on that and hammered it into place.

♦ **AJ:** *How did that feel?*
♦ **BF:** I was mostly thinking about the video . . . I didn't want to have to do this again! My penis throbbed, but once the nail was in, it was *in.* Anticipation was the worst part—once you do it, it's not so bad.

♦ **AJ:** *What did you worry about?*
♦ **BF:** Missing the nail. I asked myself, "Why am I doing this? What's the pain going to feel like?" This is a supreme act of momentary self-mutilation, whereby you transcend everything screaming at you: "Don't do this!" At that moment the yin and the yang really cross; the sparks fly!

♦ **AJ:** *Once the nail goes in, what do you feel?*
♦ **BF:** A tremendous relief and a real high: "Wow, I did it!" I wouldn't even call the throbbing *pain.* The most painful part is placing the nail where it just lightly touches the skin. I'm concentrating so much on the physical act of putting the nail in that I don't feel the pain; I'm just thinking about being *accurate.* That's why I do this to myself, because if somebody else were doing it, it would just be the pain. Here, because I'm both the dominant and the submissive, I get the best of both worlds.

Auto-erotic SM, when I'm in the mood and it works, is in many ways much more explosive than being submissive to anybody else, even though that's really great on a long-term basis. When it works, auto-eroticism is the best of both worlds; the electricity is intense. When masturbating is over, you want somebody to share it with. Sheree videotapes my auto-eroticism so we can re-live it, and she's excited by watching it, so with her I get the best of both worlds.

Doing something for video is weird, because it's not a matter of doing it when you're "in the mood." There's a challenge to it that I like. I really am an exhibitionist, so I love the fact that it's on tape and I can watch it a million times and send it to people and freak them out. I want to get up the nerve to nail my dick to a board during a *live* performance—the scrotum is passé (it's too easy for me to do). The scrotum is just a flap of skin, and *guys* will respond to it being nailed, but for me it's like doing a magic trick—*I* know it doesn't hurt, but everybody else thinks it does (I'm giving away a secret!). Mr Lift-O in the Jim Rose Circus Sideshow hangs weights from his nipples and tongue, and I'd like to offer them my services doing penis-nailings! When my art career's over, I'll join the circus.

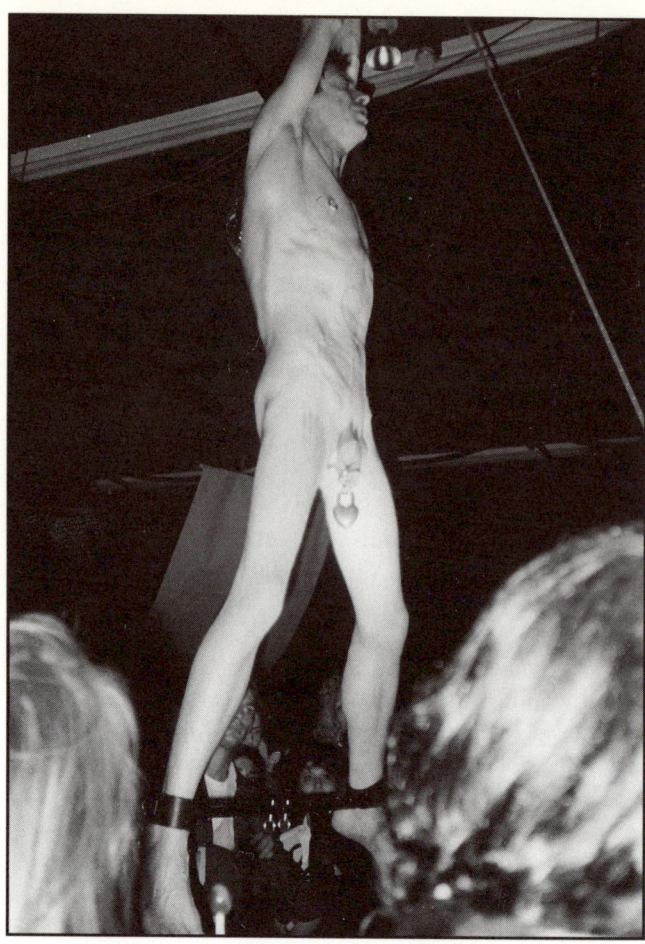

LACE Valentine's Day Benefit: Sheree suspends me above the dance floor as I recite the words to "Why." Los Angeles, 1990. Photo: Monica Rex

♦ **V:** *Again, how does penis-nailing feel?*
♦ **BF:** The scrotum doesn't bleed, but since the penis is basically just a sponge for blood, it bleeds. And there's definitely a throb going on. But it doesn't bleed until you take the nail out; if you leave the nail in, it's "fine."

♦ **AJ:** *Do you start to get a hard-on?*
♦ **BF:** No. When making a video, there's a lot of fear involved, and fear definitely shrinks an erection. First we nailed the penis, then we re-set up the camera with a plexiglass reservoir to collect all the blood. The camera focused on the penis to record me taking the nail out; then I bled and the entire screen filled up with blood.

♦ **V:** *How do you stanch the blood flow?*
♦ **BF:** You *don't!* You just let it go. It stops within five minutes. If you're naturally coagulating, then you should be all right. Any ampallang will bleed, and if you leave the ring in it won't bleed, but it will bleed if you get an erection at night because that enlarges the hole. However, that only happens for a day or so. It's just like getting a big cut: it'll bleed for awhile and then stop. For this video we also used footage of me getting a Prince Albert and giving a urine specimen in a cup—that was a medical joke.

The video for the other parts of the body involved basic bondage, syringes, rubber gloves, and Jesus getting his hands

nailed to the cross (excerpted from different movies).
- **AJ:** *What movie scenes did you pick?*
- **BF:** For my earlier "Bob Flanagan at the Movies" shows I collected film clips that had been erotic for me as a kid. Today, kids have MTV and I don't know what kids eroticize because things are so naturally erotic—there's nothing hidden, it's all there. But when I was a kid sex was all veiled, so I derived more eroticism from things that weren't *supposed* to be erotic, like *Cinderfella*—to have been imprinted with Jerry Lewis was really bad! [laughs] I saw that in 1960 at the age of eight. Recently I rented it and only two scenes are still a turn-on: the beginning, where his godmother is yelling, "Fella! Fella!" and he answers, "Yes, mother—I mean *stepmother!*". . . he's a slave to this woman and her three sons. There's a lot of veiled homosexuality: the sons are leather boys (without the clothes) who order him around and make him light their cigarettes.

There's one lengthy scene at a long dinner table in an elegant mansion (later, it was used for the *Beverly Hillbillies* set). The stepmother and her three sons are at one end of the table, and Jerry Lewis is at the other end, and every time they want him to do something like pour the wine (which is right in front of them), he has to get up, change into his waiter's outfit, go all the way down to their end of the table, pour the wine, and then go back and change clothes—it's absurd. This is a long, stupid scene, but it inspired me to want to be a slave. After this, the film degenerates into sentimental bullshit and becomes really bad.

That same year I saw Roger Corman's *Little Shop of Horrors,* and there was Jack Nicholson reading *Pain* magazine. I identified with the weirdest, creepiest, sleaziest people in the movie—
- **AJ:** *But these films are also slapstick and funny—*
- **BF:** As serious as I am about SM, I never lose my sense of humor about it, because imprinted with it was also this weird ridiculousness . . .

In the mid-'60s my dad would take my brother and me to drive-ins every Saturday night. He took us to films like *The Boston Strangler,* and there's a scene where a character based on the psychic Peter Hurkos is trying to find the strangler (played by Tony Curtis). Hurkos holds the dead women's underwear to his head to get visions—it's a great scene. This was before VCRs, and unless a film was shown on TV it became just a vague memory. I'm really glad, because if I'd had access to them whenever I wanted, they wouldn't have had the power they have.

One of my most vivid memories was of *The Nun's Story,* which all my lesbian friends love. Audrey Hepburn plays a nice Catholic girl who decides to become a nun. She's very intelligent, questioning a lot of the church doctrines, and has a lot of trouble with her vows. The whole regimen she undergoes to become a nun is so lesbian-dominant; she has to follow all these *rules:* vows of silence, poverty, shaving of the head . . . in fact, there are many parallels between *The Nun's Story* and the *Story of O.* They both go to one place and then another; both have a master [or god]; in both films the submissive gives her whole life to Sir Stephen (or Jesus); both characters have to wear special clothes and do special rituals; and both are doing this out of love (they don't *have* to do this). So there are parallels all along the way. One scene in particular had Mother Superior showing her a whip, and I always remembered Audrey Hepburn whipping herself with it. But when I rented the video recently, it turned out that she never even *touched* it. Mother Superior just flicked it this way and that while saying, "Too much is as bad as too little!" That line always stuck with me because I wondered, "*Why?* What would happen if you did it too much?"

- **AJ:** *Nowadays, not only is everything out there, but nothing's veiled. Where's all this leading to?*
- **BF:** It can only lead to more repression. I don't know. If everything's out there already, what do you discover inside yourself? Actually, it's out there more but it's also dumped on more. Earlier there was more of an interest to *find out* about SM; now there's more of an interest to laugh about it or trash it.
- **AJ:** *When were you first on a TV talk show?*
- **BF:** In '84 Sheree and I were on "Hour Magazine" with Gary Collins. We appeared with a writer named Jeannie Scott, and were shown in shadows because Sheree was still raising her kids and didn't want to embarrass them at school. We were identified as "Bob, submissive male, and Rose, dominant female." Of course they were on the attack: "What about the restraints? What about the *kids?*" We said, "This is like any other sexual act; you don't do it in front of the kids, but I'm her submissive all the time; the kids see me cleaning the house . . ." We put it in language like I was just her house husband and they got really frustrated; they wanted to hear more *juice.* Gary's co-host was some woman from the *Dallas* TV series who was a born-again christian, and before we appeared Gary asked her, "Are you ready for this interview?" [as though it were some big, scary thing; they made all the schoolkids in the audience leave so they wouldn't be "exposed" to us] and she replied [southern drawl], "Ah've *prayed* about it." [laughs] Shirley MacLaine was also there doing three days of taping; she was a real *bitch*—she wouldn't talk to anybody. [laughs]

Later Sheree was on the Sally Jesse Raphael show (I wasn't) and all they wanted to do was to sensationalize everything . . . the audience was screaming and yelling about how horrible this was. So it's odd: now SM is much more public and more dumped on at the same time.
- **AJ:** *Years ago, a book like* **Peyton Place** *(which barely*

Photo: Monica Rex

sketched a few sex scenes) was billed as so erotic. Now anybody would go, "So what?"

♦ BF: People with a few clothes on are a lot more erotic than naked people. That scene in the *Boston Strangler* of Peter Hurkos holding this woman's underwear to his head: "He's dirty! He's a priest—no, he works with priest! He sleeps on bedsprings; he washes in toilet"—the next scene cuts to this little hole-in-the-wall apartment with just bedsprings; the police are there looking at this closet full of handbags and shoes—apparently the killer opens these handbags and masturbates on them. Then this masochist appears who isn't the strangler, but by coincidence he has these ropes with all these knots tied in them, and he feels really guilty about what he does and wants to stop it. When he finds out that the police think he's the strangler, he goes [wizened voice], "I never hurt anyone in my life . . . except myself!" and starts crying. The first time I saw this I was cringing; I thought about this for months. During the rest of my life, in the middle of some weird sexual scene (all tied up, doing something alone) I would flash on this character and think, "Jesus Christ—am I *him?!*" Because I too would sleep on bedsprings or the floor; sometimes I'd sleep on a plank of wood in my closet for days with no mattress, pillow or blanket. And this came directly from that movie!

So many things I did later came from movies. Jon Reiss's *Nine Inch Nails'* video, "Happiness In Slavery," is built around this torture chair. I take my clothes off, get into this chair and suddenly clamps come around my wrists and legs and the chair eventually tortures me to death! It pulls me apart; there's all this blood and guts, and I'm screaming and having orgasms. This reminds me of an old Warner Bros cartoon, *Pigs Is Pigs* (1937). In it, a little pig who is obsessed with eating has this nightmare. He's fat and wears no pants—another influential detail. He's also pink like a human and has no penis, but has a little corkscrew tail which is like a reverse penis.

The cartoon begins with this pig in front of a house. A hiccupping fiend opens the door and invites him in; the pig sits in this chair and before he knows it, clamps come out of the chair over his wrists. Then he's lowered into this weird basement (this is total child-molesting) where he's force-fed all this food while crazy music plays. What adult mind came up with this scenario?

The little pig is forced to eat giant sandwiches, and there's a pie jukebox that shovels pies into his mouth. There's also a clamp on his nose which forces his mouth to open and close. A machine swivels over and forces bananas down his mouth (they look like penises)—this is the most erotic, sex-driven weird cartoon ever made. Finally, the evil guy lets him go. By then he's bloated up to twice his size (really gross; basically it's a metaphor: he's just been fucked by this guy . . . used and abused and then kicked out the door). Then he sees a turkey leg, grabs it and eats it and explodes—which is the orgasm! Of course he wakes up; it's a wet dream. But he doesn't change; the final scene shows him eating breakfast like there's no tomorrow. No lesson has been learned; there's no moral to the story; it's not like the pig ends up being more respectful of food—no. My theory is: the pig *wants* to have that dream every night!

I was obsessed by this cartoon, and now I was able to star in Jon Reiss's version of it. I'm sure my eroticism regarding automatic machinery torture couldn't have come from any place but this cartoon. I just realized that I'm reinforcing Tipper Gore's idea that you shouldn't let little kids see certain things—although actually this made me a *better* person!

♦ *AJ: If it were more blatant, perhaps it wouldn't have been eroticized—*

♦ BF: Yes; I never even looked at *Playboy* until I was well into my teens. So basically I eroticized what was intrinsically dopey, light-hearted stuff: who would eroticize Jerry Lewis? Whereas anything that was *really* sexual I wanted to avoid; I didn't want to be caught thinking sexual thoughts. Maybe this was just natural Irish embarrassment; my grandfather was really prudish and my Catholic Irish parents had a sexual shyness in the '60s. I knew other kids who were more sexually crude and blatantly sexual, but I didn't get that way 'til my twenties—and even then only in select company. But in the meantime I

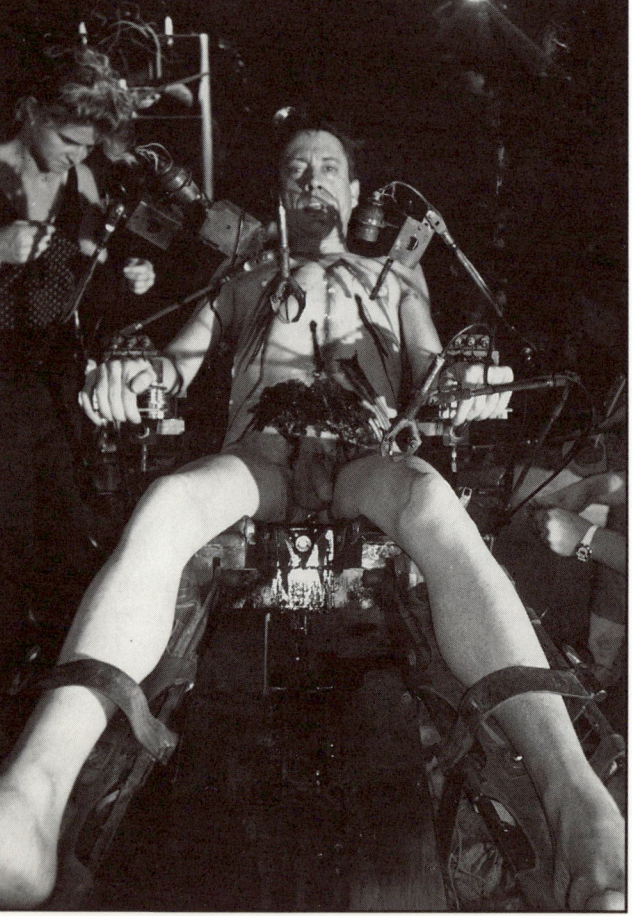

Strapped into "THE CHAIR." On the set of the Nine Inch Nails video, *Happiness in Slavery*, directed and written by Jon Reiss. Los Angeles, 1992

had this private erotic life going on that I didn't even know was erotic...

Earlier I mentioned another influential movie: *King of Kings*, starring Jeffrey Hunter as a blue-eyed, blond, sexy Jesus. There are some pretty graphic whipping scenes and some good torture scenes. *Mutiny on the Bounty* with Marlon Brando had that really graphic whipping scene with Richard Harris, who gets whipped with a cat-o'-nine-tails. I remember my dad telling me, "Butch, a cat-o'nine-tails is a whip with lead at the end so it rips a guy's back apart!" I went home and tried to make one; I got shoelaces and tied little nails to them and whipped myself in the bathroom and covered the walls with blood (and had to clean it off). Nice influence!

♦ **V: Religious movies should be banned!**
♦ **BF:** Definitely. And Catholicism is great for cultivating young masochists. Most of the people I meet in SM clubs are either Catholic or Jewish. Both religions have a lot of rituals, and there's so much ritualism in SM. What do Protestants do—they become swingers! Baptists are hopeless; they're child-molesters and burn records; they become Jimmy Swaggert.

♦ **AJ: They're real perverts in the truest sense. They're so repressed, and they don't even have a ritualistic set-up—**
♦ **BF:** They're crude; their ethic is: "Fuck 'em and leave 'em and lie about it afterwards."

♦ **AJ: You mentioned having guilty flashes about the masochist in The Boston Strangler—**
♦ **BF:** Several times in that movie Tony Curtis looked into the mirror while strangling a woman and got this cold sweat, just like I'd look into the mirror and think: "There's me, the masochist, doing this weird stuff to myself."

♦ **AJ: You don't still think that?**
♦ **BF:** No, this was before I started to turn things into art and relate to another person. This is from the time I was doing auto-erotic stuff and didn't have anybody else to share it with, except on a professional basis where I'd pay somebody to whip me. Everything changed when I met Sheree and we helped start Janus in L.A. I realized, "Here are other people just like me." Sheree and I became teachers and performers and started documenting what we did ... there was no more wondering why we were doing it—we *knew* why: because we *liked* it. Meeting Sheree in 1980 totally flipped my life around; my identity became cemented: "Here I am and there's *nothing wrong* with what I do." Also, I got to explore completely different realms with Sheree that I'd never even *thought* of when I was doing things alone—that was really great.

♦ **V: Did you see Billy Budd, in which Terence Stamp gets whipped?**
♦ **BF:** I know there's some good scenes in it but for some reason I've never seen it. Sheree found a video recently called *Against All Flags,* in which Erroll Flynn gets whipped (and he loves it!). There's a close-up of his face while he's getting disciplined with this bullwhip, and the guy whipping him looks just like John Rechy—pretty funny. [John Rechy is a gay writer who wrote *City of Night,* the first

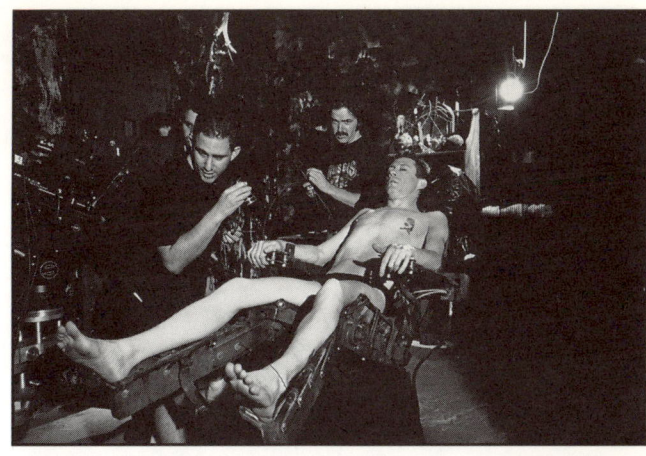

With Jonathan Reiss (director), and Michael Burnett (special effects), on the set of the Nine Inch Nails video, *Happiness in Slavery.* **Los Angeles, 1992**

mainstream best-seller about gay life.]

♦ **AJ: What did you do with Sheree that was groundbreaking?**
♦ **BF:** Most importantly: I was her slave 24 hours a day, which I'd never done with anybody before. And since Sheree was more interested in our art career than our SM

On the set of the Nine Inch Nails video, *Happiness in Slavery.* **Los Angeles, 1992**

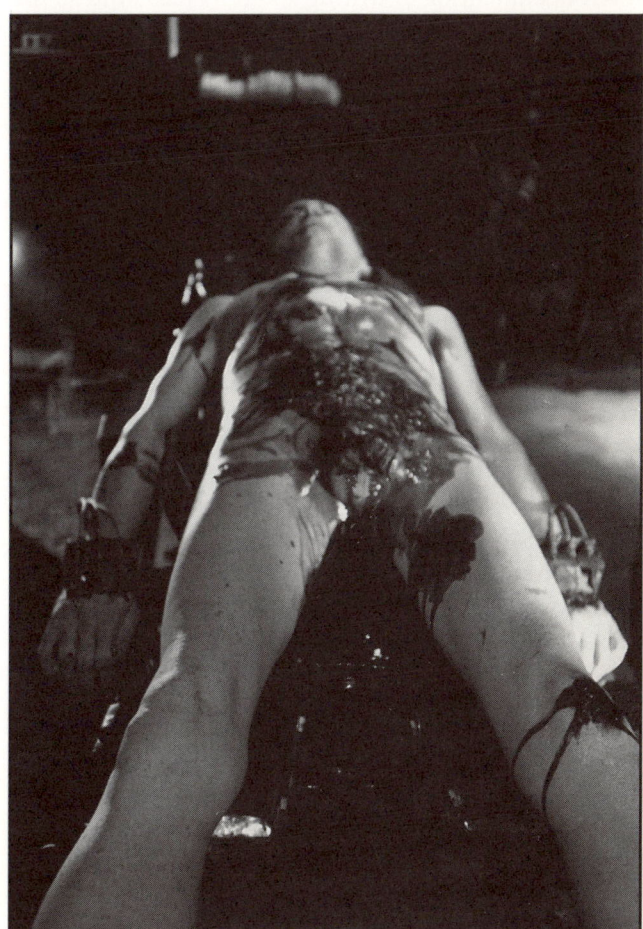

View of "Visiting Hours." Santa Monica Museum of Art, 1992. Photo: David Familian

career, she started documenting everything we did and wanted me to write about everything we did, so all these performances have happened as a result of being with her. But just on a sexual level, what I enjoyed the best (forget about documenting or writing about it) was: I did all the housework, I cooked meals for her and the kids, and at parties I waited on everybody and cleaned up. Those first two years, especially, were sheer bliss.

When Sheree and I first went to professional SM parties (before Threshold), we found them to be really creepy. They were run by dominant men, and the women who worked there weren't really into it, but there was good money in it so they were pretending to be submissive. Most of them had adjustment problems or drug problems; the professional scene by and large was pretty creepy—but it was all there was. Earlier on, I would go see the *Story of O* with girlfriends just to see what they would think of the subject of SM and remind them: "I want to be the *woman!* I don't want to be Sir Stephen; just call me 'B'!" That usually didn't work.

When I met Sheree, we started meeting people who'd been into SM before I was even *born*. That was especially great. We met a dominatrix, Mistress Nan, who had been into SM for twenty years—at that time this was almost unheard of. Her personal experiences had been similar to Sheree, except that she had already been everywhere and done everything. This was a bit intimidating to Sheree: "I could never be like that!"

♦ *AJ: Try to give us portraits of these individuals. What kind of people go to the Threshold Club?*
♦ BF: It's the kind of cross-section of people you'd find in any group: doctors, lawyers, housewives, machinists, entertainers—even a rabbi or minister or two. The Janus group started out as 40 people and now, as Threshold, it's up to 750 people (on paper)—200 might get together for a party and about 100 for a demonstration. They have a mailing list and charge dues of $30 a year which just covers expenses. Parties cost $20 a person. It's basically non-profit.

There's a lot of emphasis on letting people know that this is *not* a sex club—there's no fucking, no penetration (we do a lot of lectures at colleges about this, because the students imagine orgies with fucking and sucking: "No, there's none of that." "Well what do you *do?*" "There's nudity, crazy clothes, bondage, whipping, and a lot of times it's just people socializing."). There's even a couple of old guys who come to every party and play chess in the corner while all this whipping and spanking is going on around them! Basically, it's a way for people to be around people of their own kind, and talk about all kinds of things. It's like a nudist park: being in an environment where people are friendly and open and not hiding things. You can take your clothes off if you want; there's both men and women running around naked. It's not a situation where all the women are naked and all the men have their clothes on.

♦ *AJ: Do you know any couples into corset-training?*
♦ BF: I know one couple where the woman has her nipples pierced (Jim Ward pierced her labia, too) and the male is the dominant. She's submissive to him, but not on a 24-hour basis like Sheree and I.
♦ *AJ: How is that different from "normal" society?*

The "CF/SM" Alphabet Block Wall (4'X8'), "Visiting Hours." Santa Monica Museum of Art, 1992. Photo: David Familian

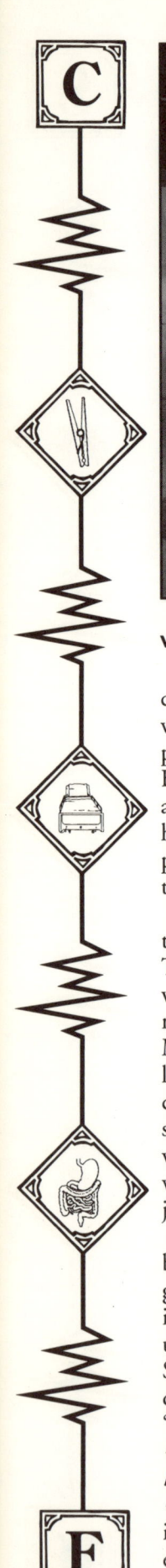

72

♦ BF: Some feminists say that all SM fantasies are male-dominated. Even if the woman fantasizes about being submissive to another woman, somehow that's to get the male off. But to me, the masochist is ultimately in control. They don't tell the dominant what to do, but they're in control because they have to want it. They have to want to be whipped, to be tied up, and somewhere down the line they have to get some good sexual feelings from that. Whereas in "real" society people aren't doing something because they want to submit but because they *have* to: because it's their job, or because they'll lose their husband if they don't. They're doing it to please somebody else, not to please themselves. That's the way society is set up: you do something because somebody's forcing you, or you're forcing yourself to do it because you don't want to lose this certain position you have, or the money.

But in an honest SM relationship, a sadist or top is not going to be turned on if the bottom dislikes what they're doing; there has to be a mutual coming together. If the person being dominated hates what you're doing, that's not good for anybody—that's not a good, healthy relationship. The difference is *choice*. You might ask, "Why would somebody desire being humiliated when society is so humiliating already?" Because for whatever reason (maybe you saw too many Jerry Lewis movies!) you're into it; you get *turned on* by it. And if you're not afraid to say, "I get turned on by being called a bag o' shit—would you please call me that?" and you meet somebody who says, "Gee, I *like* calling people a bag o' shit!" . . . that's a simplistic example of two people doing what they *both* like.

However, in real life almost every relationship gets fucked up. The top says, "Oh, I don't want to be doing this." Usually it's the top that's burdened; usually it's the master who says [groan], "Oh, I gotta whip her *again*." [laughs] Or, "I'm so sick of giving orders!" Because a real masochist *never* gets enough; they want it to go on 24 hours a day (and that's *me;* I never want it to stop. When it does end, I think, "Oh, I wasn't good enough! I didn't take it enough! Try it again; hit me *harder* this time!" And you're telling the person where to hit).

There are SAMS (smartass masochists) who say, "Oh, you're not hitting me hard enough!" They try to make the dominant mad so they'll hit harder or hurt more. SM relationships have all the same pitfalls of regular relationships [laughs], except you feel guiltier because you have this high ideal of wanting to be submissive, and here you are trying to order and orchestrate the whole situation. The top perhaps has high ideals of being real macho or butch, and then finds that sometimes they just want to be gentle. In some ways you have the opposite things working against you . . . every committed relationship I've ever seen goes through that.

♦ *AJ: Back to that corseted woman you mentioned—*
♦ BF: That couple is into fashion. There are all these little subcultures within SM. There's the piercing subculture where people might not be into whipping or even into pain but they're into the adornment and manipulation of the body—that's what's most popular now. A lot of people wouldn't even call it SM; in many ways they think it's more spiritual and it has become real New Age. It's weird—it's gone backwards and is more ancient for a lot of people, and sexuality has been removed from it—it's strictly body manipulation, changing the body, tattooing the body to symbolize some other life force—I don't want to say a higher power, but a *different* power—a significant, other power.

♦ *AJ: Unfortunately, there's a lot of pretentiousness, too—*
♦ BF: That's true. Some people have taken that "other power" and turned it into performance art, which is really a pitfall! [laughs] Somehow ancient religions and performance art have a hard time matching up . . .

♦ *AJ: The incredible ego and ethnocentricity of American white culture to actually think they have any deep understanding of what ancient cultures were about, and then to rip out of context "natural, pure, primitive" social practices—that's just another form of colonization. It's ironic that as Western industrialization is genociding most indigenous peoples, there is now a white American sub-group imitating a smorgasbord of romanticized "primitive" practices. To take some ancient, inadequately reported "primitive" practice out of its deep community context and impose some New Age Shirley MacLaine patina over it—*
♦ BF: I was raised in New York and Orange County—no way is something like the Lakota Sioux sun dance in my system . . . but Porky Pig strapped in a chair *was!* That is my god, my mythology. And those images of Jerry Lewis submissive to a stepmother—

♦ *AJ: —and Cruella (from* 101 Dalmatians*)?*
♦ BF: I saw *101 Dalmatians* but that film just didn't stick in my head. Obviously, it'd be perfect to see it again. Perhaps the day that I saw it, I was in a bad mood or was sick—maybe I went to the bathroom during the best scene!

♦ *AJ: You couldn't put the movie on "pause."*
♦ BF: Back then, whatever came your way came fatalistically, and it either stuck with you or it didn't—you're like this snowball going through space catching these things as they come along. My job now is to go back and dissect that snowball, seeing what did stick to me . . . what changed something else to change something else . . .

"Visiting Hours." Santa Monica Museum of Art, 1992

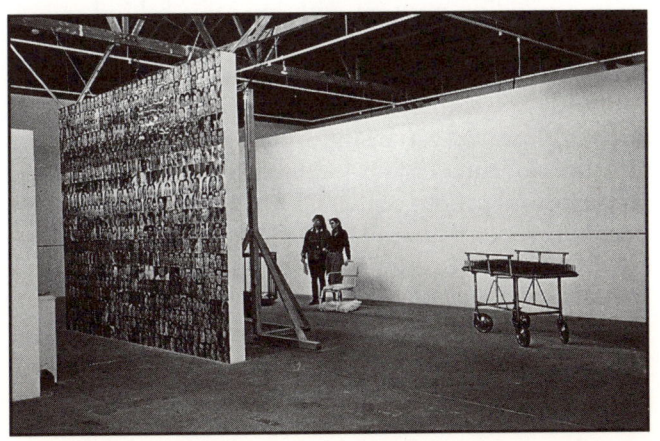

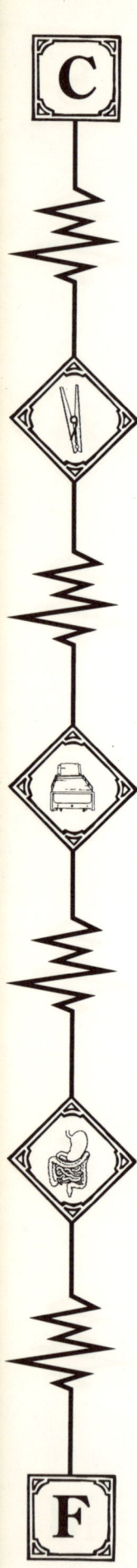

adding catechism to all that. I used to believe that thinking bad thoughts was punishable (you would go to hell), plus I loved Lent: I gave up things I loved the most for Lent. I still have that mentality of forced commitment or bondage: "I really love chocolate, so I'm not going to eat chocolate for forty days and nights." As a kid I'd give up chocolate, but Easter ends Lent, so we'd get all this candy on Easter to break the chocolate fast.

Sheree is Jewish, but Lent really appealed to her for the same reasons it still appeals to me—

♦ **AJ: *Yom Kippur corresponds to Lent—***
♦ **BF:** Yes, this arbitrary period of time for fasting, etc. As I grew older and no longer believed in god, I still kept observing Lent. Since I was a television addict and lived alone, television was sort of my pacifier, so I'd put the television in the closet for forty days and nights.
♦ **V: Now *that's* *a modern-day deprivation!***
♦ **BF:** Yeah, I did that successfully—against all odds!
♦ **AJ: *How do you feel after you've finished? A sense of accomplishment?***
♦ **BF:** Well—what have you accomplished after you've had sex?! It's not like building bridges or something, but you've completed a task and maintained a certain discipline. It's better if you have a partner, because if you're fasting, for example, it's easy to come up with reasons why you should stop: "Oh, this isn't good for me—I'd better eat now!" But it's really disappointing to quit—you feel guilty: "Guess I'm not a masochist anymore!" [sob] "I'm a terrible slave; I'm not *really* into SM." Sometimes I'll do these things (because I haven't thought about SM for a long time) just to *prove* I'm still into SM! When Sheree's out of town, I'll go back to that auto-erotic space . . . .
♦ **AJ: *Explain that—***
♦ **BF:** I'll do things like handcuffing myself up and mailing the key, so I have to wait for the mailman to deliver the key to the handcuffs. Once I mailed the key on a Saturday and had to be handcuffed all weekend, hoping that the mail would arrive safely on Monday. I could walk around the house, but I couldn't drive. On Monday I put a jacket over my wrists, walked outside to the mailbox and hoped that the neighbors wouldn't notice. I've never had an apartment where the mail gets delivered through a slot in your front door—if I had one, I would have tied myself to something right by the mailbox and waited. One of these days I'll get to do that!

Dennis Cooper has a closet I would die for—you walk into his apartment and to the left is a closet, and the mail slot is right in his closet! I'd love to go *there* for a three-day weekend; then I could chain myself inside the closet and just wait . . . What I love about that is: there's nobody to plead to (even if Sheree's dominating me, if I whine the right way and cough hard enough, eventually she stops: "I don't think I'm feeling well enough for this!" [cough] Since she's really worried about my health, she'll always unlock me. Then I feel horrible: "I ruined it! I didn't maintain the discipline. I wasn't *that* sick—I could have stood it!" And it's a double guilt, because also I lied by pretending I was sick . . .

One time Sheree was away for three days. She had a patio in the backyard, and somehow I arranged to be tied up all night spread-eagled on the cement. I had keys embedded in ice tied above me—I had to wait all night for the ice to melt and drop the keys into my hand. I also had suspended above me a can with my own shit in it and some piss mixed in. This can had weights attached in such a way that it was slowly tilting—at some point it was going to spill all over me and I had no control over it because I was completely tied up. If you're masturbating and think up this plan, it sounds really erotic . . . but the actual reality of doing it makes me go, "Oh, this is so sick!" That's when I feel the sickest—like that guy in *The Boston Strangler*. I guess I *like* being that person, though! Whipping and nailing—I've stylized *that* through doing performances, so the only way I can really humiliate myself is through using piss, shit and bodily fluids. It's too absurd to call myself names or look in the mirror and yell, "Douchebag!" But I *can* make myself eat shit, or drink my own pee . . . and do it in such a way that I go, "I don't want to do this!" yet I *have* to do it.

I usually manage to escape from anything. In this particular situation [described above], after four hours, this can of shit and piss was just about to fall on me, but in a really bizarre Houdini way I escaped from all these padlocks (without waiting for the keys to drop). Somehow, with my toe, I kept moving this bar up so I jostled the ice and got the keys to drop and then contorted my body in such a way that I got access to them. On one level I felt really horrible that I hadn't maintained the discipline, but I rationalized, "My new rule is: if I *can* get out, I'd *better* get out!" If I've forgotten to think it all the way through, or am so masterful I can figure out how to escape—then that's like Houdini; that's as good as or even better than the discipline!" So the getting out of it was as exciting as having gone through it all.

♦ **AJ: *Plus—didn't you feel a heightened sense of urgency to escape before the can fell on you?***
♦ **BF:** It was like a movie: watching the sawmill blade come closer to your head while you're waiting for someone to release you . . . Another thing I did was: I filled up a one-gallon milk bottle with urine I saved during the day (I made sure to drink a lot of water), then tied myself up in a standing position with my arms behind me. A long tube from the carton went into my mouth; the keys were on a string above, and they would only drop when the bottle was sufficiently light . . . and the only way that could happen was by me drinking all the pee! I could stay there for three days if I wanted and take my time, or suck a lot and get out of there. I had a leather hood on so I couldn't see anything. It took a couple hours for me to drink enough so I could finally escape.
♦ **AJ: *How did you feel?***
♦ **BF:** It was *thrilling*. You feel a lot of different sensations. First I get a huge erection; I'm really excited. Then panic sets in: "What if there's an earthquake? What if a helicopter drops in through the ceiling?" Sometimes

Sheree would tie me up and drive off to run errands for hours. I'd start screaming, "Sheree, this is too tight!" After the panic, a kind of erotic feeling takes over. I have a tape somewhere which is really embarrassing, recorded when Sheree left me tied up all night long. I had to pee all over myself—that's another kind of thrill: to let everything loose no matter where you are—on a table or a patio or wherever. Then the smell takes over!

The first hour spread-eagled isn't so bad. But as the hours pass, it becomes more and more painful. The muscles can't move so you start to cramp. I've read SM articles warning against that, but I *want* all that to happen—that's when it's real and not "play" bondage; when there's nothing you can do about it and you can't beg your way out of it. The articles tell you to be on a soft surface, but I want to be on a hard piece of wood, totally tied up and left there.

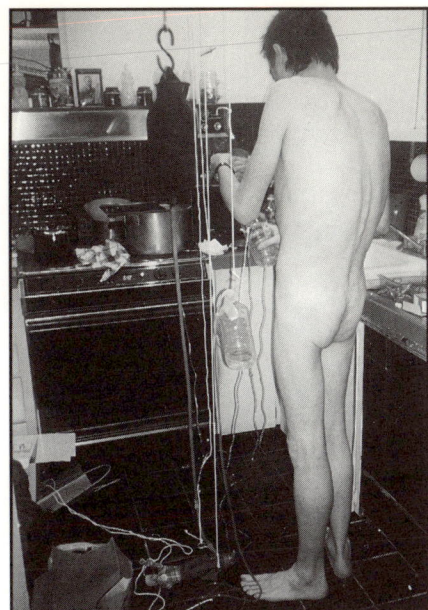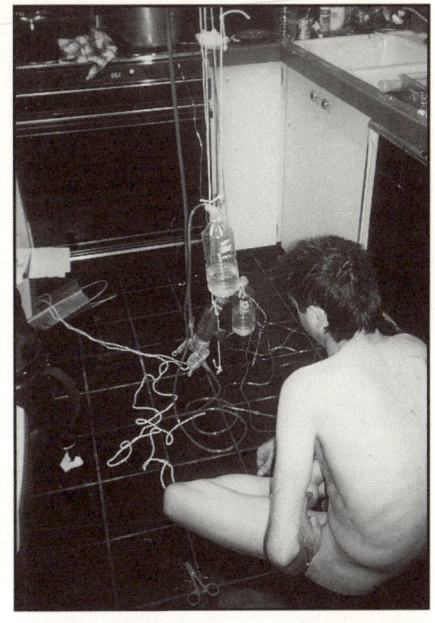

Working in the kitchen on the hydro-dynamics of how I'm going to lift myself out of my hospital bed for "Visiting Hours." The laws of physics were against me, however, so Sheree had to do the lifting, which only added to the drama and poetry of the whole thing. Los Angeles, 1992

Not long ago Sheree tied me up and went out for four hours. Then you have to come up with ways to pass the time; there's nothing to do. I don't want any distractions; I don't want the TV on; I want to just be left alone in this position blindfolded, gagged if possible, and have to deal with this position which will get more and more painful. I wind up counting so I can keep track of the time: "Is this an hour? Two hours?" Sometimes I'll be pretty accurate. I guess this is close to meditation, which I've never done in any formal way, but the numbers probably become a mantra—I just keep counting the numbers over and over again.

♦ *AJ: You're forced to be alone with yourself—*
♦ BF: If there's anything in SM that comes close to an out-of-body experience, it's those kind of bondage feats . . . where you do something for long periods of time with no distractions, no bargaining—you're just *there*.
♦ *AJ: It sounds like it's the opposite of "out-of-body": you're actually feeling and truly being* in *your body.*
♦ BF: For my Santa Monica show I plan to be in a hospital bed where people will visit me. But I'll be tied up by the ankles to this ceiling pulley which is attached to a big Sparkletts water bottle with water dripping into it. When the bottle gets filled, it'll be heavy enough to pull me up toward the ceiling! I'm still trying to work out the mechanics. I didn't want to press a button and have some motor do it; I wanted gravity to be the motivating force. I wanted to be at the whim of fate, where I don't know how long it takes before this bottle fills up (perhaps an hour). Then suddenly, out of the blue, I'm being pulled up by my ankles. Maybe I'll be talking to somebody and then: "Whoops—gotta go!"

♦ *AJ: Go back to how you feel when an endurance test is over—*
♦ BF: There's that weird sense of accomplishment over something that in some ways means *nothing*.
♦ *AJ: But what, ultimately, do our accomplishments mean* anyway?
♦ BF: You think, "Oh, what would it be like if I tried *this*?" They're *events,* and once you've done them, there's no need to do them again: "Okay, I did *that*. What's next?" You set a goal, reach it, and it's discipline. But actually it's not even discipline because I *have* to do it. Dealing with pseudo-life-threatening SM challenges ties in to how I've had to deal with my illness. I remember thinking, "Now I'm spitting up blood—I've got to deal with this." My sister had cystic fibrosis much worse than I, and toward the end it seemed like every six months a new complication was added: diabetes, heart problems. She would cry a little bit and go, "Well, I've got to deal with *that* now." So these mechanical situations I put myself in mirror that experience.

Right now I'm on IV-antibiotics for the next three weeks, so every eight hours I have to stop whatever I'm doing and do these drugs. If I miss, I feel bad, and if I do it, I feel this weird sense of accomplishment. I think this is what my show is about: SM makes fun of what I *have* to do. This is why I never lose my sense of humor about SM—in some ways it's dark and serious, but in other ways it's the goofiest kind of activity, like any kind of sex that human beings do. There's no way to make fun of an illness that can make children die at an early age—that's serious, but SM mocks it all. So even if I *did* die in the throes of doing SM, it would be no more sad and awful

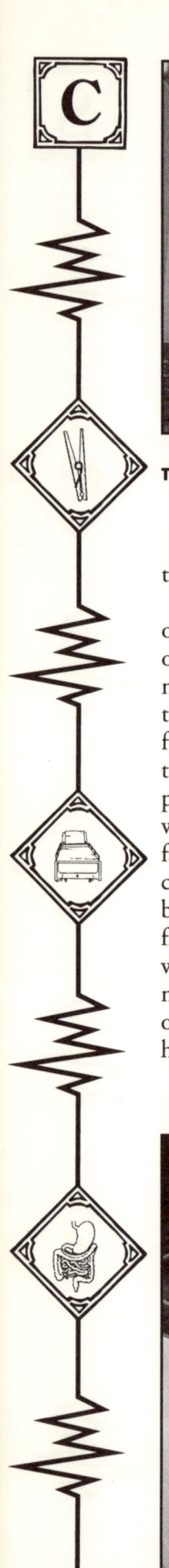

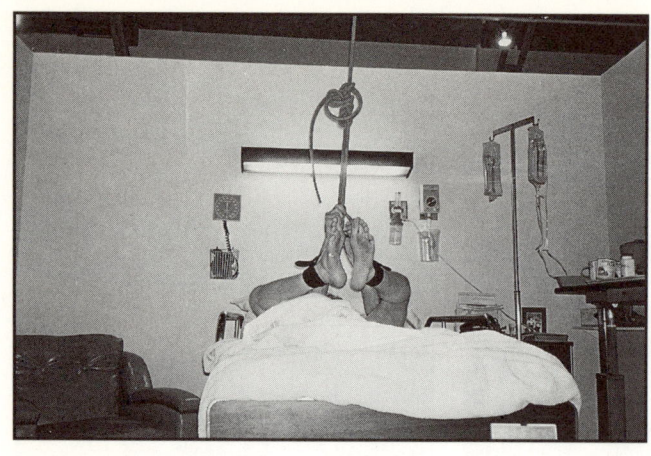 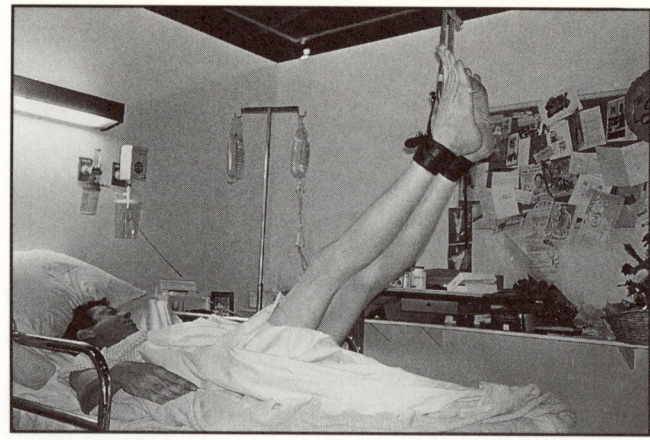

The "ascension" from my sickbed during "Visiting Hours." The Santa Monica Museum of Art. All photos: Scott Boberg

than dying of this stupid disease.

In my show there's a quotation describing me as a kind of Superman character—Superman was another influence on my life (the TV show starring George Reeves). I remember the episode where Clark Kent as a kid comes up to his mom and asks, "Mom, how come I'm different from everybody else?" That's the same thing *I* would say to my mother. But he was different because he was a superhuman person who could fly and see through walls, whereas I was different because I was this weird kid who farted all the time and whose farts smelled bad, and who coughed all the time and whom kids made fun of. So I become a sort of SM-Superman! My hospital gown gets flipped around into a cape, and I have rubber pants on, weights hanging from my balls, and an oxygen mask on my face—all the SM and medical equipment I could put on my body at one time. Sheree's going to create this huge portrait of me in front of clouds.

In the show I also have this text about me being this superhuman character fighting sickness with sickness. This echoes Superman's speeches about the battle over truth and justice, ending ultimately with the discovery that I learn to fight sickness with sickness.

♦ *AJ: This is a great metaphor—*
♦ BF: Sometimes I live from event to event. As things get harder to do, the event gives me a surge of energy. Even though I might be sick that particular weekend and not want to do anything, I'll drum up enough energy to at least get through this bondage event (or whatever). I was in therapy for a little while and this subject kept coming up: there are lots of things I can't compete with or do as a normal person, but in *this* area I'm a superman: I can nail my dick to a board and I can endure long periods of bondage. I can't do sports and a lot of other things, so I'm not able to do what a lot of people do, but I have this area where I can soar and definitely excel. My big joke at the

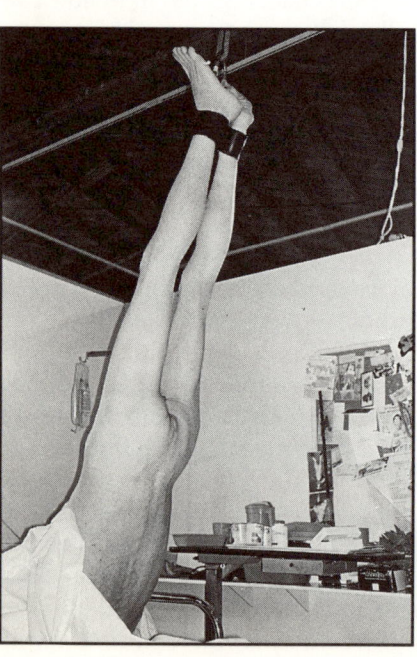  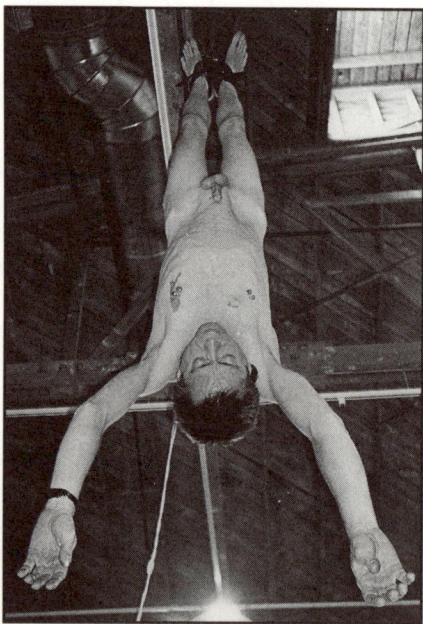

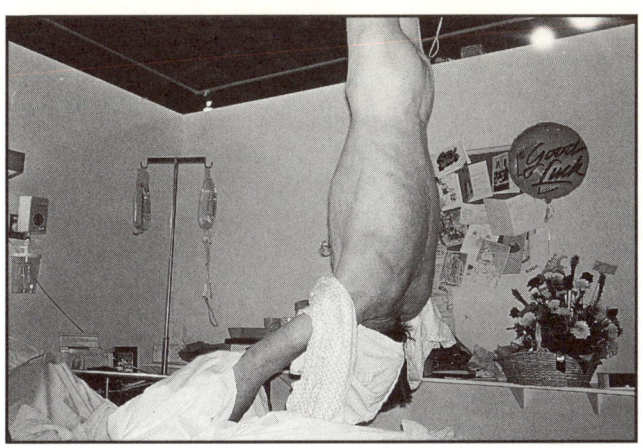

"Nailed" show was: I come out with ten pounds of weights on my balls (and I'm obviously a skinny guy) and I say, "Let's see Arnold Schwarzenegger do *this!*" [laughs] Well, maybe he hangs weights on his balls—I don't know.

♦ *AJ: Also, at your show there was absolutely no trace of embarrassment or guilt; here you are doing what most people feel guilty (or at least secretive) about. Very few people have an acceptance of things they do naturally, like masturbation, having sex, shitting, farting, etc. Yet here you are stark naked, and the only people who feel embarrassed are the audience—*

♦ BF: It's odd, because I'm basically shy about showing my body. I would never take my shirt off at the beach—I don't *go* to the beach! I never go to the pool because I'm very shy about my body. But in the context of a performance, I have this attitude: "This is it!" That's part of conquering the image of me as an ill person, going, "This is the hand I was dealt"—total acceptance. A lot of people bemoan something about themselves, like, "Why was I born this way? Why can't I be thinner? Why can't I be more muscular?" Whereas I think, "This is everything I can possibly be at the moment—that's *it*. I'll do what I can; I'll hang weights on my balls; strap myself up"—to me there's a real freeing aspect to this. Even on the *Nine Inch Nails* movie set being naked with a whole crew, I thought, "I'm this skinny guy—why try to hide it?" So I just walked around naked.

♦ *AJ: Did you write any special text for your Santa Monica show?*

♦ BF: Like I said, I have the "Why" poem spiraled around the room, so people have to walk all the way around to read it. The toy chest has this text that's all about how my penis became the center of my battle with illness: "From the very beginning, when the pediatrician spanked my ass to get my diseased lungs sparked into life, that also sent a shock wave through my sphincter, up my tiny rectum and into the shaft of my shiny new penis which ever since then has had the crazy idea that sex and pain are one and the same." That text is wood-burned into the open lid of the toybox. The chest will be filled with weird

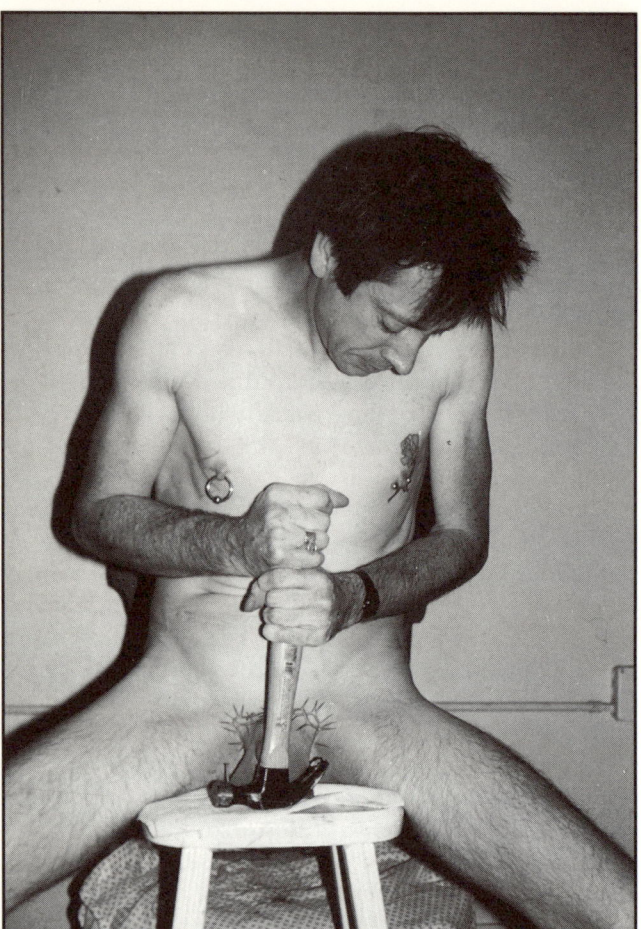

"You Always Hurt the One You Love," an SM performance and demonstration for QSM. San Francisco, 1991

Taking a breather while the audience watches "Pigs is Pigs." QSM performance, San Francisco, 1991

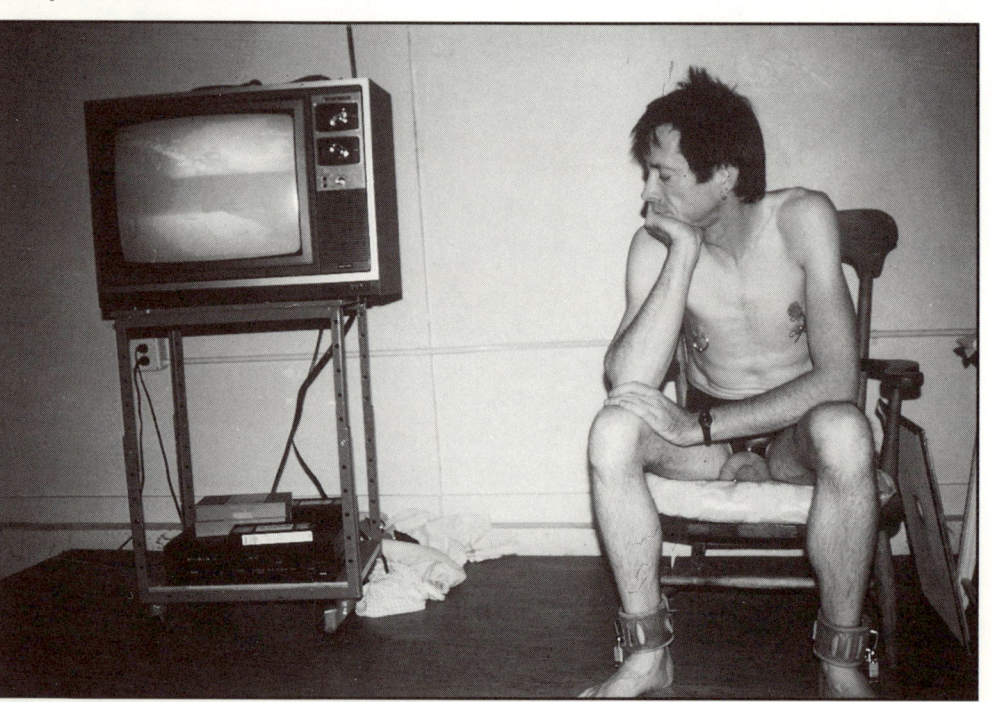

sex toys. At the Living Leather SM conference in Chicago, Sheree found this giant black rubber penis (nothing you could *use;* it's too huge) and that's thrown in. There are wooden hammers and wrenches in a little kid's workbox inscribed with the name "Bob." There's a dildo with wooden nails through the head of the penis; it looks as though a kid made it.

I also have real lung specimens in a jar, and hope to get this penis in a jar which a friend has—it's pierced, too! I think a medical student got it from a cadaver and then gave it a Prince Albert. To me, those organs are the two centers of my existence: the lungs and the penis. That's what "S M C F" is all about. People have to walk between these two specimens to see me.

I also bought a big Jack-in-the-Box which I want to turn into a Jack*off*-in-the-Box. I want to replace the clown with a big pierced penis, so when you open the lid this giant erection pops up at you!

My only hope is a lung transplant, yet Stanford turned me down—my right lung is so scarred they think surgery's too risky. When I was an infant, the doctors pierced my chest with big needles to draw out the infected fluid (that's pretty ironic, I think). Doctors have always questioned this whenever they see the scars on the x-rays, and I've had to explain it. San Diego would do it, but it would cost me $250,000.00 for the operation—that's a lot of fund-raising. Right now there's a two-year waiting list. You have to wait for the right donor, too. If I ever get a transplant, I'll have my own lungs preserved in a jar.

Right now I'm on steroid pills so I feel much better—before this, just getting off the couch was an effort. However, I can only do steroids for a short time; after awhile, it fucks up your body and makes you psychotic—

♦ **AJ: Like James Mason in *Bigger Than Life*—**
♦ BF: I've *got* to see that movie! That reminds me, in my Santa Monica show I'm going to have video monitors, and all the film clips will be related either to sex, SM or medical footage—like commercials of kids coughing, excerpts from *Boy in the Bubble* (with John Travolta; that has some great lines).

♦ *AJ: Do you have any more writing projects?*
♦ BF: You know those *Highlights* magazines you read as a kid? They're always in doctor's offices. I wanted to imitate an issue but only include SM and sickness articles—just appropriate the whole thing and have it printed.

In the Santa Monica show we're including a

fake waiting room with huge phallic cacti; posters of the genitals, chest and digestive systems (the three main areas of SM and CF); cystic fibrosis pamphlets and books instructing parents how to deal with CF children; and also SM catalogs. I have books with illustrations of kids going to the doctor, and I wanted to substitute myself (with big penises, etc) but I didn't have enough time to do this. I'm going to try to get the *smell* of the waiting room, too—that faint combination of Lysol and alcohol. I also want sound effects: "Dr So-and-so wanted in emergency . . ." I want a toy ambulance with a siren wailing constantly circling the room, too.

I've always written autobiographically in my journals, but people turn their noses up at autobiography—

♦ **AJ:** *What do you mean?*
♦ **BF:** Most writers I know make up characters and write stories—the *artists* I know certainly don't do self-portraits.
♦ **AJ:** *But you're almost inventing a genre—what you do is so deeply self-revelatory and genuine, and there are so many levels to it that—*
♦ **BF:** I tried to write prose and make up characters but they were always obviously *me;* like "Joe Hanigan, whose sister is sick with a disease." They were consistently awful failures.
♦ **AJ:** *But there's a very rare transparency in what you do. It's almost cathartic for other humans to hear your confessions or see you, like at the "Nailed" show—*
♦ **BF:** That's when I first realized this might be viable. Before, I just did demonstrations for SM clubs, but to see how a more general crowd (many of whom aren't even into this) responds, was really an eye-opener. The same with my *Fuck Journal,* which was meant to be totally private, but when that got published, I couldn't believe it. Before, I'd read from *Fuck Journal* about drinking Sheree's pee, etc, and people walked out—one woman yelled as she left, "You got *problems!*" [laughs] I said, "Well, thank you very much." People would just stare at me like I was some sort of freak; they wouldn't even talk to me. You have to have a lot of people accepting you and saying you're "good" before you start to think differently . . .

What I feel about this is: I'm just *driven* to do it. I never asked to do any of these shows; somebody has always asked me.

♦ **AJ:** *If you listen to what other people say, you'd never do anything—especially if you have a creative vision. Most people are incredibly negative and lack imagination; they're very threatened by other people's creativity—*
♦ **BF:** I'm secure about my writing, but not the visual art component. All my friends are like Mike Kelley and Jim Shaw [famous L.A. artists], teachers, and I was *rejected* from Cal Arts when I applied out of high school. So I come to "art" through the back door. I was originally going to be an artist in high school, but gave it up because I was painting self-portraits like Van Gogh and the hip artists of the time were doing neon art and conceptual art. I had no *ideas* at the time; I didn't know *what* to do, so I started writing. Now here I am in a museum—if a year ago somebody had said I would be here, I wouldn't have believed 'em.
♦ **AJ:** *A lot of artists who show in big museums and make a lot of money are just reinforcing the status quo. Most of what they do is boring, facile, and meaningless. It's an old-boy network, too (and I do emphasize "boy"). And the machinery of publicity and fame can corrupt—*
♦ **BF:** Like Fakir; it's real sad what's happening to him. I met him ten years ago when he'd come to the Gauntlet and he was just Roland _____; we called him *Roland,* not Fakir. Recently he brought his whole show down to Highways [art space] in L.A., and everybody who's ever been pierced was invited to do the kavandi dance, to have balls sewn to their bodies, and to dance and go into a trance. But nobody called me; nobody invited me. People are so competitive, I guess—
♦ **AJ:** *The whole "modern primitives" idea was not a defined subculture when we put out our book,* Modern

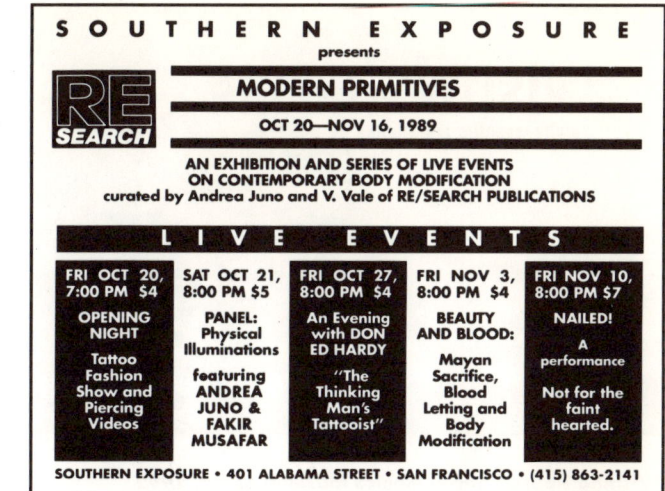

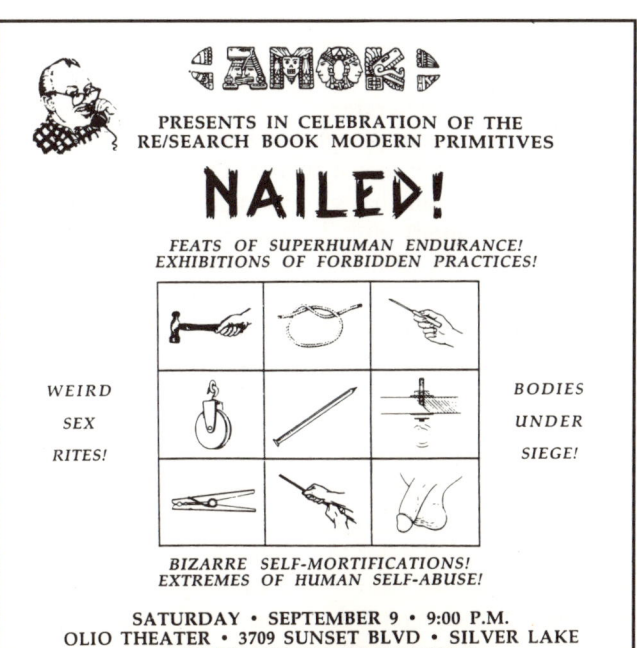

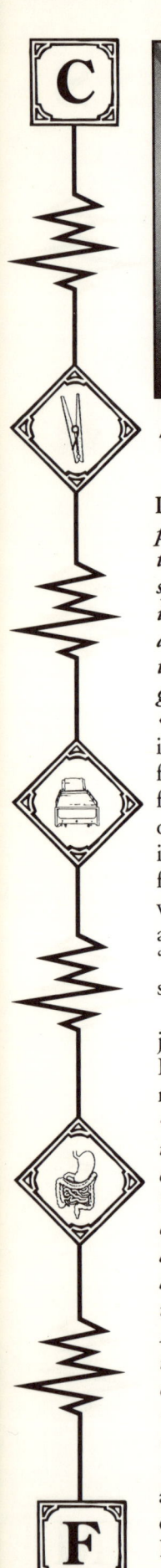

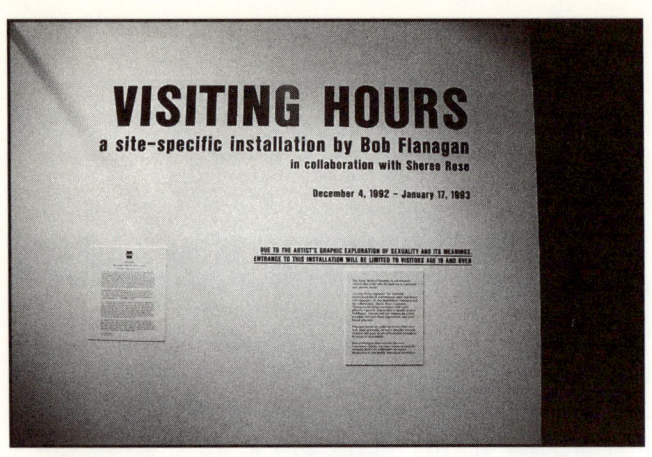

"Visiting Hours." Santa Monica Museum of Art, 1992

Primitives. *These were individuals who were exploring personal visions. Then an underground emerged, and after that the masses almost get the "forms" right but not the spirit. It became this fashion, often with a fake spirituality overlaid. It's nice to see so many tattoos and piercings as a personal expression of symbols that are meaningful to that person, but unfortunately a pretentious pseudo-religion lurks in the background.*

♦ BF: The guys who started Club Fuck in L.A. were genuine and sincere like Fakir. They started this *scene*—no different than I created with my work, but things just get further and further from their original source. Ron Athey, one of the founders of Club Fuck, has a background which is really amazing—he was raised Pentecostal. So to turn from a "holy roller" into what he became today—*that's* what intrigues me. Now he's breaking into performance art and I hope it won't be this uniform, pseudo-Nazi power "lick my boot" fantasy stuff—that's so boring and I've seen it a million times at Threshold meetings.

I never wanted to call myself a "performance artist," I just went out and did these things from an honest place. I developed certain skills as an actor and comedian and now they just emerge naturally.

♦ AJ: *I think that Fakir, in building up a "guru" image, is actually trying to create a religion—exactly the opposite of what we wanted to encourage in* Modern Primitives. *The whole concept of a "guru" is usually the perpetuation of authoritarian male control (and 99% of the time they are* male.*) Hopefully we are entering into a more mature age where people have enough self-respect and consciousness to not blindly follow anyone; just learn from many. Piercing, tattooing, or pain in themselves don't necessarily bring enlightenment; that notion can be very dangerous and fascistic—*

♦ BF: And there's so much money involved now.

♦ AJ: *It is like joining some kind of church or cult.*

♦ BF: At the *Highways* show, there was a guy walking around in a centaur costume who was the worst—apparently he's actually a nice guy, but he was dressed in this Halloween outfit and saying things like, "Oh, great spirit, call on us! Come to us!" The only true moment came when people gave a eulogy for Cliff Diller (a founder of Club Fuck), who had just died of AIDS, and when people started dancing with the balls hooked into their skin—that seemed more like a ritual; then it meant something. But then Mr Centaur had to ruin it and interrupt the *possibility* of them going into their trance, by doing something totally wrong.

Regarding these practices borrowed from India and other places, my reality check always is: I was never raised with this. In my shows I have some Catholic imagery because I was a Catholic; I have cartoons because I watched cartoons.

♦ AJ: *Humans from time immemorial have had a desire to engage in rituals in which the defense mechanisms that keep us from confronting death and our aloneness are stripped away. It's really all about fear. The trap is in identifying the ritual as something other than a mere process; in overlaying a metaphysical essence. The irony is: thus you escape deeply confronting yourself.*

♦ BF: The best part of Fakir's show is when he talks about his personal history as a kid and shows slides documenting what he did. But to take that extra step and become "The Fakir"—what do you mean: "You're *Roland!*" It's much more interesting to be Roland working in an ad agency and coming home at night and suspending yourself by hooks in your chest—that's *beautiful*. But "Fakir" is silly! You're a cartoon now! You're the new Jim Jones!

♦ AJ: *Also, there's the assumption that unless you like pain, you can't be enlightened. Yet all this is very personal, having to do with very personal imprinting and desires from childhood upbringing, etc. We all have different erotic needs and different spiritual needs. I tried lying on a bed of nails and it was nothing—it was not my personal thing. But when somebody tries to tell you, "This is the only route to enlightenment—"*

♦ BF: Exactly. I hope that getting into pain is not going to become commercialized . . . that you'll go into Thrifty's drugstore and see a "Pain" section with all these SM toys. Maybe it would be fun if they started selling pain *inducers* as well as pain relievers—

♦ AJ: *But this is your personal desire, not everyone's.*

♦ BF: The message is not to run away from anything that's there. Everyone has something that may be bizarre to them and nobody else. There are *reasons* why I went into SM, and I'm looking at those; I'm going toward those reasons instead of away from them: "Oh, I can't do this! This is wrong!" I mean, *why* do I sit and think about drinking my own pee from a bottle? It's not something everybody thinks about; why do I think about it? There's a reason for it. This all comes from some source. All religion was *invented;* it's not real.

My youngest brother and his wife are full Southern Baptists. On the surface he's not judgmental about me, but I got this weird letter from his wife about why I don't believe in god. She thinks that I hate god because god gave me CF and invented disease. But I *don't* hate god, because I don't believe in it. Besides, I wouldn't know who I would be without CF; I'm *proud* to have it and I've used it to my advantage. What would I be doing otherwise: playing baseball?! I never had that "Woe is me; I'm in such horrible straits!" attitude. Religion is bad because people use it to kill other people, but that's not "god."

♦ **AJ: Right. Go back to when you were exploring why you would drink piss—**
♦ BF: It keeps coming back to inventing ways to deal with the illness, just like people want to find out why they're on this planet. And this is minor and tiny; it's not big. What I'm doing is not for everybody; it may be for twenty other people on the planet. But it's my own mechanism for me, and I wouldn't dream of saying, *"You* should do this. This is enlightening for *you."* My performances are autobiographical; I'm saying, "Look at what I've done to myself, with myself." And hopefully that's enough to spark people thinking in *other* terms and other directions—

♦ **V: —*getting* inspiration *from it, not imitation.***
♦ BF: I suppose that if you go more and more into the personal, then by being so open it becomes more and more universal.

In high school my big influence in art was Van Gogh (that's a cliche now) because I stumbled onto his show in L.A. and couldn't believe what I was seeing. In person, his paintings are almost psychedelic. But he's like Dylan was for me in music; it was a watershed breakthrough *then,* but no longer. I especially liked the self-portraits in which Van Gogh looked at every aspect of the torturous pain he went through, and painted himself exactly the way he saw himself, not hiding the bandages or the scars.

♦ **V: Do you want to talk about your white sheep brother?**
♦ BF: I think John has his own sense of guilt, being the youngest and the healthiest in our family. He's the only family member into sports. I'm painting this picture of him as this horrible guy into religion and sports, but he's not—he loves us all. He never judged my brother for being gay, and he doesn't really know the extent of what I'm into. He was closer in age to my sister who died of CF, and he was really affected by her death. He made sure he didn't cause any trouble, whereas my other brother Tim went through his marijuana stage and had screaming fights with my mother when she flushed his stash down the toilet. I was the oldest and was sick all the time, but my sister was even sicker, so my parents certainly had their hands full. But they were careful to give Tim and John as much love and attention as they gave my sister and me. John wasn't raised with Catholicism; by the time he was born, my parents had given up on that. Ironically, since I was the first-born and the only one to go to Catholic school, I had that Catholic guilt in me, but when John came around, I was still going to catechism and realized that John didn't even know who Jesus *was!* My parents never talked about religion, and John didn't go see *King of Kings,* so . . .

♦ **AJ: How much younger is he?**
♦ BF: He was born in 1960, so he's eight years younger. I was imprinted by the nun punishing me for sharpening my pencils on the first day of Catholic school—she made me stand in front of the class for the entire period (I had the *nerve* to sharpen my brand-new pencils while she was talking; I didn't know this wasn't allowed, and I'd never had a pencil box before). Somehow this memory is tied to the smell of the new leather briefcase I had. But John didn't have any of that; he's a person who had no religion at all. Even my sister had gotten religion on some level, and my gay brother had gone to communion with me.

But now it's all flipped around: my brother John is a preacher who works for the Southern Baptist church. His wife was his high school girlfriend; then they didn't see each other for years; then he went to see her and she was heavily into this religion, and it all just seemed to fit and solve a lot of his problems about where he fit into this world. After all, he was the healthy one, the survivor of his sister who died, the one who never wanted to make waves. He thinks I criticize him but I don't; I realize that this is *his* way of dealing with the big questions.

John's wife was pregnant last year and the baby died—it strangled on its own umbilical cord. We attended the funeral service and when I saw the coffin I thought it was

The Toy Box, "Visiting Hours." Santa Monica Museum of Art, 1992

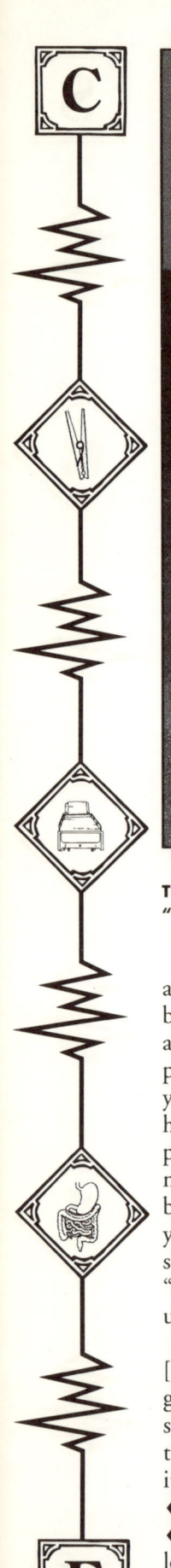

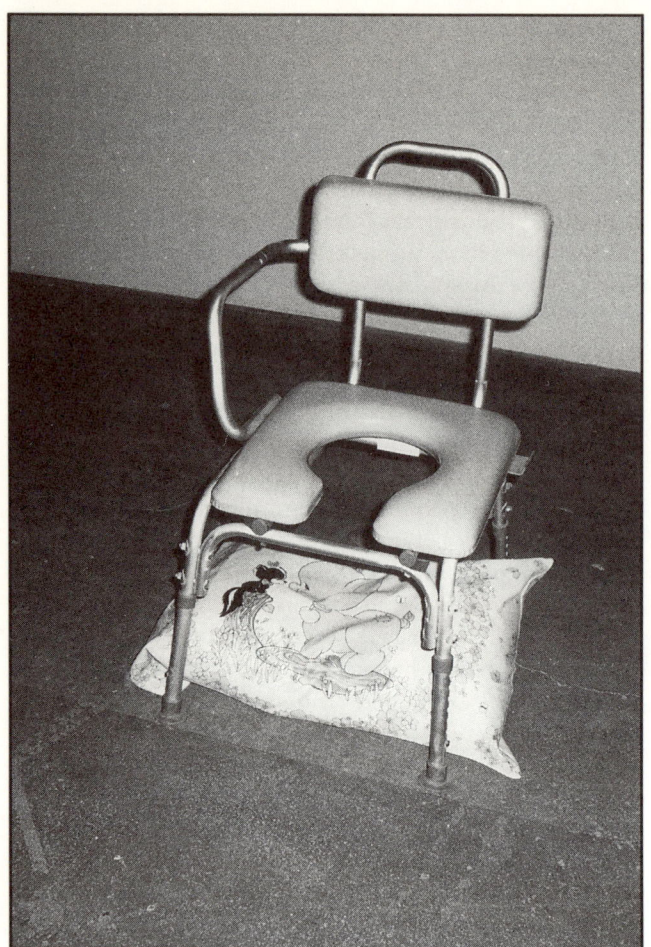

The Porta-potty with pig pillow for someone's weary head. "Visiting Hours." Santa Monica Museum of Art, 1992

The Gurney of Nails, "Visiting Hours." Santa Monica Museum of Art, 1992

a styrofoam ice chest! I wish I had a picture of this church, because there was a big flannel board showing a ship with a caption underneath: "We are all on a ship called Discipline"! The preacher talked about why this baby died—you gotta invent reasons, you know. If god is all loving, how could it take this innocent little baby? And the preacher came up with, "Well, Jesus just decided that he needed another little baby in heaven." Sheree and my brother Tim were with me, and—this is a funny scene: you've got the homosexual, the masochist and the Jew sitting there in this Baptist church! We were wondering, "What kind of Jesus is *this:* 'Hey, we need another baby up here! Go down and get that kid.' "

The preacher also said, "It's *good* that this baby died." [then confidentially] "It's a *blessing*... because he didn't grow up to be a sinner!" [laughs] He continued, "You shouldn't feel bad, because this baby lived a full life. It got to know Jesus through its mother, in the womb, and now it's with Jesus."

♦ **V:** *You call that a full life?*
♦ **BF:** Me drinking piss out of a bottle makes a helluva lot more sense than believing in this Jesus in heaven who wants your baby—dead or alive.
♦ **AJ:** *And this attitude: these people can't stand life; what they really want is death.*
♦ **BF:** This intense belief in some "after-life" . . . to me that's really frightening. My mother came from a family of ten kids who suffered lots of abuse—I wonder if abuse is passed on through the genes? She used to tell us stories of being beaten with sticks and belts by her older brothers. The girls in the family were treated like slaves, and the boys participated in a pecking order—the older you were, the more power you had over the ones below. Now they're dropping off like flies from weird blood diseases, liver diseases, intestinal disorders . . . one died in a fire. And they all think they're going to heaven. Saturday night they get shit-faced drunk and beat their wives, and on Sunday they're in church taking communion. That's one of the reasons my parents left the church and their family behind—they couldn't stand the abuse or the hypocrisy.
♦ **AJ:** *How much do your parents know about what you do?*
♦ **BF:** Well, the idea of my mother sitting in front of a TV seeing my dick being nailed to a board—no matter *how* great we relate [laughs], no matter *how* understanding they are, I just think that would make her feel bad. Yet she's always been supportive of everything I've ever done. And I'm getting more and more fame for things I can talk less

and less about to her. Last week in the hospital I was spitting up blood and getting scared, thinking, "This is the end." So I try and talk to them about what I do: "Oh, it's a little like what Madonna's doing now," [laughs] and relate it to what they know. I gave 'em a copy of my poem "Why," but I *didn't* give them *Fuck Journal*. I think they know there are things they shouldn't ask about, and that's fine with me. I'm not into the sexuality of children or anything like that at all, but I'm really into analyzing my *own* childhood. I was a real sexual kid but nobody knew about it. From the earliest age I was doing things that had some sort of sexual resonance; it seems like I was having erections from Day One. I'm turned on by my own recollections of being a kid who was sexually turned-on.

♦ *AJ: Every child has a very active sexuality. Most of our eroticism can be traced to childhood experiences, yet most people and society don't want to talk about that—*
♦ BF: And you'll never recapture the sweetness of what it was originally like: the first orgasms, the first fantasies. As violent as I may have made them, there was a sweetness to them that I always want to go back and try to re-experience. Why, when I would not allow myself to masturbate to orgasm, would I call it "going overboard"? Back then I didn't know the word "orgasm," I didn't know the word "cum." The first time I came I went, "What's *this*?" After that I thought of it as "going overboard," and I told myself, "You can't go overboard. Don't go overboard." There was a sweeter taste and innocence as to what it was all about; my auto-erotic activities go back to that. In fact, that's what I always hope a new auto-erotic activity will do: evoke that feeling. I always want to do something different, like: instead of drinking piss, maybe I'll drink expelled enema juice. That's even *more* powerful and repulsive! I haven't done that, but I've thought about it many, many times!

♦ *AJ: Then you can purge yourself of that fantasy, literally! [laughs]*
♦ BF: Yes. Literally and literarily, too. It's all infantile. Another thing I'm putting into my show is a hospital commode, but replacing the bedpan underneath by a kid's pillow with a little indentation for the head. And there'll be a Porky Pig-type motif on the pillow. So someone seeing it might think, "Why would somebody put their head there?"

♦ *V: A modified ready-made sculpture . . .*
♦ BF: I'll have a little cage set up with a kid's blanket inside, and my hospital gurney of 1,400 nails—this is part of the torture environment built around the scaffold.

♦ *V: This is a post-Duchamp installation with a kick to it, what with all these potent, sexually-charged objects—*
♦ BF: Duchamp is a good person to be in league with.

♦ *AJ: Also, when you were on that gurney it probably felt like a torture bed—*
♦ BF: As something to endure. Being in a hospital bed is an endurance test. A gurney is something they use to wheel you into surgery, and that feeling when you're still awake being wheeled in, before the drugs take effect—well, you may as well be on a bed of nails. Last time when all this fluid collected around my heart (pericarditis), I thought, "This is really serious." Some music was playing and at first I didn't know what it was because I was fading away as the drugs took effect. But just before I went "out" I realized it was *Pink Floyd*. I thought, "Oh fuck—I'm going to die, and the last thing on my brain is gonna be *Pink Floyd's* "Another Brick in the Wall"! NO!"

♦ *AJ: That would not be fair—*
♦ BF: Although . . . I built the alphabet block wall after that, so maybe it inspired me!

♦ *V: Your show is a retrospective which includes all of the "props" from previous shows, right? It will show stages (literally) along life's way. That reminds me of the Liberace museum, which shows his past costumes and his 200-pound gold-embroidered cloaks—*
♦ BF: Exactly. This will be the beginning of a little museum . . . ■ ■ ■

The Cage, which was actually a birthday present, was designed and built by my friend Bob Evans eight years ago. It fit so perfectly in "Visiting Hours," I had to use it. Santa Monica Museum of Art, 1992

BOB FLANAGAN  SUPERMASOCHIST

Interview Four

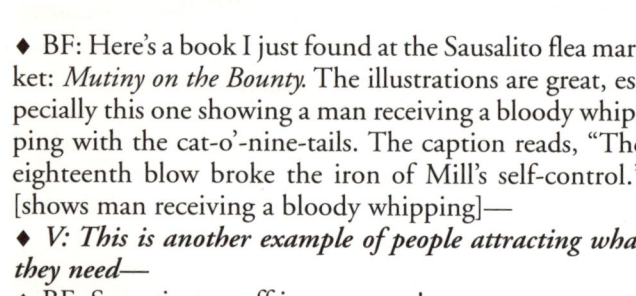

♦ **BF: Here's a book I just found at the Sausalito flea market:** *Mutiny on the Bounty.* The illustrations are great, especially this one showing a man receiving a bloody whipping with the cat-o'-nine-tails. The caption reads, "The eighteenth blow broke the iron of Mill's self-control." [shows man receiving a bloody whipping]—

♦ *V: This is another example of people attracting what they need—*

♦ **BF:** Sometimes stuff just pops up!

♦ *V: Can you talk about your family dynamics a bit more—*

♦ **BF:** Like I said, my parents were really supportive of us kids growing up. In my whole life, we've never missed Christmas together. That's a special holiday; my parents give us a lot of presents, and even though they've never had a lot of money, they're generous to a fault with what they have. So we've always gotten together to celebrate the fact that we've made it through another year (for me, against all odds). And since my birthday falls on the next day, December 26, this time of year has a double significance for me. Knowing how odd we all are, I think my mother thinks that if she'd done something differently, we'd all be "normal." Of course, I think being normal is the worst thing in the world. At our get-togethers we're all tolerant in the sense that we don't *talk* about our differences . . . even though everyone probably knows more than they let on.

Cystic fibrosis has made me the person I am, and I can't even imagine how I'd be without it—it's impossible to think in those terms. I recognize that it's a struggle, but since at camp I work with kids who have much *more* of a struggle, I think that my life isn't that bad.

♦ *AJ: When you described that preacher talking about the dead baby, I got the feeling that christians really view life as something to get over with as quickly as possible . . . zoom from fetus to corpse—*

♦ **BF:** "Get me outta here!" Whereas I don't believe there *is* anything after life, so I better make the best out of life now.

♦ *AJ: You seem quite creatively fulfilled—*

♦ **BF:** I used to think, "I could die tomorrow and be happy." But now I want to finish my book before I die. When I'm in a creative mode I get very opinionated and almost vicious: "It has to be my way or no way!" It's hard on the people you're collaborating with. Especially if that person is supposed to be your Mistress, and you're supposed to be her slave. I revert more into my nasty older brother mode, a side of me that my brother Tim never lets me forget. When we were growing up I was constantly teasing him and playing pranks on him, or just being mean for the sake of being mean. We had a rivalry going; I didn't want him to be like me, and he didn't want me to be like him. He was the actor and I was the painter, but then he started painting and I started acting, and it was like: "Why is *he* painting?" We had this territorial contest all our lives, although thankfully we've advanced beyond that. We went through a five-year period where we didn't talk that much.

Tim has told me stories—he was incredibly sexual and did weird, bizarre things (although nothing to do with SM). I remember building forts with my friends and camping out in the backyard with no thoughts of sexuality; I was nerdy and straight. But it turned out that these same friends were sucking Tim off! It's funny to recall these parallels: "You did *what* with Lenny?" Lenny and I would go into the fort and just sing the lyrics to "Big Bad John" by Jimmy Dean, but Tim would go in there with Lenny and they'd be giving each other blow jobs! [laughs] Me—I was a freak on the *inside,* but totally innocent and nerdy on the outside.

♦ AJ: *You were an actor with the Groundlings?*
♦ BF: Peewee Herman, Laraine Newman, and half the people in *Saturday Night Live* have come from the Groundlings. It's an improvisational theater, although most of it isn't improvisational by the time it hits the stage; the skits have all been worked out. Only rarely are they political; it's pretty white bread conservative material.

The way I got into acting was: I was doing poetry readings and liked being in front of an audience. As always, I'm really slow at writing, so in order to do more readings, I started drinking lots of tequila and reading poems off a blank page—improvising, but trying to make them *sound* as if they were written down. And the reaction was amazing—people would go, "Wow, is that a new poem? Can I hear that again?" And I'd hand them a blank sheet of paper.

Then I tried to tape the improvisations and type them up, but they were nothing—they were garbage. I realized that what was happening was mass hypnosis—you set up a rhythm and say, "I'm reading a poem about a girl in a chair and her feet are painted red" and people go, "Oh wow!" but if you read it on a page, it's absolutely nothing.

On my birthday, at my parents' house. Fremont, 1982

As "Icon Ike," owner of "Ike's House of Religious Icons," displaying the "Magic Tortilla of Turin." The Groundlings, Los Angeles, 1988

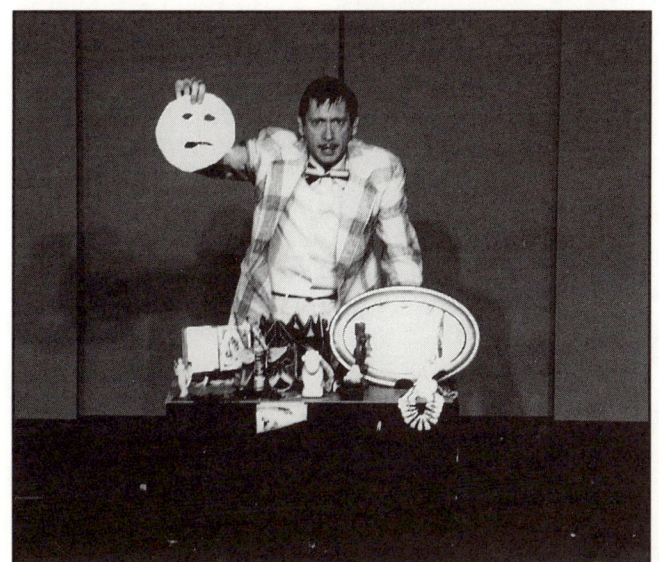

In those days, all the poetry seemed to have this same cadence: *da-duh, da-duh, da-duh, da-duh . . .* [laughs] It was the rhythm that lulled people into the idea that they were hearing this fabulous work. I think that when I realized the nature of this "gimmick," I stopped writing poetry so much. But I loved the excitement of being on the *edge,* improvising.

♦ AJ: *There's always that threat of humiliating yourself in public—*
♦ BF: Very much so. And it's exhibitionism—taking your clothes off mentally. Being in the Groundlings was great training for that. By the time you get into actual shows, you're basically writing skits—and I don't like that as much. After three years I made it into their "Sunday" company, which is just a step away from their main company. Then I started getting sicker and sicker. It takes a lot of energy to be onstage, and if somebody wanted me to be screaming and hysterical, I'd have to hold back because I didn't want to have a coughing fit. I couldn't really commit to what was needed. Plus I realized, looking at the people around me, that it was largely a dead end: you're in the Groundlings but only rarely do you get on television—it *could* happen, but most of the time you're in the Groundlings for ten years. I'm glad they didn't accept me, because literally weeks after I left I started doing

these art performances, and that's when everything took off for me. But I learned a lot about improvisation there; I can always fall back on that training. Plus I learned a lot about staging, setting up and pacing a show.

♦ *AJ: It's impressive, seeing you on stage, because you're doing all this shocking stuff but you're also a master—it feels like you're comfortable. And you're funny. To be able to deliver funny jokes while nailing your scrotum to a board—that's something!*

♦ BF: That's the only way to combat the nervousness. People knew what was going to happen (after all, the show was titled "Nailed") and most of the time their expectations are far worse than what's going to happen. Before our Southern Exposure show in San Francisco, I attended a reading by Dennis Cooper and William Gibson the night before at the Victoria Theater, and overheard someone saying, "Bob Flanagan's going to crucify himself tomorrow!" And someone else said to me, "Bob, I hear that for your fortieth birthday you're going to nail your dick to a friend's wooden leg!" I think that was a joke that Brian King [of Amok Books] made up, but now it's become a myth that people believe. However, a leg has no symbolic meaning for me—if it were another part of the body, I might do it, but a leg doesn't have enough symbolism for me to nail my dick to it. I'm not going to waste my energy on that.

♦ *AJ: How about a wooden lung?*

♦ BF: It's funny how people's expectations are even more extreme than what will happen. Then when I come out and tell jokes, they don't know where to turn. They think they're going to get scared but then they laugh, but then they get scared again—it's like snaking through their emotions, which I think makes people faint more, as well as get into the show more.

♦ *AJ: I like the fact that your shows don't have any phony spiritual allusions—*

♦ BF: I'm not invoking Kali or other Great Spirits.

♦ *AJ: Or putting on some Halloweenish spook and freak show, or performing like a Svengali with a pretentious seriousness that is "dark" or "eerie." You act so "normal" doing these weird things—*

♦ BF: Anybody who's not into the scene does do that: pretends to be a deep, dark, scary guy and puts a mask on and does an act. My idea isn't to do that, but to give a demonstration and talk about what I'm about. When I do these things for myself, as scary as it might be to do them, it's done for some supreme kind of ecstasy or joy—something that will lead toward a positive emotion, not a negative or dark one. It's moving toward light rather than darkness. And to turn it all around and pretend like it's dark (even though it deals with things that are scary) is the opposite of my intention. I don't think anyone would describe an intense orgasm as "going into darkness"—it seems the total opposite direction. And that's why I did those things.

There are SM scenes where people delve into foreboding areas, but they always ends with something happy: people laughing, hugging, being warm and gentle with each other—when the scene is over, something happens that's positive. When I lived in Long Beach I had a room painted black that was a dungeon with bondage furniture which I built—all the windows were painted black, and sometimes it was scary to be in there alone. But I loved it!

♦ *AJ: People don't go see*

In the "Bridal Falls Suite" at the Madonna Inn on my 38th birthday, patiently awaiting my 38 birthday whacks from Sheree (plus one to grow on!). San Luis Obispo, 1990

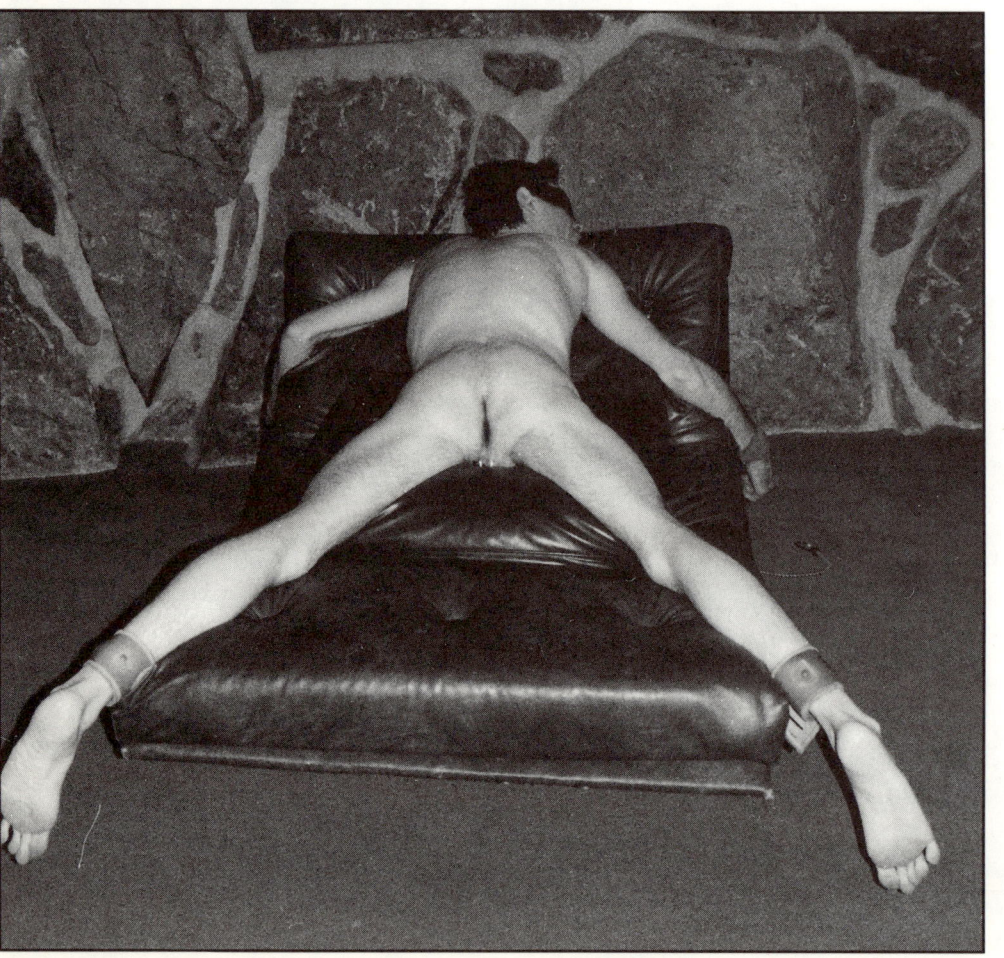

horror movies to feel worse, but to exorcise their own dreads and fears—

♦ BF: Yes. Whenever we go to colleges to lecture, the first question we get is: "Do you believe in satan?" (as if there *were* a satan, anymore than there were a god to believe in). There's an underlying assumption that you can't just be a regular "person" doing what people have done for thousands of years; everything you do has to be done for a reason other than *yourself.*

♦ *AJ: People also assume that if you do what you do, you must be very "immoral" . . . whereas you're a very moral person—*

♦ BF: I am. Even the people I know who are well-adjusted and who happen to get really turned on by sadism only do it

New Year's Eve, 1983

with people who *like* it. Then that becomes a positive experience: you're not overpowering someone, you're *melding* with someone. To overpower somebody is wrong, but to meld with somebody is a pleasure-bonding which . . . if you crank up the juice with SM, you get more enjoyment out of it. You're winding the rubber band a lot tighter, so the energy that gets released afterwards is a lot more intense. Having experienced this kind of intensity, I could never go back to a non-SM relationship!

Unfortunately, Sheree and I don't have that kind of relationship at the moment . . . my health is one reason, and I also have a hard time getting into this space when I'm working. It's ironic, because the work is all about SM and going to the *source* of where these feelings came from, yet to get the work done I can't do the SM that inspired it!

♦ *AJ: The source?*

♦ BF: Yes, the illness, the movie images, the childhood games . . . reworking hospital equipment into torture devices. As a young boy, I remember the humiliation of medical procedures I'd have to endure: being on this electronic table for two hours getting a barium enema while I was a kid, and before you learned to demystify and get past it, you're just naked in front of people on this Frankenstein table, and they're turning you upside down and doing all these things to you. And it wasn't erotic at the time, but I notice that now we do erotic enemas—that was never a thing for me, but Sheree came home from this professional place she worked for awhile, saying, "Look what I got!"—she had this huge black enema bag.

Then she gave me a wine enema, which was one of the best experiences of my life!

♦ *AJ: The wine gets absorbed through your large intestine?*

♦ BF: Yes. You mix one cup of wine with two cups of water—cheap port wine will do. Sheree would come in while I was lying on the bathroom floor, and within five minutes I'd be singing and the room would be spinning—it's a very pleasant drunk because you're not bloated from drinking all night. It wears off relatively fast—in an hour or two you sober up.

♦ *AJ: The Mayans used to give tobacco-and-wine enemas—*

♦ BF: They used coffee enemas, too, which I tried once—it speeded me up. Enemas are another crossover, because as a kid my biggest problem was digestion—lots of pain in the stomach . . . which is why I started masturbating: to distract myself from that pain.

♦ *AJ: Have you been on TV recently?*

♦ BF: We turned down an invitation to be on the Maury Povitch show. A woman called me and I said, "No, I'm too busy" and I felt really clean and great doing that. But she was really seductive—she said: "Oh, can't you come out for a day? It'll be *really fun!*" I said, "You know, one day of programming really means at least a week of anxiety beforehand, and I just can't take it." I felt so good. Plus, there's the anxiety of: how many people are going to see this, where will it show, what will they think, how will they edit what I say—

♦ *AJ: You can get conned into thinking that you can ac-*

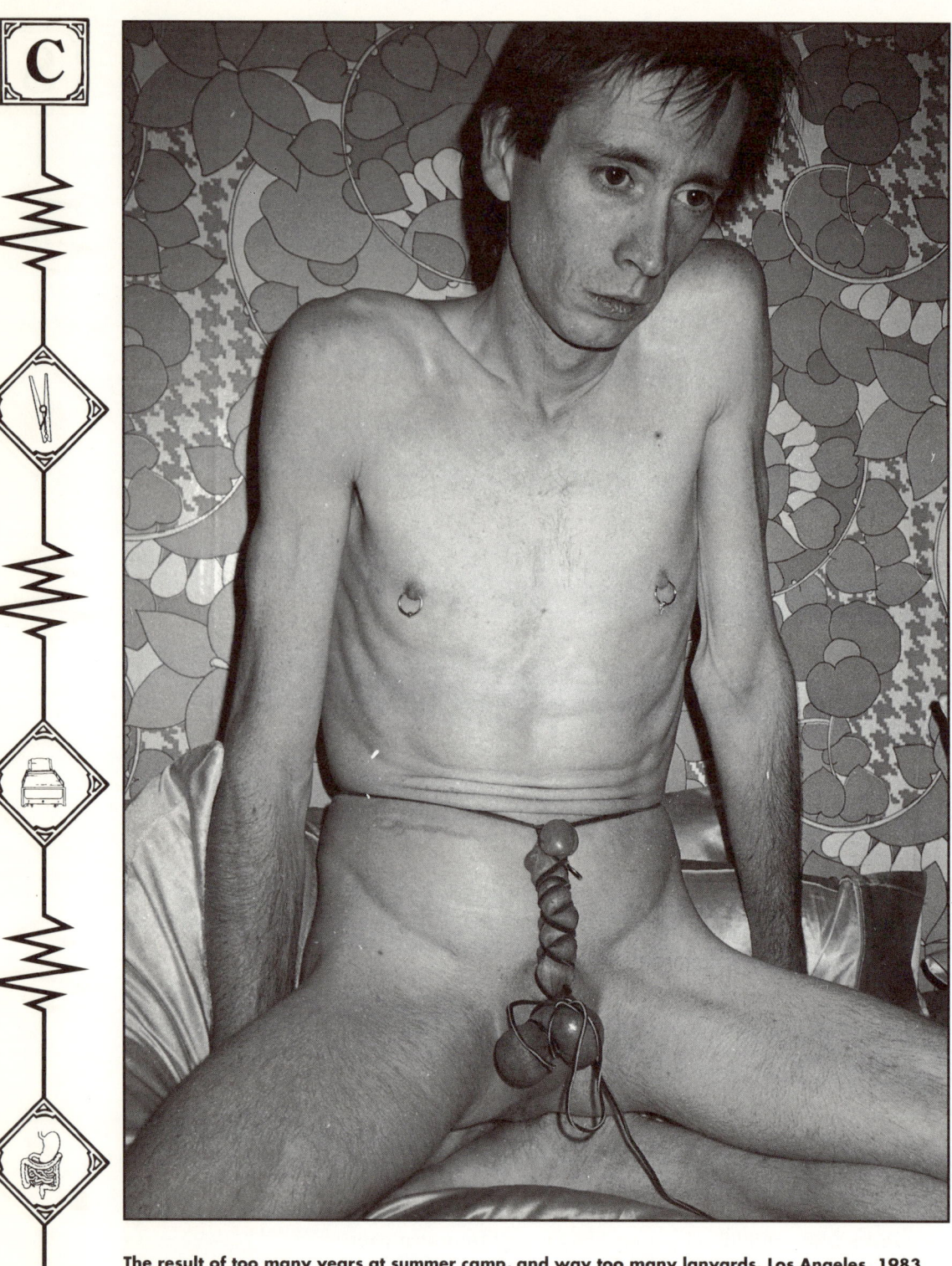

The result of too many years at summer camp, and way too many lanyards. Los Angeles, 1983

♦ **AJ:** *—some kind of evil freak. They're not going to let you explain, "Look, I'm actually a nice person. I'm normal in a lot of other ways; I'm highly ethical and moral in what I do." They won't show that. It's a foregone conclusion that they will portray you as some sort of monster; they can't show you as a nice guy. They want viewers to think: "There should be laws against this."*

♦ **BF:** There's no way to win. Maybe a few people come up and say, "I think you're really brave for coming on the show," and they'll have the perfunctory psychiatrist come on and say, "What they're doing is quite healthy." But it's all completely programmed and formularized—

♦ **V:** *—the shows exist to show conflict and then reach a conservative, christian-approved conclusion.*

♦ **BF:** For the past eight years with the Janus Society and the Threshold club, Sheree and I have been giving talks and presentations to various college "human sexuality" classes. Some students are barely out of high school, and they're hearing things they've never imagined: "Hi, I'm Bob. I'm a full-time slave, I was branded by my Mistress, and I've got a ring in my penis." One person thought we were satanists because of sadism—she thought that the word "sadism" derived from "satan"! I had to tell her, "No, there's *no* connection."

We always give a little explanation as to where "SM" came from, and who the Marquis de Sade was, and who Leopold von Sacher-Masoch was, and how the behavior spectrum goes from people who get off being tickled . . . to people who get turned on by being branded, pierced, severely punished and disciplined (and everything in between); and how some people stay down here, some people

tually promote your position but in those kinds of TV shows it's like wearing a dunce cap for a half hour—it's total humiliation. Whatever "cause" you think you're going to advance—forget it! There's no opportunity to discuss any ideas or actually have a constructive dialogue on any of those talk shows.

♦ **BF:** They're all ratings-driven. And no matter what they *say,* I know what they're *really* going to do with the footage: edit it so you look like—

graduate up to there, some people hop around on the spectrum of SM, and that not necessarily are you driven to do every single thing in between. Basically, we're dispelling all the myths, and if they listen to us it's great.

You get some antagonism from religious ones, for instance. They assume we're satanists and say we can't believe in god because "the body is a holy place"—

♦ *AJ: If it's so holy, why do they hate sex, nudity and natural bodily functions so much?*

♦ *BF:* And naturally, when Sheree mentions she has kids, and that I helped raise the kids for five years, that gets them *crazed!* You can't have a deviant existence and raise kids. We always ask them, "Do you fuck in front of your kids? It's the same thing with us." Sheree's kids just saw that I was a man who does what a woman says—as opposed to the opposite way, and it was a different thing for them to see; it was good for them. It may not have influenced their lives, but it told them that there were other alternatives out there that they might not have been exposed to. And as they got older and got more open, they heard about the whips and chains, but it was never anything that *they* had to witness. Her son did walk in on us once, but—even kids sometimes walk in on their parents having sex; sometimes that happens no matter how much you try to be private. Actually, you have to be pretty *civilized* to have a healthy SM relationship between two adults—you can't be out of control or whimsical or really mean: you have to really be in control of what you're doing. If you're just uncouth and uncivilized—well, that's where the *real* rapes and brutality and abuse come from.

People always ask (with regard to the SM clubs), "Aren't you afraid you'll have weirdos and rapists trying to join?" Well, they don't *want* to be in our club; they don't want *consenting* adults. We have very strict social rules—much stricter than your average bar. If you ask somebody to do something in an SM club and they say "No," and you don't hear it the first time—you're *out*, no questions about it.

At the Janus Society parties there's no fucking, there's no drugs—that keeps us free from legal hassles as well as AIDS. The rules center around total consent for everything. If you see somebody in a restaurant whom you know is in the club, you don't go up to them and say, "Hey Joe—you did a great whipping scene last week!" if his mother's sitting there. The main thing is: you don't interrupt people's scenes and you don't force yourself on people—it's not a singles' pick-up scene.

One of the most frequent complaints is: "There are too many people looking!" But I say, "That's what you're here for. This is a party. If you want to do private SM, go home!" Why would you come to one of these parties and then expect a lot of "space"?! When I first joined Janus, I answered all the phone membership inquiries, and really felt sympathy for the single guys who wanted to join this club for thirty dollars a year, so they wouldn't be ripped off by the professional houses. They'd ask, "Will I be able to find a dominant woman there?" and I'd tell them, "Chances are—*not*. There are lots of masochists but very few dominant women to go around. Think of this as a 3-D magazine you walk into—you'll see all the things you ever wanted to see in your life, and you'll be able to talk to everybody about anything you ever wanted to talk to, and you'll make friends. And out of this friendship you'll never know what might develop (and things do develop). In the meantime, just look around, learn, have some food and talk to people."

It started out with parties of from thirty to seventy people, but nowadays the average party is at least two hundred people—and that's why I rarely go anymore. There's a lot more women now, which is good (earlier on, it was eighty percent men and twenty percent women). And there's also a lot more couples. What's happened since AIDS is: this is a perfect place for ex-swingers who don't want to fuck but still want to be exhibitionistic and voyeuristic. There's great costumes, nudity, and sexual play . . . then they go home and have private sex parties (and intercourse, if they want it) that they *can't* have at Janus or Threshold. And these swingers are not real SM'ers. In the early days, most of my friends were into it as a lifestyle; they'd been into it for twenty years and had, if not committed relationships, committed *sensibilities* about it. In some ways things have gotten more theatrical.

Sheree finds a new use for leftovers. Los Angeles, 1981

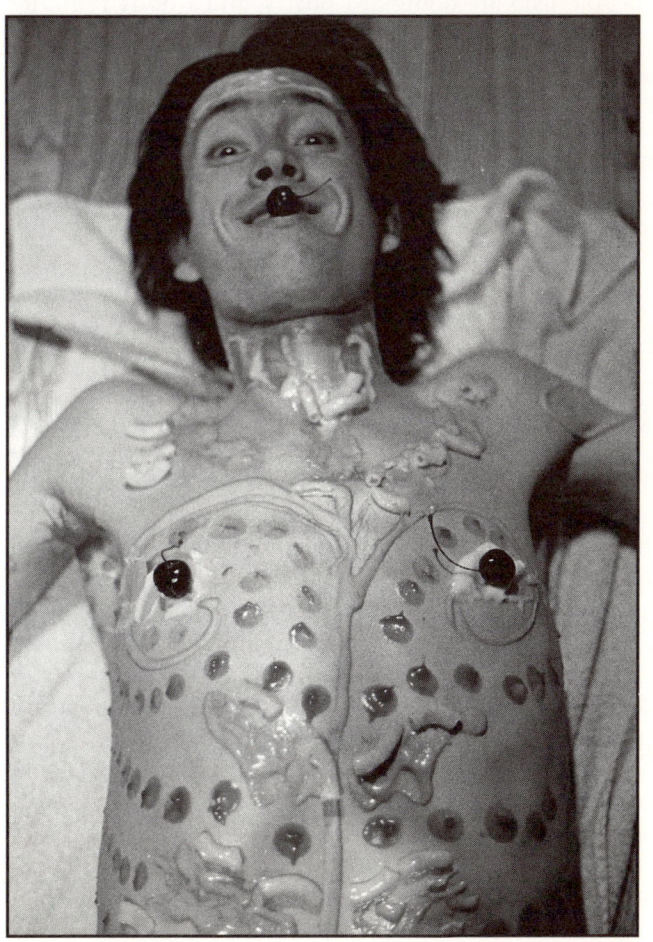

◆ **AJ: Are most of these women submissive?**
◆ BF: A lot of them are, but I don't know if I'd say most. Many women start from a submissive place and become dominant—that happens a lot. And the ones who are dominant are that way because 99% of the time they met a masochist who told them, "I would like to be submissive to you"—that's what happened with Sheree and me. It wasn't her thing, and that creates problems because she's dealing with me and my fantasies of a lifetime, and she never had these fantasies. So sometimes she walks out of it because it's not what she wants. Her basic connection to it is social—*that's* what she likes. Whereas I want the privacy of the dungeon—I don't care if we *never* go out, but that really has no attraction to her, so we have a lot of conflicts over that. She really doesn't get the charge out of being a mistress that I get out of being a slave.

◆ **AJ: So are there a lot more male submissives?**
◆ BF: Most males *are* submissive at these clubs. Many of them call themselves submissive, but they want to tell the woman exactly what to do and how to dominate them . . . they're really controlling. There aren't that many *truly* submissive men. Basically they want their fantasies played out (which I'm not putting down); they want a certain kind of woman who will meld with their fantasies. If you find someone who gets off doing that, it's really great.

I teach a weekly poetry workshop at *Beyond Baroque*. I write about SM pretty openly and read my work, and notice that over the years we've gotten more and more people who are doing SM poetry, and I don't think it's because they know me, either. They're writing about having clothespins on their nipples, about being pierced . . . there's a whole resurgence of people who are into body manipulation and piercing.

◆ **AJ: Even in academic circles there's been a literary resurgence, including the publication of works by Bataille and de Sade. Mapplethorpe has been accepted and—**
◆ BF: The stigma's been removed. In the early days we were ignored and even maligned, but *now* it's the thing to talk about it. Jesse Helms turned a lot of people's art around; they thought, "Now I can do this; now I can be open about what I do."

◆ **AJ: In your college presentations, what else do you say to defend SM?**
◆ BF: We describe how the imagery of the Catholic church and the tortures of Jesus influenced us. In Catholicism, torture was considered something beautiful and spiritual: something to rise above and change your life. And as kids those influences stuck with us . . . we never shirked from torture or pain *because* of the church. So it's not a reaction *against*, it's a reaction to. The Catholics teach the Stations of the Cross, where whipping and scourges ending up in crucifixion—death by torture. Jesus always has this great smile on his face and this expression of *release* when it's all over. Sometimes Jewish people present will talk about guilt and all their past histories of torture . . .

◆ **AJ: But how do you tie in earlier religious indoctrination into SM?**

◆ BF: Basically, we say that we don't believe SM is against god. We don't believe it's a bad thing to do. Of course, you can't change somebody's mind—if they believe that SM is against god, that's just the way it is. Whenever serial killers are mentioned in the press, they're usually linked to satanism or sadism. But when *we* talk about sadism, it's not in that context of overpowering somebody, but of two people in a consensual relationship. Our rituals have nothing to do with any deities, or with torturing animals. Basically, we talk about how everything we do stems from our personal lives, and is done for personal reasons—not out of any group thought or religious mentality.

We also aren't trying to proselytize; we don't say that "SM is the greatest thing in the world, and you should do it." We say, "Don't put people down." We try to dispel the whole idea of making judgments against people, when you don't even understand what they're doing. Somebody listening might think, "Well, that's interesting, but *I* don't want to do it." And that's exactly what we want you to think. Someone else might react, "Hmm—now I know how I can get into it." And that's great too. Basically we're against anybody who says, "This is the only way; *everyone* should experience this!" NO—there are people who shouldn't come anywhere near this!

◆ **AJ: It's more about going to the deepest levels of your own desires. Our culture's concept of sexuality and the body is so puerile and shallow; there are so many levels of childishness and ignorance. People don't even know what their own desires are, but I think, "Hey, go get in touch with your own sexuality, your desires, check deeply into your childhood (going through therapy helps, too). Maybe if you release your sexuality in a way that isn't going to hurt anyone, you won't be a serial killer, wife beater or a rapist!"**
◆ BF: People ask, "How can you get turned on by being in pain? How can you like pain and get sexually turned-on?" I reply, "Context is everything. If you're in bed with a lover and your lover scratches you on your back in the middle of the orgasm, it feels pretty exciting and you might not register it as pain. But if the person behind you in the middle of a class scratches you with a pencil, it's gonna feel awful and you might turn around and hit the guy! If you kiss somebody and bite them on the lips, that's a form of SM. It's just that we've identified it, we've talked about it, and we're not afraid to go to that place and admit that that's what we like. Whereas somebody else might go, "Ohmigod, why did I do that? That's awful. I shouldn't like that!" and then try and run away from that, and make up all these religious rules to guard against these feelings. So religion becomes just a safeguard against having these feelings: "Dear god, I was turned on by that. I better go back home and pray." [laughs]

Of course, many people want to know exactly what Sheree and I do. So we tell stories about nailing a dick to a board—piercing stories drive 'em nuts! Even now, I expect that after all the press built up around piercing and tattoos, people would be used to it . . . but if I stick my tongue out or lift my shirt up, they start to groan.

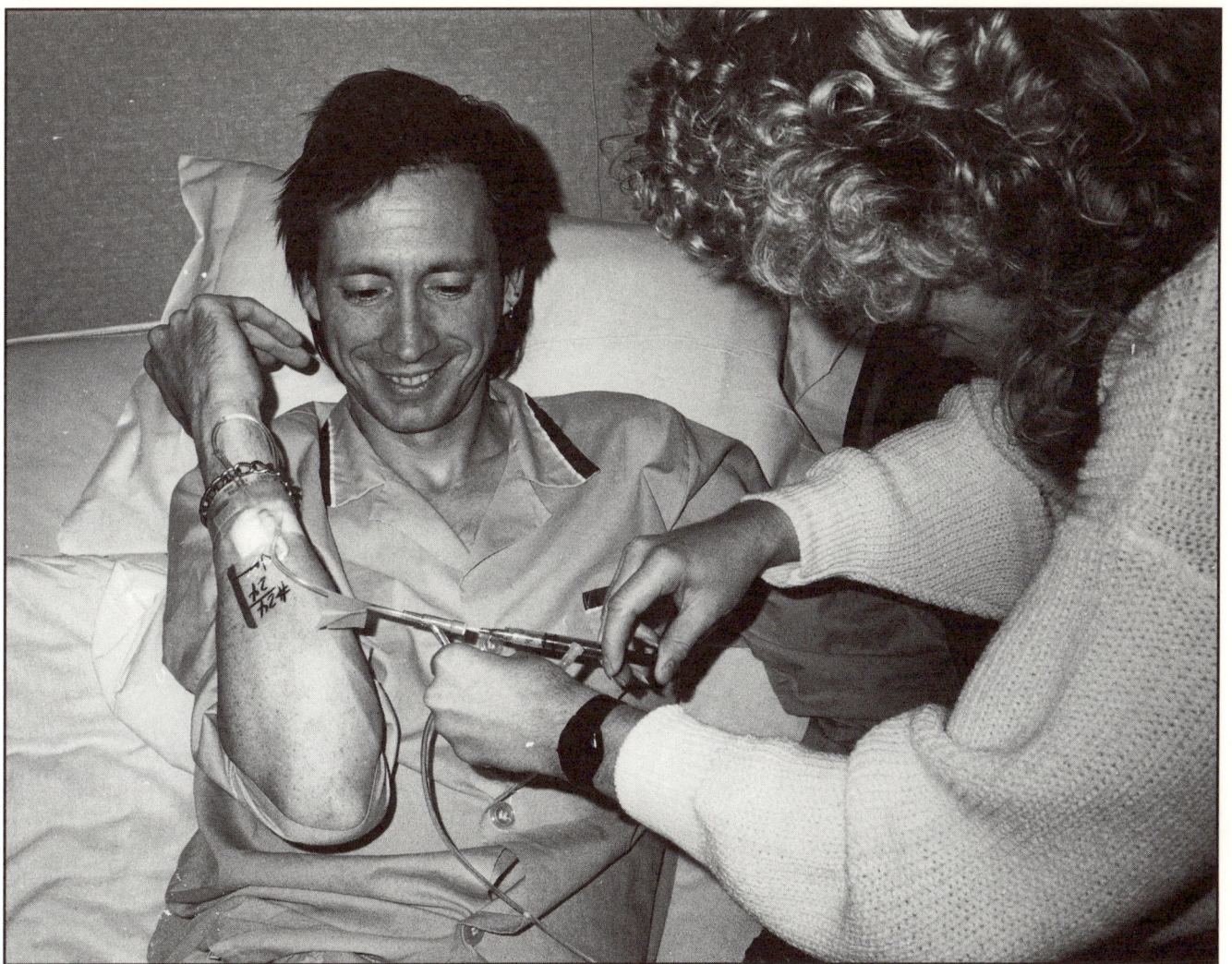

Another hospitalization, another nurse, another shot. I'm enjoying this just a little too much. Los Angeles, 1983

The main reason I got a Prince Albert and a guiche piercing was so they could be locked by a padlock all the time—it was a big, heart-shaped brass padlock which we still have, and Sheree has the keys. I couldn't even masturbate or have erections for weeks on end unless I was unlocked. To me that was blissful and exciting: walking around during the day doing what I had to do, and knowing this heavy padlock was between my legs—this was just great! And whenever Sheree and I would explain this to a class, they would just go crazy.

Lately, I end every lecture or panel with a reading of "Why." Now audiences see SM turned into "serious art." I always ask the audience what their jobs are, especially at the panels, and you see this whole spectrum: some people work in aerospace or computers or therapy or are artists. Sometimes Sheree shows her slides and I read my work, which they've never heard before.

♦ V: . . . *Do you want to read any more excerpts from your journal?*
♦ BF: Here's an excerpt from my 1978 journal when I was dating this nurse I met at cystic fibrosis summer camp. She was a very strict Catholic, yet we did everything (she used to suck me off while I hung suspended by my wrists in the bedroom) but we couldn't fuck. *Now* I would have thought that was great, but then I was upset that we didn't fuck. I knew the relationship wasn't going to go anywhere, because the whole masochism thing bothered her.

"12:30 AM, July 4, 1978. What's happening? Is it happening all over again? Have I gone too far, expecting too much? I'm home now unexpectedly. Our differences have bubbled to the surface. One too many jokes about masochism, one push too much to see how much Julie would be willing to get involved with. But that's not what started it; it just brought it out. The masochism is a small part of my total make-up" [that's not true anymore]. "I want someone" [this is at the end of my romanticism] "to love, to be with, to share with, to give to, to touch, to sleep with, to wake up with" [garbage—Jesus!]. "I don't want Julie to do *anything* that she would feel uncomfortable doing. Masochistic sex is nowhere near as important to me as she is" [that's not true!]. "Making love with her is the most important and the best thing—masochism is"

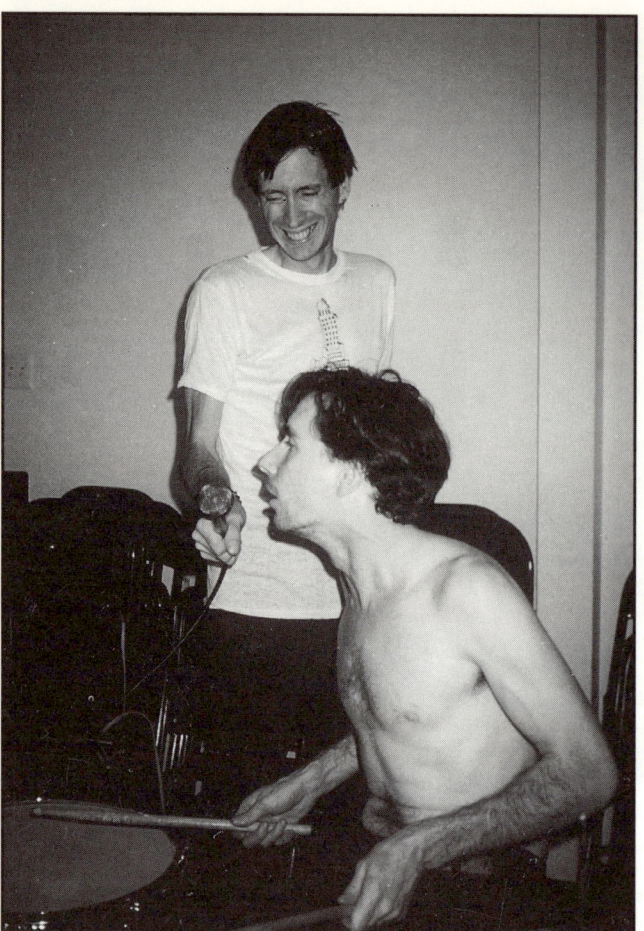

With Mike Kelley and our improvisational noise band, Idiot Bliss. Los Angeles, 1984

that's more out of dissatisfaction with the church than it is out of infatuation with me. If she doesn't think of her prayers naturally, would they be any more valid if she freed herself to say them? Things are changing too fast for her and she's panicking. Her values are threatened but they shouldn't be . . ." Basically I'm saying that she won't fuck me—that's the whole thing! Because fucking was only for marriage and for children. But what's weird was: she was doing everything else.

♦ **AJ: How about your diaries during the Sheree years?**
♦ BF: A lot of those entries are just *whining*. Here's one from April '84: "Had to get away from Sheree and her crying and her craziness, sadness. I'm no good for her anyway. She was in such a bad state when she left, but I followed her, afraid of what she might do or where she might go. She keeps talking about dying. I'm thinking about getting on a plane and going to Las Vegas." [My big plan was always to go to Las Vegas and gamble—I love playing blackjack. I've never done it, but I've thought about it many times.]

♦ **AJ: It's funny: that *would be your rebellion!***
♦ BF: That's it—I don't want to fuck at all, I just want to go to Vegas.

♦ **AJ: Have you ever been there?**
♦ BF: Yes—I can sit at a blackjack table from sundown to sun-up, and I love that feeling. I don't care if I win anything, I just love seeing the money going back and forth. The first time Sheree and I went there, she took me

[I'm trying to sell something to myself; I sound like Ross Perot] "just a small thing that I talk a lot about" [that's true].

"This thing started with Julie in church this morning. It's the differences that blew up tonight, ignited by my stupid mind-playing, asking Julie to punch me in the arm. This would have come out anyway. I sensed something different in the car today on the way to my parents. It all came out tonight in her bed. Guilt is a big part of it. She talks like she's guilty about feeling so good with me, about neglecting other people, about neglecting her religion. Guilt, retrospective guilt. What's wrong with feeling good together? We feel whole together" [that's all bullshit. I'm trying to fool myself that masochism wasn't the Number One thing—of course it was!]

♦ **AJ: Your commentary makes it great; I think we can all relate to reading diaries from our past: "Ohmigod, how deluded I was!"**
♦ BF: [continues reading] "We make others around us feel good—how can that be bad? Where is she neglecting other people? I look at her and see nothing but dedication. I've see her with [kids who died of cystic fibrosis]—how can god fault her for that? Maybe she is neglecting her religion; maybe she has forgotten her prayers. But

Finding SM messages wherever we look. Los Angeles, 1984

to the Valley of Fire and made me take mushrooms and I had a really weird time—she has some great photos of me out in the desert naked with a huge erection, standing on these mountains. I like the coolness of the hotels; I never leave 'em if I can. We're really old fogeys; we play bingo—"Bob and Rose play bingo in Las Vegas"—that's what *we* do for fun!

♦ **AJ:** *So you like bingo better?*
♦ **BF:** No, I like blackjack better, but you lose money slower at bingo . . . Here's a typical journal entry, dated August '84. "Pissed because Sheree's being so wish-washy. Where's my dominant? All of a sudden now it's not good enough—what the fuck happened to the rules? I enjoyed it too much—that's what. So now I'm going to sulk." [That always happens: it goes really good, and then it stops.]

"My place. Sheree on the couch. Tons of work to do but I don't want to do it. Bought some torture things at the Supply Sergeant. Sheree uses them on me, ties me to the chair and fucks me, and then says she's not really into torture. Can't figure her out, but I'm into rebelling right now." This is when I kept an hourly journal; I did that off and on. Once in a while something interesting would pop up, but usually it's just every boring thing that happens instead of anything good happening.

♦ **V:** *When it gets good, you're too involved to write it down—*
♦ **BF:** Right.
♦ **AJ:** *Besides, if you have to stop every hour to write it down, how can anything develop? Journals are an artificial slice of life. God forbid if you die and someone reads your journals, because the life they read is not your life—it's mostly whining and complaining. I never write when I'm happy.*
♦ **BF:** Exactly. If what Sheree and I were doing was *good*, then we were just doing it. Usually the journals get written when I'm in the hospital. Once as an SM thing I had to write a letter to Sheree every day.
♦ **AJ:** *By the way, how many times have you been in the hospital this past year?*
♦ **BF:** Five times. It used to be about every three months, but now I'm getting a complication in between those three months, so I'm having to go more often. I'm on IV-antibiotics right now and I'm still not doing that well. I usually go in for a week at a time—it used to be three weeks, until they perfected home IV care, because you have to be on IV drugs for about three weeks to knock these things out. Now I go when I can't feed myself anymore and can't stand taking care of myself anymore—I go there for five days to a week and come home and recuperate and do drugs for two more weeks at home. That's where I'm at now. I went in because I started spitting up blood. Fortunately I can only be treated at a CF clinic, and they're usually good—I don't have to go to county hospitals. Since I have CF, not only am I eligible for MediCal but also a genetically-handicapped persons program that California has (covering epilepsy, sickle-cell anemia, etc) which pays for whatever MediCal doesn't pay for. I'm sure there are

A break in my journal writing, for another photograph by Sheree. Los Angeles, 1984.

certain rightwing persons who would say, "We don't feel our tax dollars should go toward keeping him alive to whip himself!"

SM relationships don't change how relationships work, *period.* In fact, sometimes it makes things harder because often Sheree and I feel pressure to live up to our own reputations or expectations. I still want to be Sheree's slave, but I can't physically clean up her house anymore. Plus, the art career is much more important to both of us than that (although secretly I would give up all the art career stuff to just have that sexual thing going, but she wouldn't). In the past, sometimes the greatest thrill was just going out to a restaurant with other people knowing I was her slave, and no matter what she said, I had to agree to it. I didn't necessarily *do* anything, but just having that agreement, that understanding, was the sole satisfaction I needed.

It's very hard for Sheree to be mean to me when I'm sick, naturally. When I went into the hospital recently that's what I craved the most: for her to be really cruel to me. But it's hard to get her to do that anymore. Now, the idea of going on a TV show and talking about SM doesn't even relate to what we're doing anymore—that's another reason I don't want to go on TV ever again. ■ ■ ■

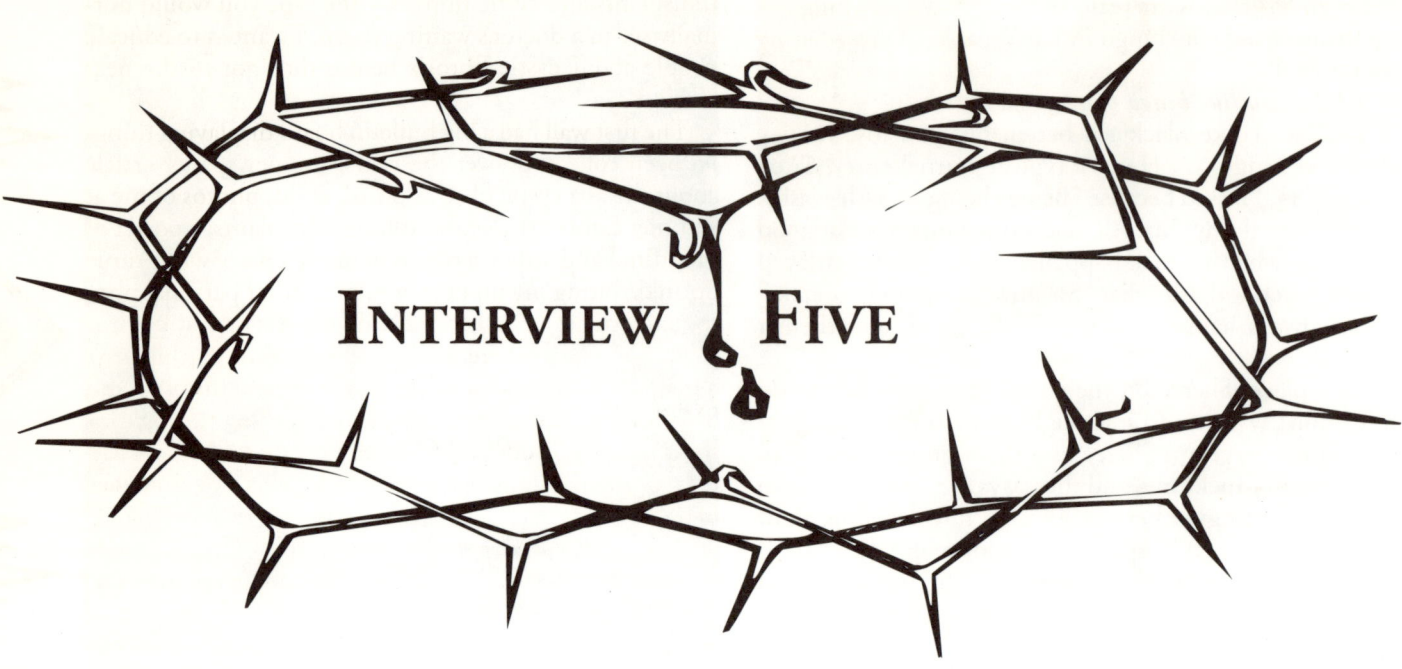

Interview Five

♦ **AJ: You've been in the intensive care ward; how are you doing?**
♦ BF: The last two weeks have been really scary, but today I'm feeling more alive.
♦ **AJ: Tell us more about your Santa Monica show, which was designed to convey the experience of being in a hospital. You walk in and there's the receptionist—**
♦ BF: The original idea was to have a museum person sitting at a desk to warn people about what they might see (especially people just wandering in off the street), because the videos show piercing, nailing and other *in-your-face* footage. They wanted to make sure visitors were over eighteen and aware of the sexual or violent nature of some of the imagery.
♦ **V: Was anyone shocked?**
♦ BF: Yes, although not nearly as many as the museum expected. First of all, I didn't want kids to come in and see me hanging around naked. The museum is in a little mini-mall behind an ice cream parlor, next to a restaurant and a record store, and people don't expect to find a museum there, neither do they expect to find this kind of confrontational performance art installation. One woman who had been dropped off at the museum while her friend got a haircut at the mall, turned out to be a born-again Christian, and she was just in tears—she literally thought I was going to hell. She was sitting in a chair crying and said, "I have to tell you: this *sickens* my heart. I hope you find Jesus Christ." I thought, "Jesus is hanging right over there—just look at that video!"

♦ **AJ: Was she just sad?**
♦ BF: You never saw a sadder person. She wasn't angry; with all her beliefs she literally thought my soul was corrupt. A number of people couldn't see anything but the sadness of facing C-F and dying, whereas what drove me to do the show was *humor:* to me it's humorous to put Jesus's head up there and my dick down there, and have a wall of blocks that spell "CF" and "SM" (sanding off the children's images and replacing them with "adult" and SM images) . . . things like that are ironic and funny to me. But a lot of people lack irony in their lives, and without irony it's hard to have a sense of humor. My *drive to survive* uses every tool at my disposal, including humor, and I tried to make the show positive and uplifting, *literally:* periodically I would get hoisted up out of the hospital bed! It would always amaze me that people could see only the sad side.

There were a *few* people who got queasy or scared, and there were a few negative comments, but usually people just walked away without confronting me. On closing night one man walked aggressively up to me and asked, "How'd you get to do this here?" I replied, "The museum asked me." He said, "Well, it just shows there are satanists in high places!" and stormed out. Satan gets a lot of undeserved credit!

When you walk in, the first thing you notice is that the walls are painted hospital green. The text of my poem "Why" starts at the left and continues as a spiral around the installation. You see a pediatrician's waiting room with

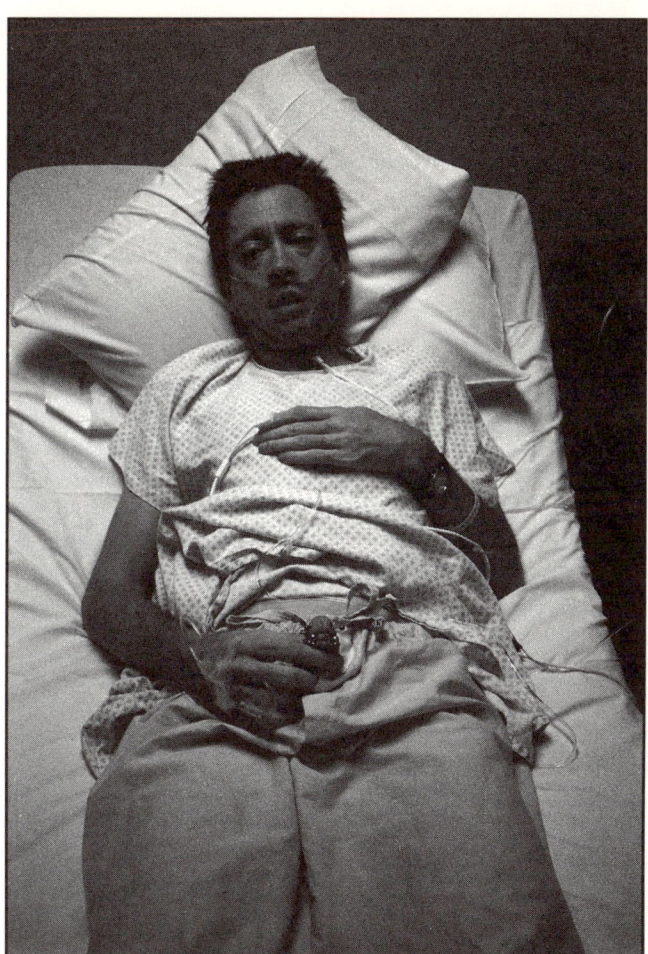

In the early days of our relationship Sheree could barely contain her anger and fear at the sight of me in the hospital hooked up to an IV and breathing oxygen through a tube. "What if I wanted us to go to the Himalayas? You can't go to the Himalayas. You can't go anywhere with that stuff." Now, twelve years later, after many hospitalizations too numerous to count, Sheree's still pissed off, but the miracle is she's still here. Long Beach, 1992

phallic cacti, toys for kids including a box labeled "Fix me up, Doc!" containing a plastic man with a big belly; you're supposed to shape internal organs out of clay and put them inside him or pull them out—I thought this was really perverse. Somebody had made penises and put them inside him. This was an area where people could sit down and play with toys as well as read magazines, and we had copies of *Highlights* [a children's magazine found in doctor's waiting rooms] scattered around, but inside the covers we had substituted SM magazines. So anybody you saw reading *Highlights* was really looking at all this SM imagery—and people were *always* on the couch reading these with rapt attention!

♦ **AJ: Right—I picked up one of those and it was a shock to discover an SM magazine inside . . . that was a subtle touch.**

♦ **BF:** Originally I wanted to produce a *real* magazine especially for the show, but I ran out of time. Actually, it's probably more of a shock to discover an SM magazine inside real *Highlights* covers. We had a *Humpty Dumpty* magazine cover that fit perfectly around a weird German SM magazine. Also, there were pamphlets about lung transplants and cystic fibrosis—the type you would normally see in a doctor's waiting room. I wanted to educate people about cystic fibrosis before they got to the next section . . .

The first wall had a big bulletin board displaying things I'd been collecting over the years: the newspaper article about me as a cystic fibrosis poster child, photos of me at summer camp, articles about lung transplants, a poster of Houdini handcuffed, a photo of me at a party with Annie Sprinkle biting my nipple rings, plus other personal photos and articles . . . all connecting aspects of cystic fibrosis to SM. Then there was a 4x8-foot wall of children's alphabet blocks that spelled CF (for cystic fibrosis) and SM (for sado-masochism), and interspersed throughout was my name "Bob" and 65 little drawings. I had sanded off the original drawings and replaced them by drawings of butt plugs, whips, chains, scalpels, syringes, dominatrix gear, etc. There were 1,400 blocks in this wall, and people could walk around it. The top three rows were loose, so nobody really knew if the blocks were glued together or just "balanced"—they looked as if they could fall over at any moment, and the ones at the top *could* fall.

On another wall were x-rays showing my nipple rings (another combination medical-SM image). Then there was the toy box, and woodburned into the lid was a funny little paragraph I wrote about my penis—about being turned on by pain from a very early age. The outside of the toybox had the same images that are on the alphabet blocks, but enlarged. Inside the toybox were all these kids' toys that have double meanings, like jump ropes, boxing gloves (things that are pseudo-violent and colorful), a crucifix, a Superman doll, and other things I'd been collecting for many years. In a lot of ways, it's all about arrested development . . .

Waiting Room for "Visiting Hours." Santa Monica Museum of Art, 1992

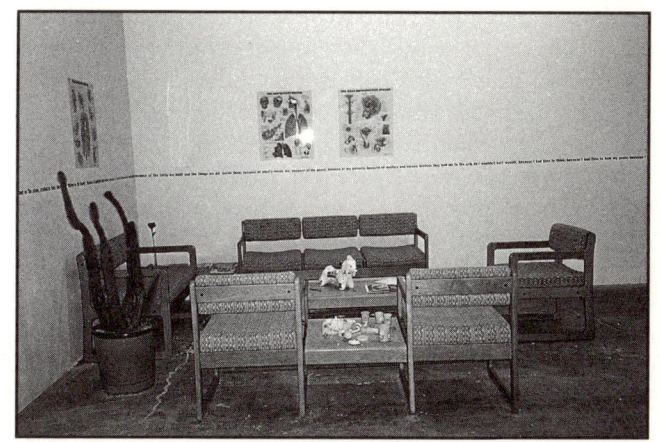

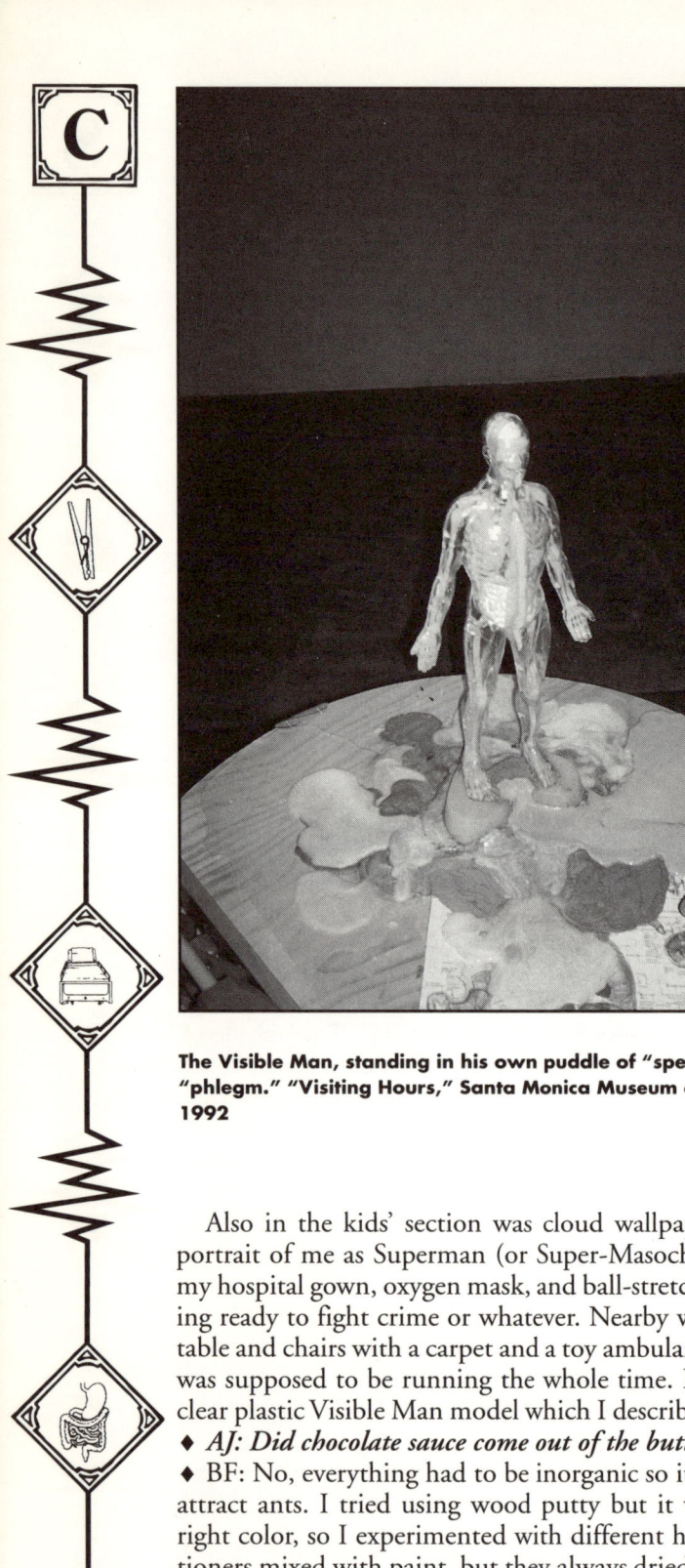

The Visible Man, standing in his own puddle of "sperm" and "phlegm." "Visiting Hours," Santa Monica Museum of Art, 1992

Also in the kids' section was cloud wallpaper and a portrait of me as Superman (or Super-Masochist), with my hospital gown, oxygen mask, and ball-stretcher, looking ready to fight crime or whatever. Nearby was a kids' table and chairs with a carpet and a toy ambulance which was supposed to be running the whole time. I had that clear plastic Visible Man model which I described earlier.

♦ *AJ: Did chocolate sauce come out of the butt?*
♦ BF: No, everything had to be inorganic so it wouldn't attract ants. I tried using wood putty but it wasn't the right color, so I experimented with different hair conditioners mixed with paint, but they always dried up. I still have to perfect that.

♦ *AJ: When you were a kid, was Superman significant?*
♦ BF: The Superman TV series came out in the '50s. Along with *Howdy Doody* that was one of the first shows I ever watched. It showed up in re-runs and has always been one of my favorite shows—I liked the comic books, too. When I was a kid, I used to dress up as Superman using a towel as a cape and pretend to fly. For my show, Superman was a good symbol because I get lifted up in the air. Plus, the SM I do belies the fact that I have this terminal illness. Even though I'm kind of a cripple, the fact that I can stand these painful activities is sort of super-heroic . . . even though I'm sick, I'm still sort of "super-human" in the things I've been able to withstand.

♦ *V: Describe the rest of the show—*
♦ BF: At the back is an ominous door labeled "Isolation." Facing that is an 11x15-foot "Wall of Pain" showing 750 photos of me in various stages of pain, taken by Sheree about eight years ago for one of our first projects together. One roll of film showed my face reacting to a cat-o'-nine-tails on my thighs, and every time Sheree whacked me, I (or she) would try to press the cable release while I was screaming, so you got my face reacting to the blow. Each roll of film was devoted to a "theme": stomach-punching, hair-pulling, and there are literally hundreds of photos.

Behind this wall was our 12-foot-high video scaffold which we used in a previous show, "Bob Flanagan's Sick." There were seven video monitors positioned where my face, chest, genitals, hand and feet should be, and this scaffold ended the whole exhibition. But whereas "Bob Flanagan's Sick" had a beginning, middle and end, for this show I cut out the beginnings and just made continuous video loops of my face, chest, genitals, hands and feet being tortured. A soundtrack of random audio clips from various movies (like, "You're sick!") played continuously.

That's a lung I'm attempting to transplant into a brand new specimen jar. I borrowed it from a respiratory therapist friend of mine and had intended to use it in my "Visiting Hours" show at the Santa Monica Museum along with a pierced penis that I got from someone else. How perfect, I thought—penis and lungs—the yin and yang of my existence. But the lung ended up looking like a giant turd, and the penis made everyone sick, so I scrapped the whole idea. —Los Angeles, 1992

I wanted to provide a comfortable place where people could sit and watch the videos, so I installed a gurney of nails, a cage which a friend had made years ago as a birthday present (it contained a kid's alphabet blanket and a rattle), and a portable toilet with a pillow underneath where people could rest their head—no one did, however! For this pillow I wanted a Porky Pig pillowcase (Porky Pig is so grossly sexual, doesn't wear any pants, and is kind of nasty; he implies the idea of gluttony) to suggest the idea of insatiability, but I couldn't find any. I called every fabric store in L.A. to locate material with pigs on it, and luckily found a pattern of a pig smelling a skunk—which seemed to be a perfect image to have underneath a toilet!

♦ **AJ: That video wall is pretty complex—**
♦ **BF:** The video monitors are arranged in an "x" to form a stand-in for my body. We first used that scaffold for the *Amok* publication party for *Modern Primitives* in L.A., and for the *Modern Primitives* show at Southern Exposure gallery in San Francisco. But I didn't want to just keep on hanging myself from the scaffold, so for the next show (I don't know where I got the idea—probably in the hospital, and from watching too much television) I came up with the idea of videoing all the parts of my body undergoing different tortures we'd already done over the years. Also, we used videos Sheree has collected of me getting my various pierces, plus different movie clips where a head or a hand is prominent. The close-up of Jesus's face dying on the cross in *King of Kings* has always been memorable, so I played that on the "head" video monitor. I rented films and cartoons so I could get Mickey Mouse's hands, etc.; I always remembered that image in *Gulliver's Travels* where the Lilliputians tied Gulliver down to the ground, so I included that. The whole video display included not just images of me, but images that inspired me to become whatever I am.

♦ **AJ: The video monitor at your left foot would show your left foot being whipped—suddenly you'd see a huge Dumbo The Elephant foot stomping on a cartoon mouse foot. It was amazing to see this cartoon and movie imagery mixed with your live SM footage—**
♦ **BF:** To me, what I do isn't scary—these are "fun" things I do to myself for pleasure. Well, *everything* isn't always funny, but ultimately it's pleasurable. The fact that I see humor in SM is unusual to other people; they're wrapped up in the "horror" of what they're watching. The videos run all day long with no order, everything is all juxtaposed randomly, so on one monitor you might see my dick being nailed to a board, while on another you might see a cartoon. Often something that really scares people is playing next to something that's silly.

SM basically is a silly thing to *watch*. When you're experiencing it—that's different. But to watch, there's a lot of silliness attached. In the show I tried to have as much as possible going on simultaneously, and there were many wonderful accidents or coincidences. When I wanted to sew my lips up for the "head" video, I found an old Betty Boop cartoon where a hippopotamus accidentally gets his lips sewn up by a machine that goes crazy! The sequence only lasted about five seconds, so I slowed the sequence down and repeated it about ten times so it lasted longer, and it came right after my own lips were sewn up on the video. That's one of the more gruesome parts of the video: watching this needle and thread going through my lips, because they swell up about four times their normal size! Sheree ties a little knot in each stitch; then suddenly you see this machine zipping through this hippopotamus's mouth sewing it right up—you go, "Whoa!"

♦ **AJ: What happened on your "genitals" video?**
♦ **BF:** The grand finale comes when I actually nail my penis to a board—I've already described how hard it was to do that. I had all these jack-off shots leading up to it,

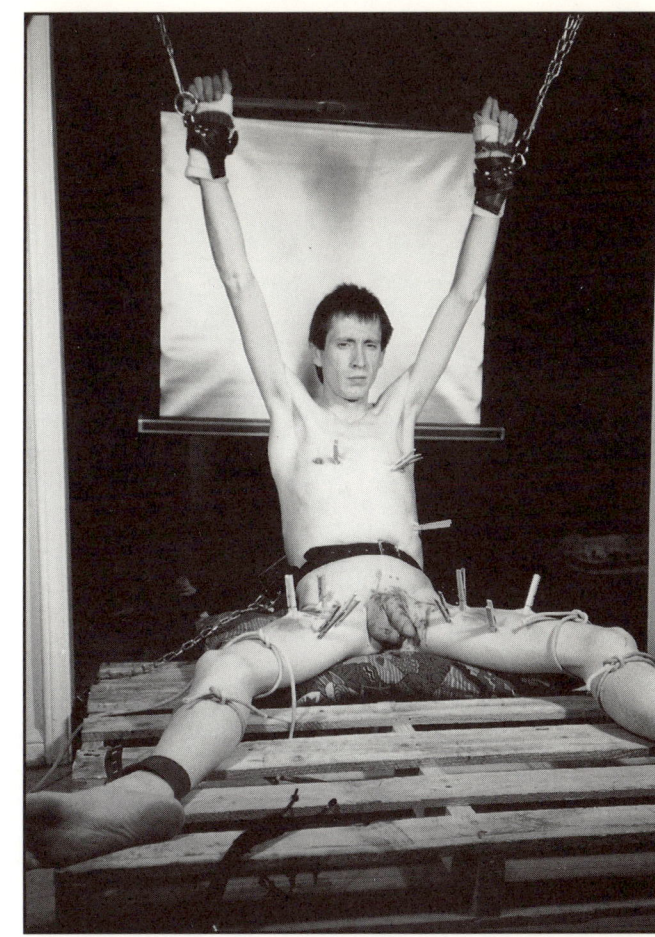

Behind the scenes for the "pain" photos, which later were used for the Wall of Pain in "Visiting Hours." Los Angeles, 1982

I woke up with this mile high hard-on which is only now descending back into the depths of my battle-scarred frame. I open the burgundy robe I am wearing to look at it again. My thighs are criss-crossed with ugly red stripes and welts where Sheree beat me with a riding crop last night for the photomontage we are making. We are taking over 500 photos of my face in the throes of pain. Last night's sesssion went very well with Scott manning the camera, Sheree torturing me, and me, tied up to the wall, squeezing the black bulb which released the shutter as I writhed in pain. The things we do for art! The point is, or the point I would like it to be, is that we are not doing it just for art. A lot more happened last night that no one will ever see in the walls of *Beyond Baroque*. But, who knows, maybe they will. Bringing my art and my strange ideas on how to live my life; bringing those two factors together is one of my goals. —Journal note from June 6, 1992

all these masturbation scenes—there was this flurry of activity that (ideally) would end up with a blow of the hammer. If I didn't do it, I knew there'd be no ending. On the day the video was supposed to premiere at LACE, I said, "Let's turn on the video real fast," and we did it. We had a plexiglass screen set up so when I pulled the nail out, it would look like it was bleeding right into the camera lens. The screen literally filled with blood—it looked real gory . . .

♦ **AJ: Was the footage mixed with cartoon images?**

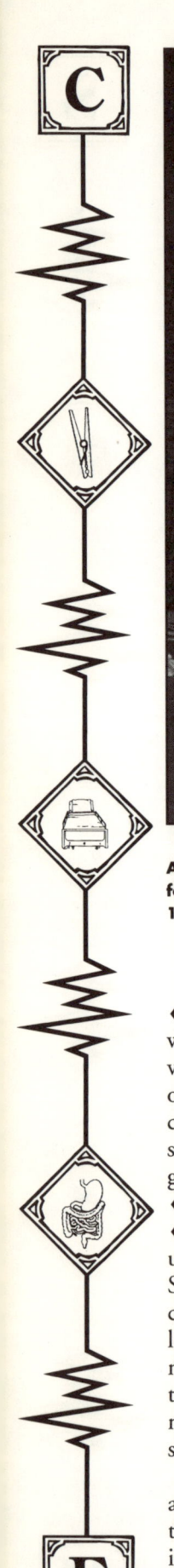
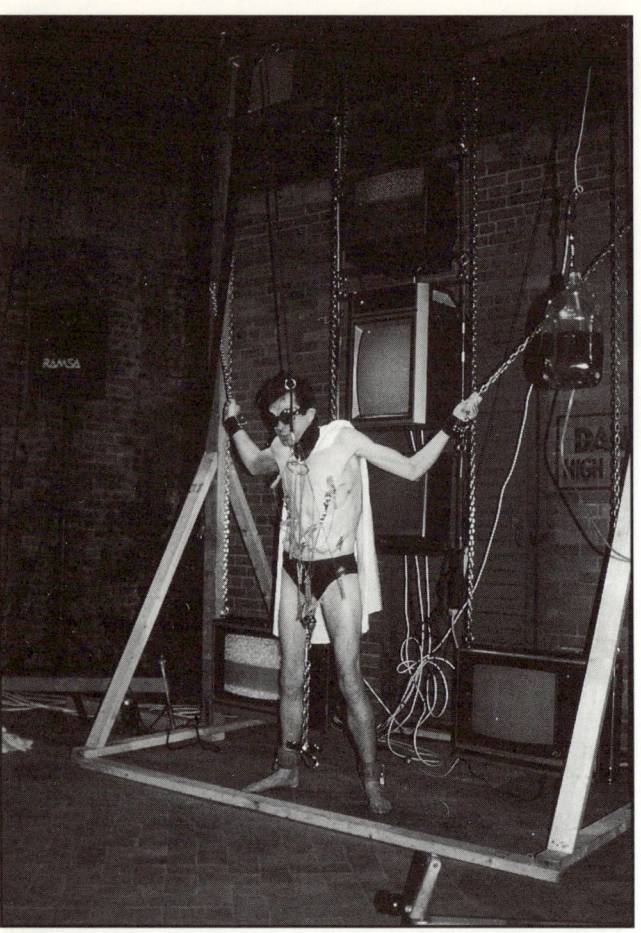

As "Superman" with clothespins, reciting the words to "Why," for "Bob Flanagan's Sick," at Art in the Anchorage, New York, 1991

Video scaffold for "Bob Flanagan's Sick" LACE, Los Angeles, 1991

♦ BF: Before my penis got nailed? Yes; leading up to that were scenes like me peeing in my pants, peeing into the video screen, a lot of ball-whacking, and Sheree's first video of me getting a Prince Albert piercing. There weren't many cartoon penises I could insert [laughs], but I did insert some footage from an instructional video cartoon of boys growing up and discovering their first pubic hair.

♦ AJ: What about the chest video?

♦ BF: That's mainly C-F, physical therapy, stethoscope usage, and being whipped on the chest. We included Sheree's video of my nipple rings being enlarged. All the chest footage was shot sideways to make the composition look better, and so you could see the chest and the abdomen at the same time (here let's credit Skip Arnold). After an intense whipping, Sheree carved her initials into my chest with a scalpel, and blood streamed down the side of the screen—that was the finale.

Also, at the beginning of the penis video my penis was all sewn up. Each stitch was removed, and the penis burst through like a flower. Then all these things happened to it until it got nailed. Whereas the chest video begins with my chest, physical therapy, x-rays showing my nipple rings, plus cartoon images like Bugs Bunny trying to get out of fighting in the army. This cartoon is from World War II, and his heart, which is pounding real hard, says "4-F." During the Vietnam war, *I* was 4-F.

There are an amazing number of slappings on TV; I taped some of them and included them in the show. I also included force-feeding, a little shit-eating and baby bottle-feeding. Most of the videos ran about 18 minutes, whereas the hands and feet videos were the shortest, about five minutes—there isn't a whole lot you can do with them.

♦ AJ: Nevertheless, they added a lot to the total presentation—

♦ BF: There were a lot of gruesome images people would be confronted with, so I figured they could always look at the hands and feet if they needed some relief.

♦ AJ: Tell us about some of your personal interactions with visitors—

♦ BF: This was something I never planned. Everything else happened pretty much the way I anticipated, but I never thought that people would actually sit down and talk to me. After seeing the entire show and reading the text of "Why," visitors could enter this "box" in the middle of the museum which was a perfect replica of a hospital room with me dressed in my hospital gown in a hospital bed. Also in the room was a TV monitor showing video loops I'd made (again, containing footage from influential movies), and chairs for people to sit in.

People would come in and suddenly begin telling their own hospital horror stories—some of them happened when they were kids. One woman brought in her ten-year-old son who'd been hospitalized with cancer (she got special permission to bring in a minor). She asked, "Can he come in and talk to you? Because he has too many memories of hospitals." He showed me the scars from his cancer operations, and I showed him my antibiotic hookups. More and more people with cystic fibrosis showed up, perhaps drawn by reviews which mentioned my C-F. One man was born without a mouth, and he showed me these incredible drawings of evil doctors with bloody scalpels. He described his different operations.

♦ **V: What did he look like?**
♦ BF: He had undergone a lot of reconstructive surgery. He just looked like he'd once had a hairlip; he didn't look bad. He talked a little funny.

♦ **AJ: How did people deal with the SM aspect?**
♦ BF: People responded very well. I was afraid they might think I was making fun of handicapped or sick people, but they seemed to understand that SM pain was a metaphor for the kind of pain they were forced to endure as illness. A few people actually were into SM. One man had been totally paralyzed in a car accident—he didn't have anything to do with SM, but he could relate to the whole pain-as-metaphor idea, especially regarding the tortures people have to go through for medical reasons.

Actually, it came down to: not being afraid to talk about pain. People would say things like, "My father's in the hospital right now; he's got cancer." Seeing someone who purposely focused on pain gave people a doorway to come in and explode about their own painful situations, whether they were sexual or hospital-related. Usually it was about relatives who'd been in the hospital, who had undergone operations, and who had died.

Most of the time people wouldn't even *ask*; they'd just come in, sit down and start talking. At first I felt a little uncomfortable; I didn't want to become this person who "gave advice." I didn't want to become a sort of guru, so I just listened and encouraged people to talk (or not to talk). I would just say, "Yeah, I know how that feels," and a lot of people came back three or four times just to talk! With all the publicity we had up to 300 visitors a day. It was amazing!

♦ **AJ: Our society has no forums or contexts to even discuss pain, death, or sex. You provided an amazing environment for people just to be free to talk—**
♦ BF: That's true: to provide a place where people could be hypnotized by honesty. We're used to keeping secrets, being lied to, and not talking about certain topics. All I ever try to do, in my writing and in my shows, is state everything that happens as plainly and honestly as possible, yet with some sort of *craft*—to be entertaining and funny, too. And in this show, people got swept up in that and wanted to just talk.

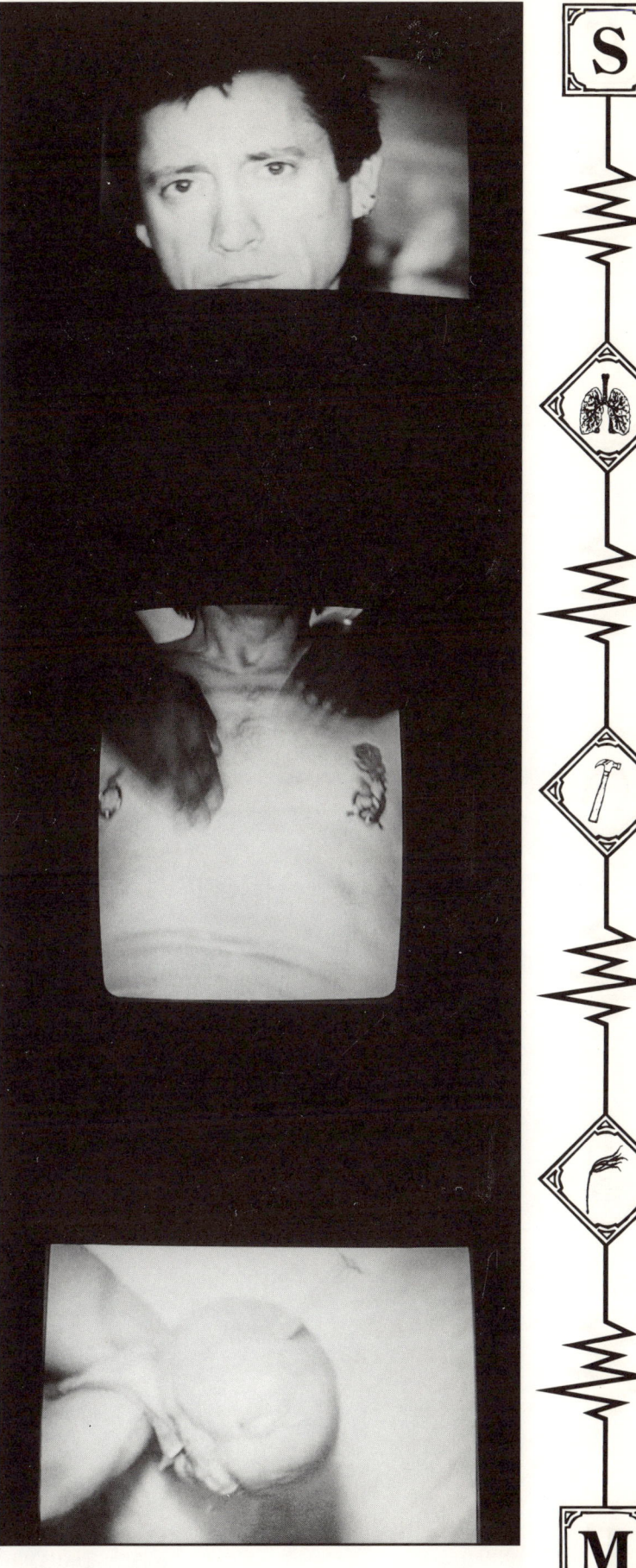

Photo: Jessica Pompei

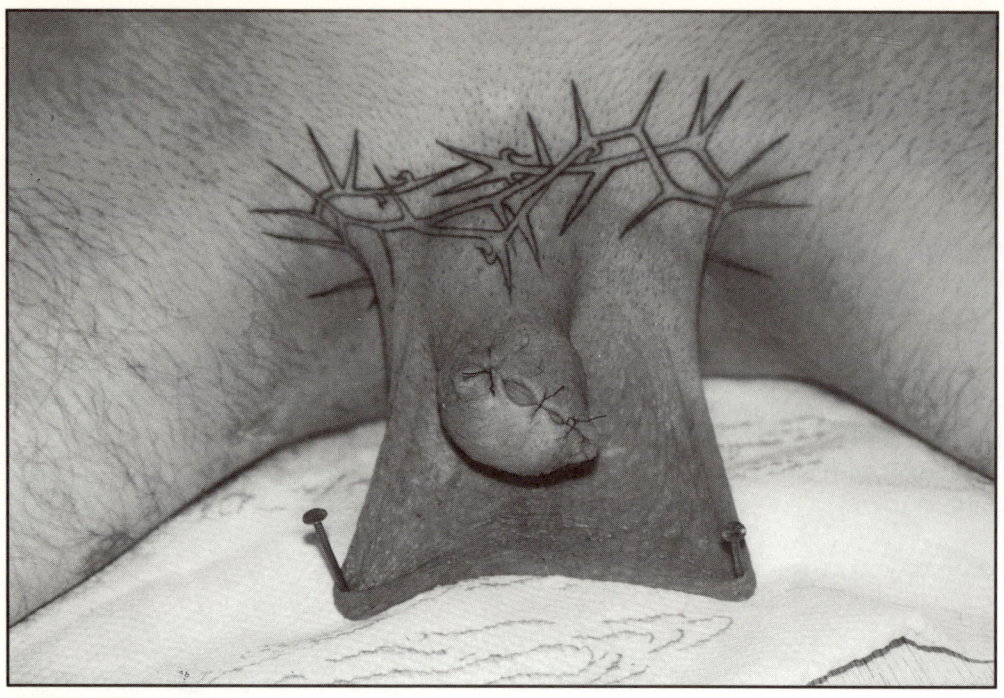

All sewn up and nowhere to go.

Leading the audience in song in "Bob Flanagan's Sick," LACE: "Old Ben Lucas had a lot of mucus, running right out of his nose. He picks and he picks till it makes you sick, but back again it grows." Los Angeles, 1991

Of course, some people were resistant. Some people were horrified about what the show made them want to do, but most people were pretty open.

♦ *AJ: When people are resistant, something's being brought to the surface—*
♦ BF: Right. And I'm not telling people to do or not to do anything; my show is strictly autobiographical. Occasionally, while people were talking to me, I'd be pulled up by my ankles. This would be done using a pulley system from a different room in the museum; nobody could see Sheree lifting me, so it was very mysterious and *quiet*, too—no ratchet wheels turning. I'd be hoisted up and my hospital gown would fall off, revealing me as totally naked. People would fall dead silent—I'd just be hanging there. Once someone called me a *piñata*, but most of the time people just stared at me in silence. After three or four minutes I'd be lowered down, red in the face and huffing and puffing. And that became a metaphor for recovery (from a coughing attack, for example) and people would applaud.

It's funny—every time I was lowered down, I felt embarrassed that people could look up my asshole. But I had to override that, and smile. As quickly as I could I'd climb into my hospital gown, get back under the covers and continue talking to people.

♦ *AJ: Do you think this was healthy for you?*
♦ BF: Who knows—I got a blood clot, although the doctors assured me this wasn't caused by hanging upside-down. Oddly enough, now there's this blood in my head that I can't get rid of; my veins are bulging in my head and chest and I feel as if I'm *still* hanging upside-down. This happened right after the show, and I assumed it was caused by being upside-down in the show. But it didn't go away—that's why I went into intensive care and discovered I had a blood clot around the IV site.

♦ *AJ: What's happening now?*
♦ BF: The clot doesn't seem to be getting any worse. Eventually I'll grow new veins (they say) that will replace the vein that's clogged. Now they're mainly treating the cystic-fibrosis problem which this time is more difficult—the mucus is a lot thicker and stickier and they're having a harder time getting rid of it. I have another week of antibiotics ahead.

♦ *AJ: I usually don't like installation/performance art because often it's meaningless or boring, but your show was so full of life, with incredible details. I love the fact*

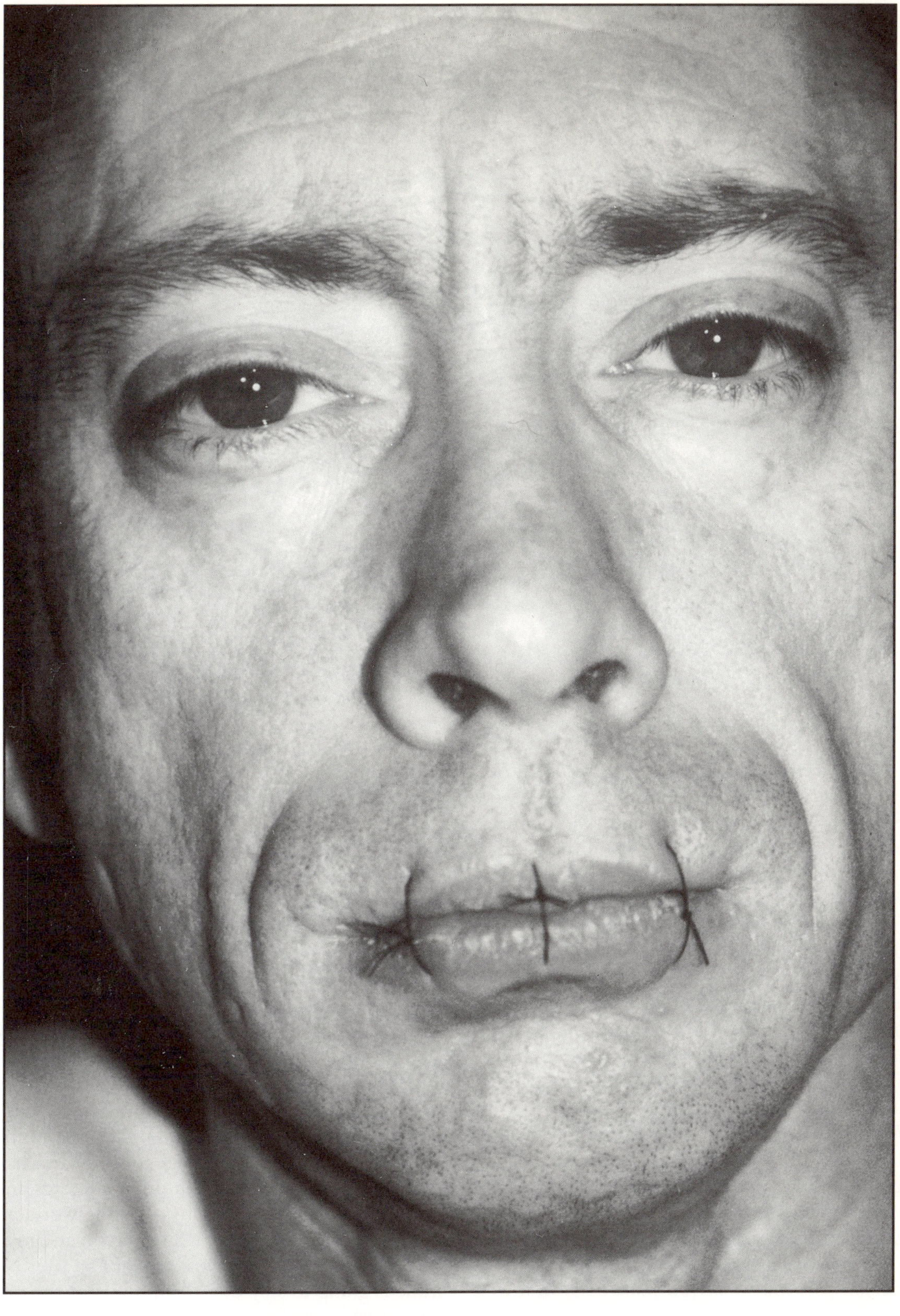

Mouth sewn up for the video portion of "Bob Flanagan's Sick." Los Angeles, 1991

that your show became a community function—
♦ BF: Me too. If I'd sat down and tried to plan that kind of intense interaction with people, it would have come out wrong. The fact that it spontaneously happened— that's why I want to try it again in New York in a totally different environment. I don't want to analyze too thoroughly what happened, because I don't want to come off as some sort of "fakir"—oops! ■ ■ ■

SHEREE ROSE

♦ **VALE: What impresses you the most about Bob Flanagan?**
♦ **SHEREE ROSE:** Bob is so strong, and everyone who knows him is affected by him one way or another, and in a very positive way—that's part of the power he has. And he doesn't do it consciously; unlike Fakir, he doesn't want to have these people around him who worship him—he hates anything like that. He's totally against anything that makes him into something larger than life. But in his soul—who he is—he *is* larger than life.
♦ **ANDREA JUNO: Because he's on a more mature level. He brings out people's best. I never feel that sleaziness that's in a lot of the SM scene—that really dark "energy."**
♦ **SR:** One of the articles written about us called us "Saint Bob and Mistress Rose." But *he* would pooh-pooh that idea; he doesn't like that connotation. He just lives his life: very plainly, very practically. And because I'm basically a neurotic Jewish woman [laughs], to be dealing with this man who faces death every day—well, this has been a learning process for me.
♦ **V: When you first met Bob, you thought of him as a poet—**
♦ **SR:** The first poem I read by him was "The Nails Go In"—that was prophetic! I found Bob really fascinating; he was thin (at the time I didn't know he had any illness) and he wasn't some regular macho guy who was coming on to me. And from the very start I loved Bob's sense of humor. After years of a traditional marriage with two kids, I had gotten divorced and had started dating. I'd been thrown into the '70s world of fast sex and "C'mon honey, let's *do* it, and if you're divorced you must *really* want it!"—that was the way heterosexual men were treating women. I was horrified at this, because I had been a sheltered wife for 14 years. Also, I had gotten into the women's movement—after the divorce one of the first things I'd done was to join *Women Against Violence Against Women.* This group was pretty popular; we would protest all these movies which depicted women as victims. At the time this was an important step for me, because it was a statement that I didn't like the *status quo* . . . of how women were treated in our society.
♦ **V: How did your divorce come about?**
♦ **SR:** Before I met Bob I wasn't into SM, but I *was* into being an independent person. The catalyst for my divorce was: I had gone back to college to study archaeology. After class I would go out with other students and discuss archaeology and philosophy—it was wonderful. One night I came home at about 11:30 p.m. and my husband was furious: "How dare you stay out so late? No wife of mine is going to stay out 'til all hours of the night!" and he started throwing things at me. I looked at him and thought, "What right does this person have to tell me what I can do with my life?" This was my first glimmering . . . I could no longer remain in the role of a wife who has to obey her husband, where the husband makes the rules and "you can't do this and you can't do that." I knew I could no longer remain married if marriage meant I was under his control. That's the genesis of my wanting

to take control of my own life, and do what I want to do.

Three years later I met Bob, a man who really wanted to totally reverse that equation so that the woman made all the decisions about what to do and what not to do. Immediately I was sexually attracted to him, and then when he told me what he was into, I had no personal experience of what that meant but I was eager to learn. Part of being married so young and having such a traditional marriage was: I felt I had missed out on a lot in my twenties. I wanted to try new things, and this seemed like a good new thing to try. And it happened because I *already* had feelings for Bob; if it were just anybody else I don't know if I would have gotten into this. But the force of Bob's personality was so strong, as well as my attraction to him, that I felt this was a good thing to do. I went purely on instinct—it was pure gut reaction; my head didn't make these decisions. We made this very strong visceral connection immediately.

At that point I was so independent that I didn't want Bob (or anybody) to live with me. But he came over quite often and spent the night. At the time he was teaching poetry to kids at a school in Yucaipa during the week, and he

The Mistress and her pet slave. San Francisco, 1992

would see me on weekends. From the very beginning he wanted me to make up rules and restrictions, and that was difficult for me because I was—not exactly a hippie, but I was more laid-back. He really wanted strict rules, like: when he was in Yucaipa staying at the motel, he couldn't sleep in the bed, he had to sleep on the floor.

We had a lot of philosophical discussions about rules and why they were important. I had some trouble with this, because as a parent my problem was: I was raising my kids too permissively. And when Bob and I made a full-time, 24-hour-a-day commitment to an SM relationship (it wasn't just play) he was really into it as a lifestyle, and I was interested in seeing how it might work when the woman really does make all the decisions: how does that *feel?* Women in our society don't often get chances to experience that (or even think of it), so a lot of my motivation was *political:* for a heterosexual woman, this was a role model of a different way of living with a man.

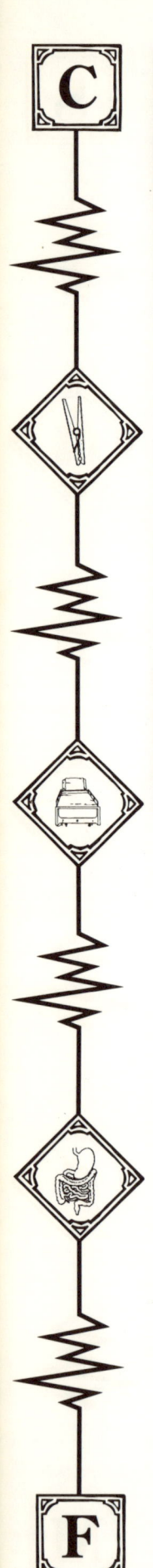

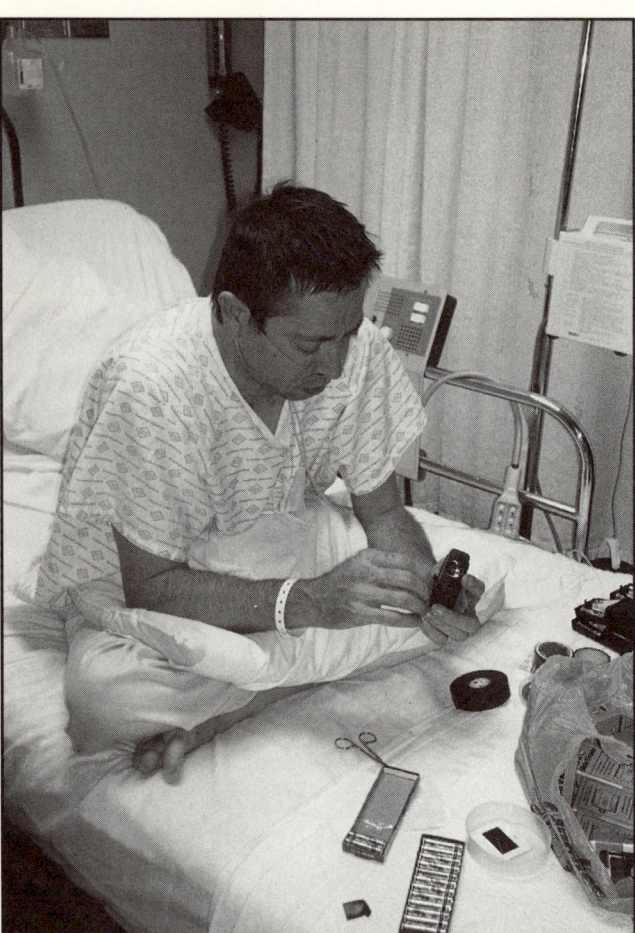

Even on my sick bed I'm still slaving away, assembling Sheree's "butt boxes" for her "100 Reasons" show at the Lab in San Francisco. Long Beach, 1993

♦ **V: So you were studying archaeology—**
♦ **SR:** When I finally separated from my husband in 1977, I went back to graduate school and got a Masters degree in psychology from Cal State Northridge. Then I worked in a women's center and met my first lesbians, got their point of view (I had never known any lesbians before this) and I ran several groups for single mothers and did counseling. The majority of women had abusive husbands or boyfriends—I heard a lot of horror stories. Many of the married women had no way out; their husband was a pig, they had three or four kids and no way of earning a living, so they were stuck. Even though I might think, "Get rid of the bum! Leave him!" that wasn't a possibility. I saw firsthand how women were affected by living with men who really were tyrants.

When you join an organization like *Women Against Violence Against Women,* you collectively try to "change the world"—which is very difficult to do. Bob said, "You can't do that. All you can do is change yourself." So in our life we created a microcosm of the world as we wanted the world to be.

♦ **V: You must have discussed the topic of "power" in a relationship—**

♦ **SR:** We had *many* conversations about this—long discussions into the night about the whole nature of consensual power, which is different from being with a dictator. Often I found that *having* power was oppressive—I didn't want it all the time. Sometimes I wanted it unreasonably. I was raised Jewish; I don't practice the religion but I definitely have picked up the Jewish value system which has been kept alive for 2000 years. Tradition breeds continuity, and continuity means the survival of your group, and that tradition is very powerful. And to try and break that and create new rules is very difficult. We're trying that right now in America and it's not going very well: having women be equals in the workplace and having men be equals in childcare just hasn't happened.

With Bob, there were many times I felt *guilty* if I had to tell him to do something I knew he didn't want to do. But he would do it because he got a sexual charge out of serving me. My dilemma was: if I had to force Bob to do something, it didn't give *me* the same sexual charge it gave him. From early on, this was the main source of difficulty.

In the bedroom, I never had any problem—I loved the SM stuff because it was like getting new toys at Christmastime: "Oh boy, what do I do with *this?"* It was a learning process, and the erotic sexual activity was very satisfying; we had a really hot sex life for several years. I loved the fact that we only had sex when *I* wanted it and *how* I wanted it . . . and I liked giving him pain and whipping him—again, because that was a part of me that had never been expressed before. I had no qualms about whipping him or tying him up or giving him pain—and the reason was: I saw the reaction in him; it turned him on tremendously. He loved it! And that's always been really important for me: I get turned on by people who really get into it.

Another component of our relationship that started very early was: because I felt that Bob was a very special person, I felt compelled to document a lot of what we did, because I had never heard of it before, I'd never done it before. Before Bob, I had photographed a number of poets and was drawn to the idea of documenting people or events that may have some historical significance later. Many of our friends such as Dennis Cooper, Amy Gerstler, Mike Kelley and Jim Shaw—whom we just "hung out" with at parties—did go on to become famous writers and artists of our generation. I never took the photographs thinking I would have this wonderful career—

♦ **V: It was your contribution to this community.**
♦ **SR:** Early on, I was very lucky to be able to photograph a lot of different scenes, including the SM community—people got used to seeing me with a camera and were very open to me. At the time our SM life was very private, although I would definitely dress the part, wear the leather, and be more "out" about my role, and Bob would wear a slave collar all the time. This was around 1980, before it became more fashionable to do this. If you were wearing a dog collar, people averted their eyes. So we were definitely ahead of our time that way.

Then we got involved with the Threshold club which at the time was called Janus. We formed a social group of SM people that was totally separate from our art friends. The art friends knew about our SM activities, but these were two separate groups, and in fact on many occasions we would have fights as to which event to go to on a particular night: an art event or an SM event?

♦ **V: You could attend both—**

♦ **SR:** Well, we did, and we missed out on a lot. Because of that conflict we started to bring the two groups together. Bob had always been someone who worked from real life; writing fiction wasn't his "thing." I have some hot, incredible letters he's written to me, because if we had a fight or disagreement, he would write me a long letter about it. From this came his *Fuck Journal*—I suggested that Bob write about every time we had sexual intercourse, so for a whole year ('82) he did that.

At the same time Bob began writing the *Book of Medicine,* which again was a breakthrough in that it's rare for someone to be so honest about their personal life, in very intimate details. At first it was hard for him to read from that in public, because it was very revealing. I was in it, and I wasn't always depicted favorably because we were having fights—

♦ **V: It wouldn't have been "real" if you were—**

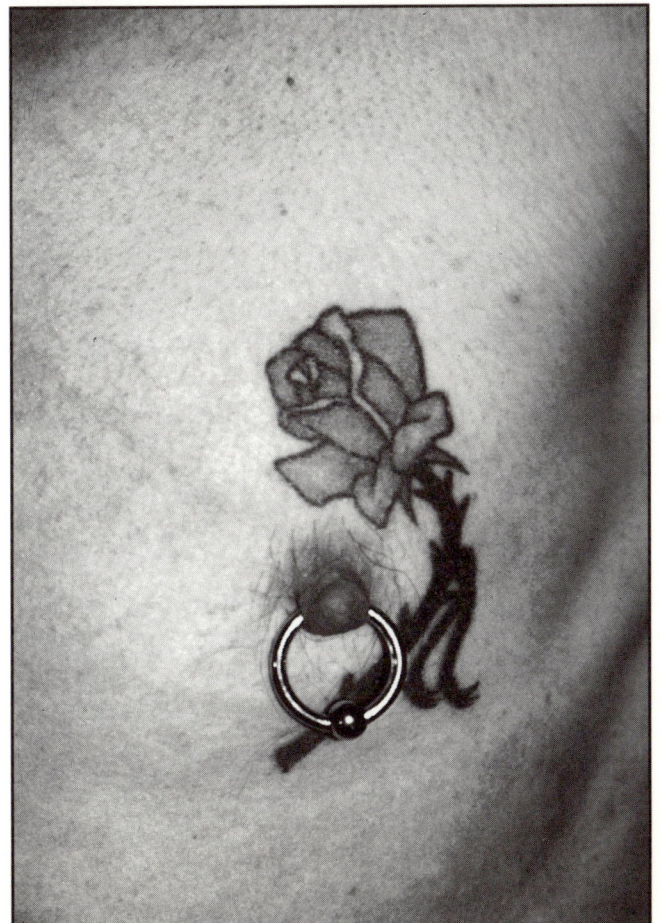

Left nipple: a rose for Mistress Rose. Los Angeles, 1991

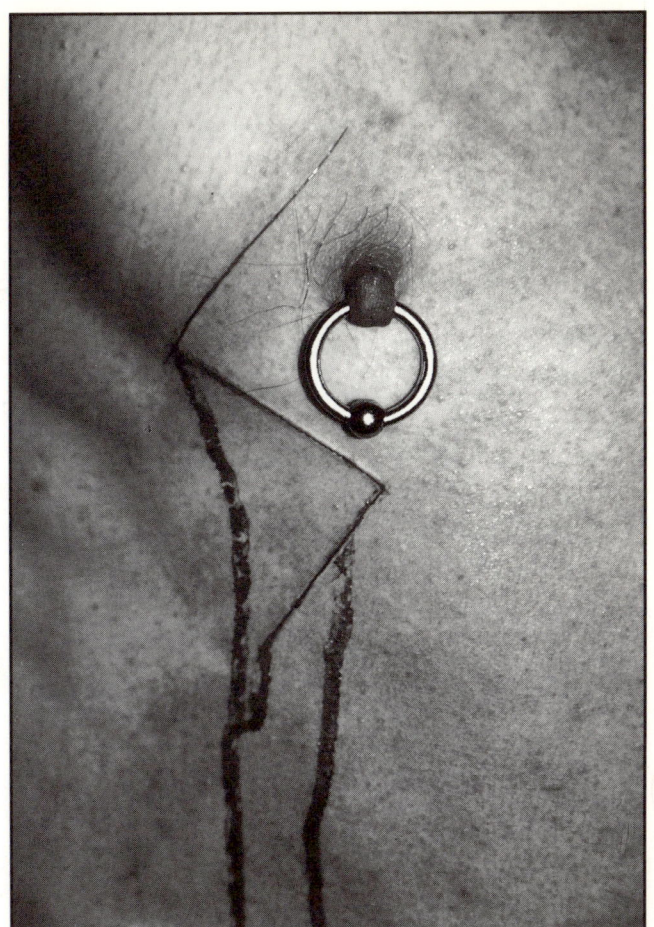

Right nipple with a bloody "S" carved into my chest by Sheree and her trusty scalpel. "S" for "Sheree," my soul-mate, sex-partner, and side-kick. And "S" for "slave," which is what I am and what I have always aspired to be. Los Angeles, 1991

♦ **SR:** Right. We started the Los Angeles branch of the Janus Society because we wanted a community. In the early years this was an incredible group of people brave enough to come out of the closet for the first time and join with others. At the first meeting there were 12 people into SM crammed into our tiny apartment. Then I started hosting meetings in Westwood, a very upper-middle-class neighborhood, and that added some "respectability." I knew how to give a party and make people feel comfortable and sociable—all my skills as an Encino housewife came into play! So from the very beginning we had this patina of respectability: of nice people who happened to be kinky. We tried to broaden the spectrum of what SM was; remove the stigma that "only crazy people do this, and end up murdering their partners."

From the beginning I made certain decisions. First, I told my children that I was involved with Bob in a "different" kind of relationship. And they *saw* it. They were ten or eleven years old when he came into my life, and were certainly not used to a man being in the house cooking and cleaning. But they learned very fast: "Oh, just tell *Bob* to do that!" [laughs] "Mom, tell Bob to pick me up after school!" They loved it; it was beneficial to them, and

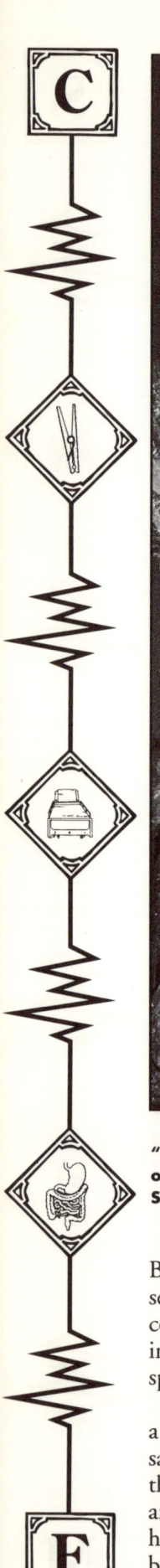

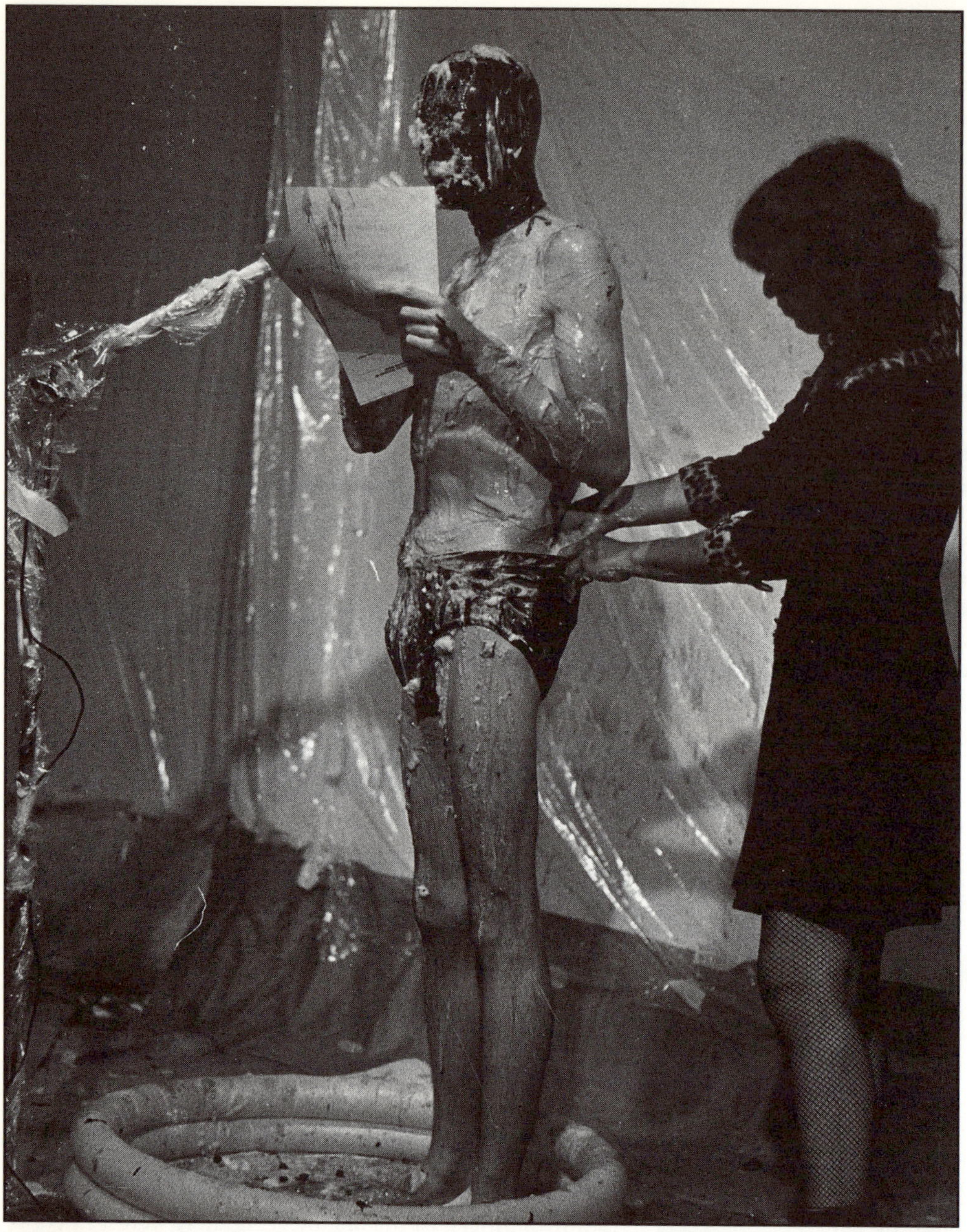

"Improvisation with Food and Poetry." I am pelted with mustard, mayonnaise, ketchup, eggs, oatmeal, and more, while attempting to read poetry. First foray into performance art with Sheree. *Beyond Baroque,* Los Angeles, 1981. Photo: Bones

throw it on him! I took some funny photos of Bob with whipped cream on his nose, etc. But I think the end result of this upbringing was: my kids are very tolerant of people's differences. They have no prejudice against gay people or people into SM, and they themselves are not practitioners. My son is 25 and my daughter is 24 and sexually they are extremely normal, but very tolerant. So that belies the idea that if you're into something weird, your children are going to be weird, too. I did not treat SM as something weird; I treated it as something matter-of-fact. Since then I've had conversations about this with my daughter and my son—

♦ **V: They're adults, now—**

♦ SR: And my daughter did not want to have much to do with this, because she wants a career as a film director in Hollywood. I use a different name than she does. However, she was up for a job at a production company that made this movie, *The New Age,* directed by Michael Tolkin, in which Bob and I have a small part. On the producer's desk was *Modern Primitives,* because he was using it as a resource. My daughter saw it and said, "Oh, my mom's in that book!" Suddenly it was *okay* that she was connected with me. However, I don't think she got the job! But that was the first time she publicly acknowledged that I was associated with her. My son has no such problems—he's very thrilled that Bob and I are doing our lifestyle. His friends love us and our work.

Bob was very funny. We were very careful to *never* have sex around them or be nude (although Bob did wear his collar around the house). They basically knew we were into something a little weird, but they didn't know the specifics for quite awhile.

One time, my daughter tried out for a starring role in a school play and didn't get it. She was despondent, so I said to her, "Let's do something to cheer you up . . . something that will get the anger out of you in a very safe way, and that won't hurt anybody." The night before we had had a party, and there was all this food left over: baked beans, potato salad, etc. We had Bob lie down fully clothed in the bathtub and had her take handfuls of food and just

♦ **V: Tell us about the first time you had to deal with Bob's cystic fibrosis—**

♦ SR: During our first date, we were having dinner and I noticed he took a handful of pills. He said, "I have this genetic disease." I said, "Oh, really—what's that?" He said, "Cystic fibrosis." This was 1980 and I wasn't familiar with that, so I asked, "What is that?" He said, "It's like a digestive problem. I have to take pills when I eat." Basically that's all he said. I think something registered, but not a whole lot—we were brand-new "getting to know each other" and I was attracted to the man.

On New Year's Eve, Bob got ill for the first time. New Year's Eve for me is always a time when I like to go out and have a good time, and he was too ill to go out. It upset me that we had to stay home. The next day I had to go to a wedding in Carmel on a private plane, so I went without Bob. One of the passengers was a nurse, and we got to talking. I told her my boyfriend was sick and she casually asked, "What does he have?" I said, "Cystic fibrosis." She turned pale, got very agitated and said, "Ohmigod—that's horrible." My heart sank (I had only known Bob for three months) and I asked her, "What is it?" She said, "It's a degenerative disease. He's going to die." Then she told me all these horror stories, and it felt like somebody had punched me in the stomach. I realized this was not just "he coughs a little bit."

Bob and I talked about it and he said, "You know what I want? I want a wonderful two-year relationship." I thought that sounded good, too. I told myself, "This is going to be a romantic experience. I'll be with this wonderful, sickly Irish poet" [laughs] "and we'll have these romantic two years together and then he'll die, and I'll go on with my life."

Of course, he *didn't* die. There were times he did more work than a healthy person, and there were times he was sick and would have to slow down and not do too much, but it got to be a rhythm or a pattern. Then he had several setbacks: a collapsed lung, a lot of infections, etc. The last couple years have been much more problematic. There are times when any physical exertion really tires him; he can't do simple things like climb stairs. So the SM aspect of our lives has not been as strong because of his health. For example, now he's on this anticoagulant, so I couldn't spank him or do anything to him even if I wanted to.

Now we call Bob a "Medical Masochist" because he has to endure all these horrible procedures but he takes that in stride, too. Whatever fate gives him, he accepts and just goes on—he doesn't give up. *I* give up more; I get depressed. At this point I'm very attached to him, and the work we do is very collaborative. The show at The Lab [performance art space] in San Francisco is a good example of how we work: I took about sixty slides of people's bruised asses, but Bob came up with the idea of exhibiting them in custom-made Viewmaster boxes.

These days I have a lot of sadness because there are a lot of things we can't do because of his health, but that's just the way it is. I can't even imagine him dead; it's really hard. We've been together thirteen years and are very close. Even though our relationship no longer has that same sexual charge, we still are heavily connected. The SM component is still there; it's just dormant. At any given moment he would like to be my full-time slave.

♦ **V: How have you prepared for Bob's death?**
♦ SR: So many of our friends have died of AIDS, including my brother's lover, but Bob's still here. It's hard for me to imagine a world where Bob isn't in it, and it's going to be a real loss for me. I also hope he'll get this lung transplant and be fine for a few more years. The only way to approach it is the way Bob does: "This is just the next step."

Fate has always come into our lives in ways that are strange and mysterious. Bob is on MediCal, and there's no way he could afford this operation which costs $250,000. But because there's a new facility at a nearby university, they had some extra money, and some doctors came and saw our show and were so impressed they decided to give Bob a free lung transplant! I told Bob, "You're the highest-paid artist in L.A.—$250,000 for your show. Not bad." When we did the show we didn't know all these doctors would troop through—the ones who could make the decision. So hopefully this new problem with a blood clot won't foul up that possibility—

♦ **V: What *new problem with a blood clot*?**
♦ SR: That's why he's in intensive care now; he got a blood clot. But they're giving him blood-thinning medi-

I'm either going brush my teeth with this toothbrush, or scrub the kitchen floor. This is a rather recent photo, and I'm not the slave I used to be, so I'm probably going to brush my teeth. But there was a time when the kitchen floor sparkled much brighter than my teeth. New York, 1989

cation, and they hope that in time it'll get better. The transplant people say they don't think this will be a problem.

When they okay him to be on the "list" for a transplant, he gets a beeper which he has to wear constantly. And he cannot be more than two hours away from the medical center. When the proper lungs become available—and this is a macabre side-effect: you have to *hope* there'll be a lot of gunshot hits to the head so that we'll get a good pair of lungs for Bob! In fact, some doctors who do transplants got very upset with the motorcycle helmet law because they used to get a lot of people who had head injuries from motorcycle accidents, but the rest of their body was perfect—they were strong, healthy young men. But with the helmet law, they no longer get so many. However, I think gunshot wounds are taking their place. Somebody said, "It's really *lucky* you live in L.A., because your chances of getting lungs are much better here than anywhere else." Hopefully he'll get on the list, and that'll be a whole new phase of his life.

So Bob has gone from the masochism which was totally private as a child and young man, to something that was shared with a few people, to something that was shared with the world, and now it's turned into this "medical masochism" . . . yet all along, the *principles* are the same. For Bob, masochism means *endurance* . . . endurance over his own limitations. It's very much (I don't want to use the word "Zen") a *meditation process* where you "will" yourself into another state of consciousness. One night I tied him to a wooden bench under a bunch of bushes rather than to a pole, because lying down is easier than standing up. However, all these bugs showed up. I can't even *imagine* it, but there he is completely bound with little spiders crawling all over his body, biting him all night long. And he endured it. He had welts all over his body, but he did it. To you and I this would probably be unthinkable; normal people could never endure that. But to Bob this was a test of his will. Also, he got a sexual thrill from it because *I* was the one who tied him up. But the fact is that most people would never be able to tolerate that.

Now Bob has to go through these incredible medical procedures, which most people would probably not be able to handle. Bob can tolerate them, but like he said, "It's not fun because it's not sexual." Now the trick is to try and bring back a sexual component and integrate it into what he has to do. He really is like the Bionic Man—if something goes wrong, they fix it and there he goes out again. And even after he's gone, his legacy will be there, and people will be affected by him. He certainly changed *my* life completely—I have no idea what I would have been doing, or how I would have lived my life—

♦ V: *Or vice versa—*

♦ SR: Yeah; he often says he would have been dead if he hadn't met me. When Bob and I first got together I formed this organization called The Matriarchal Society and thought, "This is going to change the world." We had several parties where the women were all dressed and the men were all naked and served the women; it was a complete role reversal.

Early on, with Bob's encouragement, I did work professionally as an SM dominatrix. But one of the negative things that happened was: if I get paid $200 to tie somebody up and whip them, then I don't feel like going home and doing the same thing for free! Being a dominatrix is like being an actress; you have to really get into the role, and you have to tie people up correctly without hurting them—it's a very intense kind of interaction, more so than psychotherapy. When I was a counselor that was easy; you sat and listened to a person for an hour. But when you do SM, there's a lot of physical activity and your brain is working constantly. They're paying you money so you want to give them

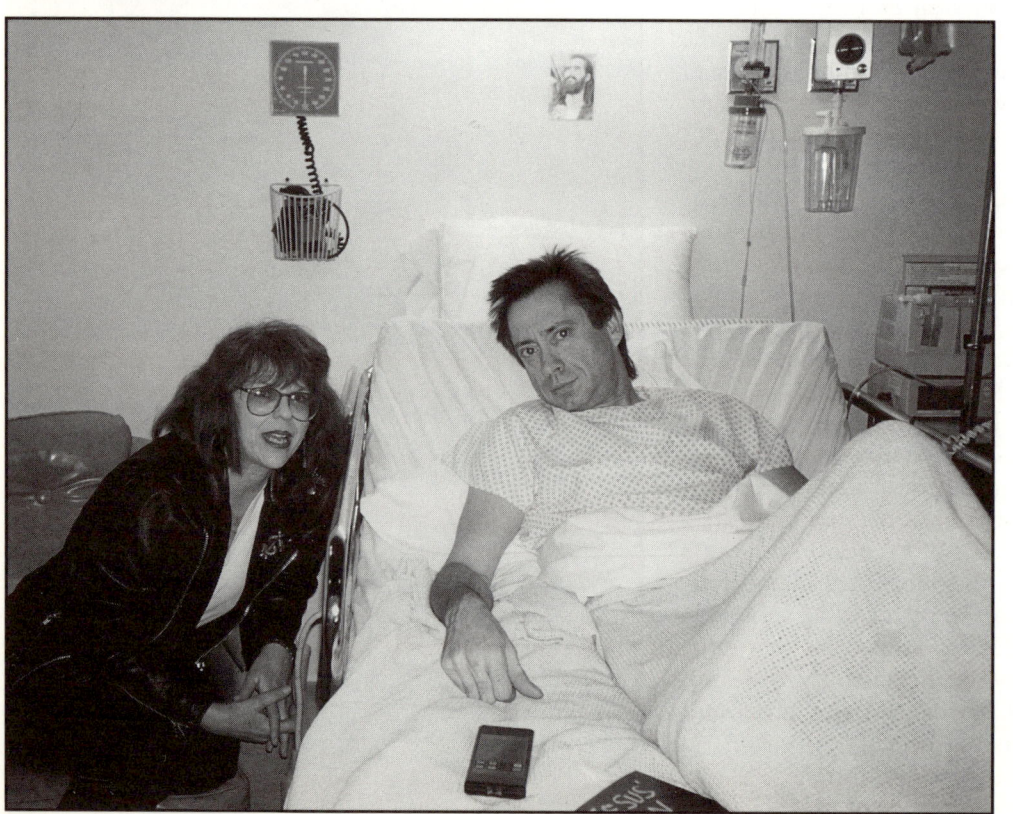

Sheree in an all-too-familiar recreation of our real life: visiting Bob. "Visiting Hours." Santa Monica Museum of Art, 1992. Photo: Molly Shore

an interesting experience.

At first I would come home and try out with Bob some of the new things I had learned. Then it became like a *job*. Now I haven't done professional SM for a long time, and Bob and I are like some "normal" couple!

I feel very fortunate that Bob and I have an intense relationship that my parents didn't have; actually, very few people I know have that. But if we're going to heal society in any way, it has to come from people forming strong bonds and *keeping* those bonds. I think it's a real challenge to do that. But when you have someone like Bob who is so special and so irreplaceable—he's worth all the trouble, because someone like him doesn't come along very often. And I was very touched by his talent very early on—I always call myself his Number One Fan, because I believed in him and what he could do from the very start. Bob also encouraged me to take my own work seriously and do more on my own.

Celebrating Halloween *and* our 11th anniversary. Los Angeles, 1991. Photo: Monica Rex

♦ *V: What are some of the philosophical motivations for your work?*

♦ SR: We want to see the world a better place—let's say, a *different* place. It sounds so pollyanna-ish, but we really do care about changing the world. And "the personal is political"—what you do in your own personal life can have an impact. That's where you have to start the changes. Like with me—it was my husband screaming "No wife of mine is going to be out 'til all hours!" that was the catalyst to get a divorce and radically change my life. Yet I'm sure a million housewives hear that and just quake in their boots and never go out again. One thing—no guy could ever tell my *daughter* anything like that! And that's what you have to hope for: that the *next* generation will be different, and that you'll have a generation of men who would never *think* of talking to their wives like that. That's a much better goal than dreaming of a future where all women will be dominant and all men submissive . . .

Linda Kaufman, who's currently teaching at U.C. Irvine, wrote a brilliant piece about Bob's work—the idea being that violence is part of the human condition, and that everybody gets off on violence in one way or another. SM has been disparaged and shunted aside as something horrible, but it is a very positive way of channeling those violent impulses—it's a constructive way of dealing with that, without doings things like murdering strangers. I don't know how SM could evolve toward being socially accepted, but there *has* to be a way to deal with this violence which is now out of control.

I've always been interested in philosophy: the concepts of good and evil, free will, consensuality—these are major issues that people really need to deal with. I'm an atheist, and I really resent the emphasis that is put on "god" who's going to come down and "save" us. I hate that false idea that takes away people's responsibility for their acts . . . that delusion, that lie, which is so pervasive and doesn't seem to be going away. I really resent all these references to god—this really makes me mad. It's so disgusting, and it's forced down our throats!

I think that until that word "God" disappears—and you'd certainly think that by now people would have figured it out, especially when all these cult groups continue to appear and commit their atrocities. Yet they're no different from the Protestants who believe in "Jesus" and the "Messiah"—they all believe that *bullshit,* and the Catholic church is the same way. Until that "God" idea is gone, we'll stay forever in the *true* Dark Ages . . . ■ ■ ■

Interview Six

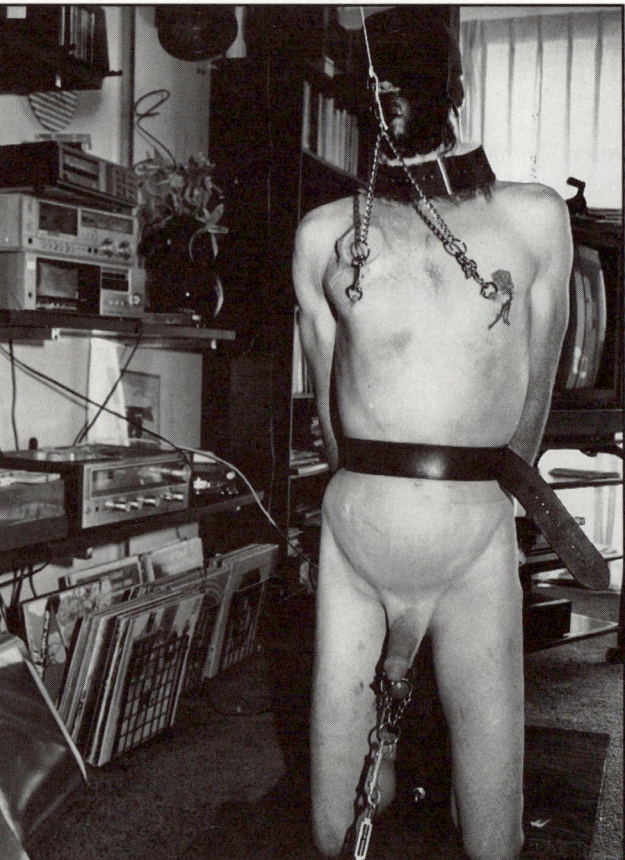

That's a Hickman catheter implanted in the right side of my chest for frequent infusions of IV antibiotics. For this 24-hour torture scene I rolled it up and taped it under a mason jar lid to protect it while I was being whipped. Los Angeles, 1988

♦ **BF:** I got some bad news today from the hospital—they won't be able to do the lung transplant on me. My lungs are too scarred and they won't be able to take them out cleanly enough—there'll be too much bleeding. They got the results of more complicated tests, like Catscans, and reviewed my case last night. Once they saw how damaged my lungs really were, they ruled me out. They're pretty good at projecting survival rates, and it's no good for them to do a surgery if they can't "win."

♦ *AJ: How you feeling now?*

♦ **BF:** Pretty rotten; sort of shaky. I didn't have my hopes up *completely*, but I *was* rearranging my life—I thought I'd get the beeper (to notify me when a suitable donor had been found) and await the transplant. Although—I had dreams last night where people were coming in my room and telling me, "No!"

♦ *AJ: A premonition.*

♦ **BF:** Now it's time to backtrack and watch the disease get worse and then a little better; worse and then better . . . My parents are going to be very upset, and so is Sheree. It's a rotten time. Now I have to hunker down and get all my projects done.

♦ **AJ: Do you want to talk about any personal turmoil you've gone through recently? Why are you in intensive care now?**
♦ BF: I'm still figuring it all out. I've been hospitalized for IV transfusions so many times that a year ago they installed a "porta-cath" in my chest. A lot of people who require constant IV therapy have these, so you don't have to keep getting poked with a needle. It looks like a little bulge under the skin. Mine got a clot in the vein—this happens with pacemakers; any foreign body can cause it. After the Santa Monica show I wasn't feeling well so I went in the hospital for a checkup, and the doctor said, "Ohmigod!" But he couldn't *do* anything about the clot—it had been there so long that it had formed a scar by itself. So now it's just a matter of waiting for new veins to grow around it.
♦ **V: They couldn't actually do anything for you?**
♦ BF: They tried to wipe it out with a couple treatments, but nothing changed it. Basically it healed by itself, but the vein itself is still clogged, so the circulation is all screwed up. That will correct itself as new veins grow; the body finds ways to get the blood around—no matter what. Aside from that, there's this C-F infection I'm trying to fight.
♦ **AJ: You think about death, no doubt?**
♦ BF: I *always* think about that, because even surgery is scary. Now I'm freed up, in a way—I don't have to worry about being on a transplant list and hanging around L.A. Now I can plan a forthcoming show in New York. Now I have no more excuses to get my own writing going—I've been stalling on that. I have to use whatever available time is left. As a

The hospital, my home away from home. Can't even piss in peace. Actually, masochist that I am, and humiliation being my stock in trade, most bodily functions have been completely demystified. So what if the doctor probes a finger up my butt, or if a nurse sees me pissing —I'm used to it—in fact, I kind of like it. Long Beach, 1992

retrospective, the Santa Monica show was so complete that no matter what happens now, it's okay! I did the main thing I wanted to do, and I did it, and I want to repeat it one more time in New York. Now I'm on *gravy time . . .* ■ ■ ■

BOB FLANAGAN  SUPERMASOCHIST

BIOGRAPHY

PERFORMANCES

A Matter of Choice
In collaboration with Sheree Rose; LACE; July, 1992

Bob Flanagan at the Movies
Artists Television Access, San Francisco, April 18, 1992

Bob Flanagan at the Movies
The Lab, San Francisco; September 7, 1991

Bob Flanagan's Sick
Art in the Anchorage, New York; August, 1991

Bob Flanagan's Sick
LACE, Los Angeles, May, 1991

Product of My Environment
Benefit for Highways, Santa Monica, April, 1990

Under Grand Music
Reading of a text on Ludwig Van Beethoven written by poet Amy Gerstler, coproduced by The Los Angeles Philharmonic Association, The Museum of Contemporary Art, Los Angeles, April 10, 1990

Why
With Sheree Rose, LACE Valentine's Day Benefit, Los Angeles Contemporary Exhibitions, Los Angeles, February, 1990

Nailed
Southern Exposure (produced by Re/Search), San Francisco, November, 1989

Nailed
Olio (produced by Amok Bookstore), Los Angeles, October, 1989

Body
Part of a group show: Mouthing Toward the Millennium, Los Angeles Contemporary Exhibitions, Los Angeles, January, 1989

Tell Me What To Do: An Improvisational Reading and Performance
Beyond Baroque, Venice, August 14, 1987

Slave Sonnets
Publication party, performance and reading, Beyond Baroque, Los Angeles, July 18, 1986

The Wedding of Everything
Beyond Baroque, Los Angeles, December 17, 1982

Gross Revisions
In collaboration with Sheree Rose as part of a group show, Poets in Performance, curated by Dennis Cooper, October 2, 1981

The Kid is the Man
Publication party, reading and performance for *The Kid is the Man* (1978, Bombshelter Press), Intellectuals & Liars Bookstore, December 10, 1978

EXHIBITS & INSTALLATIONS

Sickness to Health Through S&M
Selections from The Book of Medicine presented as part of a group show, Up with People, curated by Hudson, Feature Gallery, New York, July 7—August 6, 1993

Artists' Writing Reading Room: An Exhibition of Visual Artists Who Write and Writers Who Make Visual Art
Side Street Projects, Santa Monica, California, May, 1993

Visiting Hours
Santa Monica Museum of Art, December, 1992

A Matter of Choice
Video collaboration with Sheree Rose, presented as part of a group show, The Adrenalin Scan: Performance and Body Movement Videos, curated by Marnie Weber, Otis Art Institute, October 2, 1982

Night Gallery
Man being slapped in a video segment of an installation by Daniel Martinez, Center On Contemporary Art, Seattle, 1991

100 Reasons
In collaboration with Sheree Rose and Mike Kelley, group show, Presenting Rearwards, curated by Ralph Rugoff, Rosamund Felsen Gallery, August, 1991

Pain Photos of Bob's Face
In collaboration with Sheree Rose as part of a group show, Visual Art By Writers, curated by Dennis Cooper, Beyond Baroque, Los Angeles, June, 1982

ACTING

The New Age
Theatrical film directed by Michael Tolkin, 1993

It's Coming Down
Music video for Danzig, directed by Jonathan Reiss, Original Film, 1993

Do You Need Some?
Music video for Mind Bomb, directed by Jonathan Reiss, Original Film, 1992

Happiness in Slavery
Music video for Nine Inch Nails, directed by Jonathan Reiss, Original Film, 1992

The Groundlings
Ensemble player in the Sunday company, October, 1988—October, 1989

Armageddon Outta Here
Numerous roles in a play written by Derek McGrath and Wendy Jewell, directed by Rene Migliaccio, August, 1987

VIDEOS

A Matter of Choice
with Sheree Rose, 1992

Story of Bob
1991

Body
in collaboration with Sheree Rose, 1991

Bob Flanagan's Sick
In collaboration with Sheree Rose; video component to performance and installation, 1991

100 Reasons
In collaboration with Sheree Rose and Mike Kelley, 1991

Leather from Home
20 minute video, in collaboration with Sheree Rose, 1984

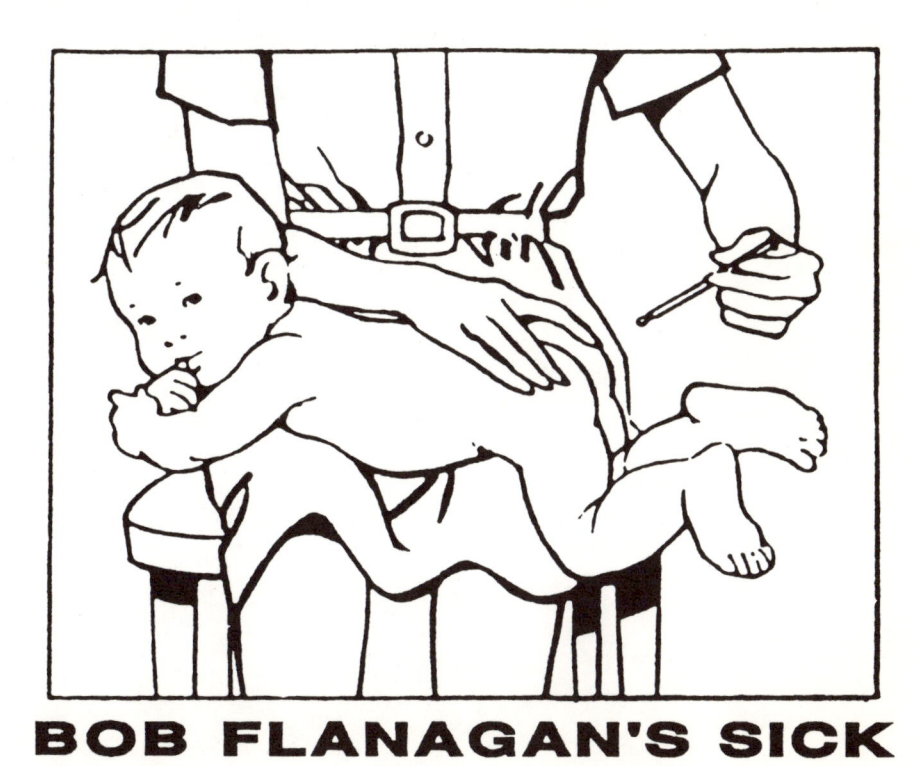

Invitation to "Bob Flanagan's Sick" at LACE

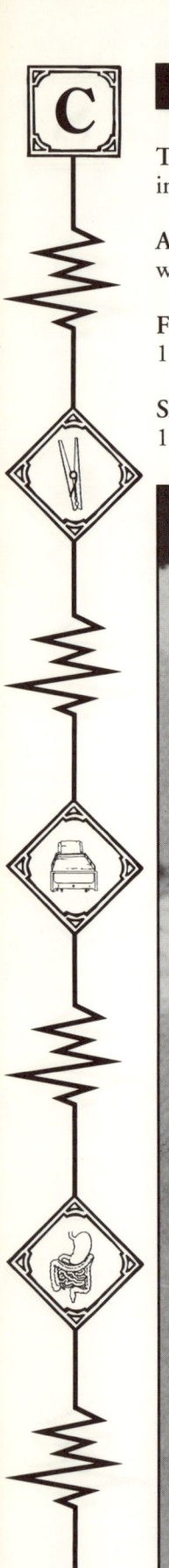

BOOKS

The Book of Medicine
in progress

A Taste of Honey
with David Trinidad, 1990, Cold Calm Press

Fuck Journal
1987, Hanuman Books

Slave Sonnets
1986, Cold Calm Press, cover art by Mike Kelley

The Wedding of Everything
1983, Sherwood Press

The Kid is the Man
1978, Bombshelter Press

JOURNALS & ANTHOLOGIES

The Best American Erotica, 1993
"Why"; editor Susie Bright, MacMillan, 1993

Film Threat Video Guide
"Mastering Machines, Meat & Movies", article by David E. Williams on the films of Jonathan Reiss, specifically the Nine Inch Nails music Video, "Happiness in Slavery." Includes interview and photos of Bob Flanagan; ed. David E. Williams, Film Threat Video, 1993

Brooklyn Review #9
"Handcuffs"; Brooklyn Review, 1992

Framework Vol. 5, #2 & 3
"S" (selections from The Book of Medicine); ed. Susan Kandel and Jody Zellen, LACPS, Summer, 1992

Dear World
"Why"; ed. Camille Roy and Nayland Blake, 1991

High Risk
"Body"; ed. Amy Scholder and Ira Silverberg, Dutton, 1991

Poetry Loves Poetry
poems; ed. Bill Mohr, Momentum Press, 1991

The Wedding of Everything

SLAVE SONNETS

Bob Flanagan

Amnesia #1
"Saint Bob and Mistress Rose: Art Criminals," interview by Monica Rex, 1990

New American Writing
"Sonnet" (I'm an instrument . . .); ed. Paul Hoover and Maxine Chernoff, Oink! Press, 1987

Forehead, Volume One
"You Boys with the Circus?" and "King of the Road," (with David Trinidad); Beyond Baroque Foundation, 1987

Spazio Umano
"Fear of Poetry" and "The Wedding of Everything"; April, 1986

Nude Erections #1
"Halloween"; ed. P. Schneidre, Illuminati, 1984

Coming Attractions
"Houses," "The World of Science," "Driving into the World"; ed. Dennis Cooper, Little Caesar, 1980

Foreign Exchange
"The Heart is a Pump"; ed. Michael C. Ford, Biographics, 1979

The Alley Cat Readings #3
"Alkies from Heaven," "Lifesize," "Spanish Stairway in Beverly Hills," "Fairfax Sestina," "From the Canal," "Lifesize Play Guy," "I Wanna Be Loved By You"; ed. Jack Grapes, Bombshelter Press, 1976

Jill Jordan hard at work, and me, trying not to get hard, as she emblazons my Godhead with a crown of thorns. Los Angeles, 1991

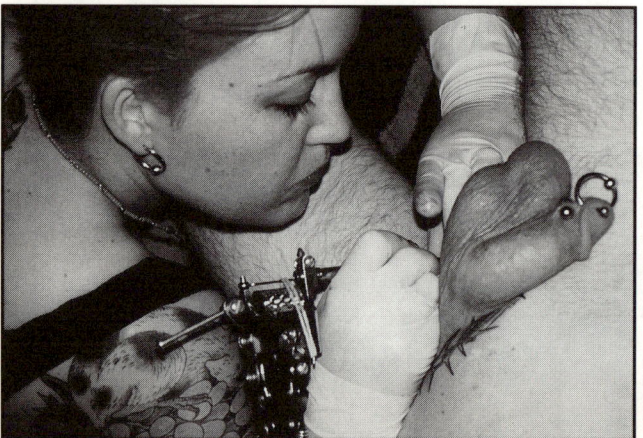

PERIODICALS

frieze
"Bizzaro Superman," March/April, 1993

Shiny #7/8
"Balladeer," 1992

Ben is Dead Magazine
"Gross? Performance Artists," interview with Bob Flanagan by Don Lewis, December/January, 1991/1992

Chemical Imbalance, Vol. 2, #3
"Why," 1991

Taste of Latex #6
"Why," ed. Lily Braindrop, 1991

Shiny #2
"February 13," "Sonnet" (The name stamped onto the lock says "Master" . . .); 1987

Das Magazin #2
"Parachute," "Handcuffs," Warten, 1991

B City
"ABC," Spring 1988

B City
"A Taste of Honey," "Shake Up, Twist and Shout, and Hullabaloo," (with David Trinidad); Spring 1987

Barney #4
Sunset Palms Hotel "2 Fuck Sonnets," 1984

Ouija Madness 2
Songs from the folk-punk bongo trio, Planet of Toys: "Vitamin Boy" (with Gary Guthrie, Rick Lawndale and Jack Skelley), "I Killed the Puppet" (with Jack Skelley), "Date with Barbie" (with Jack Skelley), plus an interview with Planet of Toys by David Smith, 1982

Snap
"New York," Winter, 1982

Barney #1
"The Arm," "The Baby," "Solid," 1981

The Modularist Review
"Just Then," 1980

Bachy 15
Portfolio of Poetry Flyers (collages), 1979

Momentum 9-10
"Dragging the Canal," Fall, 1977

Nausea 10
"Bukowski Poem," Spring, 1976

Bachy
"Spanish Stairway in Beverly Hills," "2 Old Love Letters, a Poem, and Journal Notes/ Cut-up and Rearranged"; Summer 1975

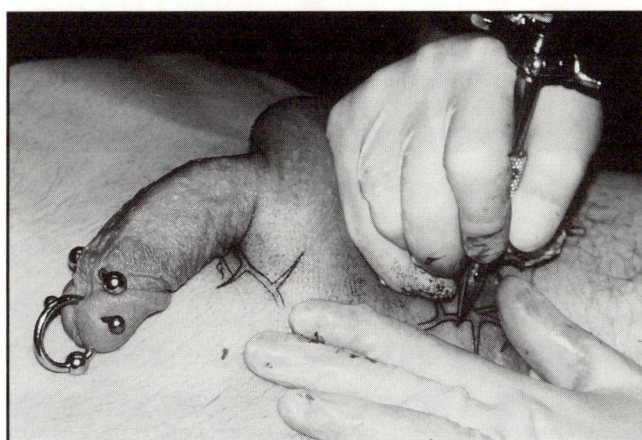

RECORDINGS

Cabin Fever
Cystic Fibrosis Summer Camp, 1990

The Wedding of Everything
Rare Bird Recordings, 1984

LECTURES

Santa Monica Museum of Art
August 1993

Rancho Santiago College
May, 1993

University of California at Irvine
1993

California Institute of the Arts
1993

Society for the Scientific Study of Sex
Symposium on Bondage and Discipline, San Diego, September 21, 1985

QSM,
San Francisco, September 9, 1991

Orange Coast College
Costa Mesa, 1983—1993

California State University at Fullerton
1986—1993

READINGS

City Restaurant, Los Angeles
Lace, Los Angeles
Gasoline Alley, Los Angeles
Oranges and Sardine Gallery, Los Angeles
The St. Mark's Poetry Project, New York
Small Press Traffic, San Francisco
Iguana Cafe, North Hollywood
Ocean Park Library, Santa Monica
Beyond Baroque, Venice
Al's Bar, Los Angeles
Lhasa Club, Los Angeles
Onyx Cafe, Los Angeles
The Kitchen, New York
The Ear Inn, New York
The Works Gallery, Los Angeles
Helena's, Los Angeles
Cafe Largo, Los Angeles
California Instutute of the Arts, Valencia
Southern Exposure, San Francisco
Otis Parsons School of Design, Los Angeles
Los Angeles Public Library
Chelsea Bookstore, Long Beach
Intellectuals and Liars Bookstore, Santa Monica
George Sand Bookstore, West Hollywood
Papa Bach's Bookstore, Los Angeles
The Anti Club, Los Angeles

MUSIC

Idiot Bliss
Anti Club, March 6, 1986

Planet of Toys
Beyond Baroque, Venice, 1981
Chelsea Bookstore, Long Beach, 1981
Al's Bar, Los Angeles, 1981
LACE, Los Angeles, 1981   ■ ■ ■

RE/SEARCH Catalog

"A series of beautifully designed volumes, each focusing on a different aspect of American life . . . [RE/Search's] mission is to stimulate creativity by providing information about marginalized elements of culture." —STANFORD WEEKLY

"A consistent standard can be applied to RE/Search: you can extract first-rate information about and thoughts of worthy artists and activists that are not available elsewhere." —BOSTON PHOENIX

"A long-term cultural re-mapping program . . . RE/Search noses out role models who show that you can be creative at any level against a society's control processes, myths and mental overlays that prevent people from expressing their individuality." —SF WEEKLY

"Obviously, the RE/Search editors are fascinated with society's fringe elements, and since most bikers also enjoy life on the edge, it's not surprising that we're gonna share some of the same interests as the fun-loving gang at RE/Search." —IRON HORSE

"RE/Search makes a study of the extremes of human behavior—saluting individualism in an age of conformity." —THE ADVOCATE

"RE/Search examines some of the most arcane fringes of subculture with a thoroughness usually found only in academia." —REFLEX MAGAZINE

◆ ◆ ◆ NEW TITLE ◆ ◆ ◆

RE/Search People Series, Vol. 1: Bob Flanagan, Super-Masochist

Bob Flanagan, born in 1952 in New York City, grew up with Cystic Fibrosis (a genetically inherited, nearly-always fatal disease) and has lived longer than any other person with CF. The physical pain of his childhood suffering was principally alleviated by masturbation and sexual experimentation, wherein pain and pleasure became inextricably linked, resulting in his lifelong practice of extreme masochism.

In deeply confessional interviews, Bob details his sexual practices and his extraordinary relationship with long-term partner and Mistress, photographer Sheree Rose. He tells how frequent near-death encounters modified his concepts of gratification and abstinence, reward and punishment, and intensified his masochistic drive. Through his insider's perspective on the Sado-Masochistic community, we learn firsthand about branding, piercing, whipping, bondage and endurance trials. Surprisingly, the most extreme narratives are infused with humor, honesty, and self-reflective irony. Bob's sharp intelligence and lack of pretense belie a deep commitment to deciphering philosophical issues regarding the body, power, sex, life and death.

Includes photographs by L.A. artist Sheree Rose. 8½ x 11", 128 pp, 125 photos & illustrations.
$14.99

RE/SEARCH BACKLIST

RE/Search #14: Incredibly Strange Music, Volume I

Featuring:
- Eartha Kitt
- The Cramps
- Martin Denny
- Amok Books
- Norton Records
- Perrey & Kingsley
- Mickey McGowan (Unknown Museum)
- Phantom Surfers
- Lypsinka
- and others...

Enthusiastic, hilarious interviews illuminate the territory of neglected vinyl records (c.1950-1980) ignored by the music criticism establishment. Genres include: outer space exploration; abstract female vocals; tiki "exotica" (featuring bird calls and jungle sounds); motivational (*How to Overcome Discouragement* and *Music to Make Automobiles By*—made for factory workers); promotional (giveaways like *Rhapsody of Steel,* produced by U.S. Steel); lurid stripping and belly dancing (which often included instruction booklets); easy listening; and experimental instrumental (which used Theremin, Ondioline, Moog, whistling, harmonica, sitar, accordion and organ). Lavishly illustrated, with reference sections, quotations, sources and an index, this is a comprehensive guide to the last remaining "garage sale" records. Volume 1 (Volume 2 scheduled for Winter 1993): 8½x11", 208 pp, over 200 photos & illustrations.

$17.99

"This book will change your life." —MIRABELLA

Incredibly Strange Music CD

This compilation of 16 of the wildest selections in the Re/Search record archive spans the gamut from beatnik "How to Speak Hip" to raucous instrumentals featuring moog, sitar, Hawaiian steel guitar, exotic primitive instruments, Latin percussion, and one-of-a-kind sound effects. Also, some of the most inexplicable (and delightful) lyrics ever recorded are resurrected on this CD, such as "Cosmic Telephone Call" (by Kali Bahlu) and "Will to Fail" (about psychotherapy). Far beyond being one-line jokes, these selections can be enjoyed over and over again.

$12.00

The Best of Perrey & Kingsley CD

Two fantastic, classic LPs (*The In Sound from Way Out,* and *Kaleidoscopic Vibrations*) combined on one hard-to-find, currently out-of-print CD available exclusively from Re/Search mail orders.

$16.00

RE/Search #13: Angry Women

Featuring:
- Karen Finley
- Annie Sprinkle
- Diamanda Galás
- bell hooks
- Kathy Acker
- Avital Ronell
- Lydia Lunch
- Sapphire
- Susie Bright
- Valie Export
- Wanda Coleman
- Linda Montano
- Holly Hughes
- Suzy Kerr & Dianne Malley ◆ Carolee Schneemann

16 cutting-edge performance artists discuss critical questions such as: How can you have a revolutionary feminism that encompasses wild sex, humor, beauty and spirituality *plus* radical politics? How can you have a powerful movement for social change that's *inclusionary*—not exclusionary? A wide range of topics—from menstruation, masturbation, vibrators, S&M & spanking to racism, failed Utopias and the death of the Sixties—are discussed passionately. Armed with total contempt for dogma, stereotype and cliche, these creative visionaries probe deep into our social foundation of taboos, beliefs and totalitarian linguistic contradictions from whence spring (as well as thwart) our theories, imaginings, behavior and dreams. 8½x11", 240 pp, 135 photos & illustrations.

$18.99

"In this illustrated, interview-format volume, 16 women performance artists animatedly address the volatile issues of male domination, feminism, race and denial. Incendiary opinions of current issues such as the Gulf War and censorship and frequent allusions to empowering art and literature make this an excellent reference source. These informed discussions arm readers verbally, philosophically and behaviorally and provide uncompromising role models for women actively seeking change." —PUBLISHER'S WEEKLY

"This is hardly the nurturing, Womanist vision espoused in the 1970s. For the most part, these artists have given up waiting for the train of sexual equality... The view here is largely prosex, proporn, and prochoice... Separatism is out, community in. Sexuality is fluid, spirituality ancient and animist. Art and activism are inseparable from life and being. The body is a creative field, the mind an exercise in liberation. This is the 13th step, beyond AA's 12: a healing rage." —THE VILLAGE VOICE

RE/SEARCH BACKLIST

RE/Search #12: Modern Primitives

An eye-opening, startling investigation of the undercover world of body modifications: tattooing, piercing and scarification. Amazing, explicit photos! *Fakir Musafar* (55-yr-old Silicon Valley ad executive who, since age 14, has practiced every body modification known to man); *Genesis & Paula P-Orridge* describing numerous ritual scarifications and personal, symbolic tattoos; *Ed Hardy* (editor of *Tattootime* and creator of over 10,000 tattoos); *Capt. Don Leslie* (sword-swallower); *Jim Ward* (editor, *Piercing Fans International*); *Anton LaVey* (founder of the Church of Satan); *Lyle Tuttle* (talking about getting tattooed in Samoa); *Raelyn Gallina* (women's piercer) & others talk about body practices that develop identity, sexual sensation and philosophic awareness. This issue spans the spectrum from S&M pain to New Age ecstasy. 22 interviews, 2 essays (including a treatise on Mayan body piercing based on recent findings), quotations, sources/bibliography & index. 8½ x 11", 212 pp, 279 photos & illustrations. **$17.99**

"MODERN PRIMITIVES is not some shock rag parading crazies for your amusement. All of the people interviewed are looking for something very simple: a way of fighting back at a mass production consumer society that prizes standardization above all else. Through 'primitive' modifications, they are taking possession of the only thing that any of us will ever really own: our bodies."
—WHOLE EARTH REVIEW

"The photographs and illustrations are both explicit and astounding . . . This is the ideal biker coffee table book, a conversation piece that provides fascinating food for thought." —IRON HORSE

"MODERN PRIMITIVES approaches contemporary body adornment and ritual from the viewpoint that today's society suffers from an almost universal feeling of powerlessness to change the world, leaving the choice for exploration, individuation and primitive rite of passage to be fought out on the only ground readily available to us: our bodies."—TIME OUT

"In a world so badly made, as ours is, there is only one road—rebellion."
— Luis Bunuel

"Habit is probably the greatest block to seeing truth." — R.A. Schwaller de Lubicz

RE/Search #11: Pranks!

A prank is a "trick, a mischievous act, a ludicrous act." Although not regarded as poetic or artistic acts, pranks constitute an art form and genre in themselves. Here pranksters such as Timothy Leary, Abbie Hoffman, Paul Krassner, Mark Pauline, Monte Cazazza, Jello Biafra, Earth First!, Joe Coleman, Karen Finley, Frank Discussion, John Waters and Henry Rollins challenge the sovereign authority of words, images & behavioral convention. Some tales are bizarre, as when Boyd Rice presented the First Lady with a skinned sheep's head on a platter. This iconoclastic compendium will dazzle and delight all lovers of humor, satire and irony. 8½ x 11", 240 pp, 164 photos & illustrations. **$17.99**

"The definitive treatment of the subject, offering extensive interviews with 36 contemporary tricksters. . . from the Underground's answer to Studs Terkel."
—WASHINGTON POST

RE/Search #10: Incredibly Strange Films

A guide to important territory neglected by the film criticism establishment, spotlighting unhailed directors—*Herschell Gordon Lewis, Russ Meyer, Larry Cohen, Ray Dennis Steckler, Ted V. Mikels, Doris Wishman* and others—who have been critically consigned to the ghettos of gore and sexploitation films. In-depth interviews focus on philosophy, while anecdotes entertain as well as illuminate theory. 13 interviews, numerous essays, A-Z of film personalities, "Favorite Films" list, quotations, bibliography, filmography, film synopses, & index. 8½ x 11", 224 pp. 157 photos & illustrations. **$17.99**

"Flicks like these are subversive alternatives to the mind control propagated by the mainstream media."
—IRON HORSE

"Whether discussing the ethics of sex and violence on the screen, film censorship, their personal motivations, or the nuts and bolts of filmmaking from financing through distribution, the interviews are intelligent, enthusiastic and articulate."—SMALL PRESS

RE/SEARCH BACKLIST

RE/Search #8/9: J.G. Ballard

A comprehensive special on this supremely relevant writer, now famous for *Empire of the Sun* and *Day of Creation*. W.S. Burroughs described Ballard's novel *Love & Napalm: Export U.S.A.* (1972) as "profound and disquieting...This book stirs sexual depths untouched by the hardest-core illustrated porn." 3 interviews, biography by David Pringle, fiction and non-fiction excerpts, essays, quotations, bibliography, sources, & index. 8½ x 11", 176 pp. 76 photos & illustrations by Ana Barrado, Ken Werner, Ed Ruscha, and others.

$14.99

"The RE/SEARCH to own if you must have just one . . . the most detailed, probing and comprehensive study of Ballard on the market."—BOSTON PHOENIX

"Highly recommended as both an introduction and a tribute to this remarkable writer."
—WASHINGTON POST

RE/Search #6/7 Industrial Culture Handbook

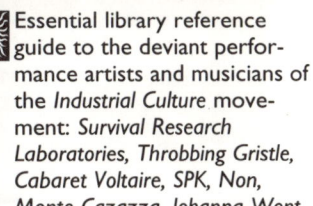

Essential library reference guide to the deviant performance artists and musicians of the *Industrial Culture* movement: Survival Research Laboratories, Throbbing Gristle, Cabaret Voltaire, SPK, Non, Monte Cazazza, Johanna Went, Sordide Sentimental, R&N, and Z'ev. Some topics discussed: new brain research, forbidden medical texts & films, creative crime & *interesting* criminals, modern warfare & weaponry, neglected gore films & their directors, psychotic lyrics in past pop songs, *art brut*, etc. 10 interviews, essays, quotations, chronologies, bibliographies, discographies, filmographies, sources, & index. 8½ x 11", 140 pp, 179 photos & illustrations.

$13.99

". . . focuses on post-punk 'industrial' performers whose work comprises a biting critique of contemporary culture . . . the book lists alone are worth the price of admission!"—SMALL PRESS

RE/Search #4/5: W. S. Burroughs, Brion Gysin, Throbbing Gristle

Interviews, scarce fiction, essays: this is a manual of ideas and insights. Strikingly designed, with rare photos, bibliographies, discographies, chronologies & illustrations. 7 interviews, essays, chronologies, bibliographies, discographies, sources. 8½ x 11", 100 pp. 58 photos & illustrations.

$12.99

"Interviews with pioneering cut-up artists William S. Burroughs, Brion Gysin and Throbbing Gristle . . . proposes a ground-breaking, radical cultural agenda for the '80s and '90s."—Jon Savage, LONDON OBSERVER

Trilogy: High Priest of California (novel & play); Wild Wives (novel) by Charles Willeford

1953 San Francisco *roman noir*: the first two novels by Charles Willeford surpass the works of Jim Thompson in profundity of hard-boiled characterization, simultaneously offering a deep critique of contemporary morality. Unusual plots, tough dialogue starring anti-heroes both brutal and complex, and women living outside the lie of chivalry: "She wasn't wearing much beneath her skirt. In an instant it was over. Fiercely and abruptly." Plus the first publication of a play. 304 pp. 5x8". 2 introductions; bibliography; 15 photos.

$9.95

"HIGH PRIEST OF CALIFORNIA—The hairiest, ballsiest hard-boiled ever penned. One continuous orgy of prolonged foreplay! WILD WIVES—sex, schizophrenia and sadism blend into a recipe for sudden doom!"
—Dennis McMillan

"Willeford never puts a foot wrong.'—NEW YORKER

RE/SEARCH CLASSICS

The Confessions of Wanda von Sacher-Masoch

Finally available in English: the racy and riveting *Confessions of Wanda von Sacher-Masoch*—married for ten years to Leopold von Sacher-Masoch (author of *Venus in Furs* and many other novels) whose whip-and-fur bedroom games spawned the term "masochism." In this feminist classic from 100 years ago, Wanda was forced to play "sadistic" roles in Leopold's fantasies to ensure the survival of herself and her 3 children—games which called into question who was the Master and who the Slave. Besides being a compelling study of a woman's search for her own identity, strength and ultimately—complete independence—this is a true-life adventure story—an odyssey through many lands peopled by amazing characters. Underneath its unforgettable poetic imagery and almost unbearable emotional cataclysms reigns a woman's consistent unblinking investigation of the limits of morality and the deepest meanings of love. Translated by Marian Phillips, Caroline Hébert & V. Vale. 8½ x 11", 136 pages, illustrations. **$13.99**

"As with all RE/Search editions, *The Confessions of Wanda von Sacher-Masoch* is extravagantly designed, in an illustrated, oversized edition that is a pleasure to hold. It is also exquisitely written, engaging and literary and turns our preconceptions upside down."—**LA READER**

Freaks: We Who Are Not As Others by Daniel P. Mannix

Another long out-of-print classic book based on Mannix's personal acquaintance with sideshow stars such as the Alligator Man and the Monkey Woman, etc. Read all about the notorious love affairs of midgets; the amazing story of the elephant boy; the unusual amours of Jolly Daisy, the fat woman; the famous pinhead who inspired Verdi's *Rigoletto;* the tragedy of Betty Lou Williams and her parasitic twin; the black midget, only 34 inches tall, who was happily married to a 264-pound wife; the human torso who could sew, crochet and type; and bizarre accounts of normal humans turned into freaks—either voluntarily or by evil design! 88 astounding photographs and additional material from the author's personal collection. 8½ x 11", 124pp. **$13.99**

SIGNED HARDBOUND: Limited edition of 300 signed by the author on acid-free paper **$50.00**

"RE/Search has provided us with a moving glimpse at the rarified world of physical deformity; a glimpse that ultimately succeeds in its goal of humanizing the inhuman, revealing the beauty that often lies behind the grotesque and in dramatically illustrating the triumph of the human spirit in the face of overwhelming debility."
—**SPECTRUM WEEKLY**

The Torture Garden by Octave Mirbeau

This book was once described as the "most sickening work of art of the nineteenth century!" Long out of print, Octave Mirbeau's macabre classic (1899) features a corrupt Frenchman and an insatiably cruel Englishwoman who meet and then frequent a fantastic 19th century Chinese garden where torture is practiced as an art form. The fascinating, horrific narrative slithers deep into the human spirit, uncovering murderous proclivities and demented desires. Lavish, loving detail of description. Introduction, biography & bibliography. 8½ x 11", 120 pp, 21 photos. **$13.99**

HARDBOUND: Limited edition of 200 hardbacks on acid-free paper **$29.00**

"... sadistic spectacle as apocalyptic celebration of human potential ... A work as chilling as it is seductive."
—**THE DAILY CALIFORNIAN**

The Atrocity Exhibition by J.G. Ballard

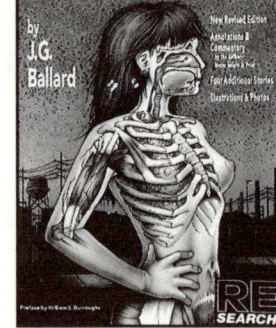

A large-format, illustrated edition of this long out-of-print classic, widely regarded as Ballard's finest, most complex work. Withdrawn by E.P. Dutton after having been shredded by Doubleday, this outrageous work was finally printed in a small edition by Grove before lapsing out of print 15 years ago. With 4 additional fiction pieces, extensive annotations (a book in themselves), disturbing photographs by Ana Barrado and dazzling, anatomically explicit medical illustrations by Phoebe Gloeckner. 8½ x 11", 136pp. **$13.99**

SIGNED HARDBOUND: Limited Edition of 300 signed by the author on acid-free paper **$50.00**

"*The Atrocity Exhibition* is remarkably fresh. One does not read these narratives as one does other fiction ... one enters into them as a kind of ritual ..."
—**SAN FRANCISCO CHRONICLE**

RE/SEARCH BACKLIST

RE/Search #1 & #3

Deep into the heart of the Control Process. Preoccupation: Creativity & Survival, past, present & future. These are the early tabloid issues, 11x17", full of photos & innovative graphics.

♦ #1 J.G. Ballard, Cabaret Voltaire, Julio Cortazar, Octavio Paz, Sun Ra, *The Slits*, Robert K. Brown (editor, *Soldier of Fortune*), *Non,* Conspiracy Theory Guide, Punk Prostitutes, and more.

♦ #2 DNA, James Blood Ulmer, P'ev, Aboriginal Music, West African Music Guide, Technology, Monte Cazazza on poisons, Diana, Seda, German Electronic Music Chart, Isabelle Eberhardt, and more. **OUT-OF-PRINT**

♦ #3 Fela, New Brain Research, The Rattlesnake Man, Sordide Sentimental, New Guinea, Kathy Acker, Sado-Masochism (interview with Pat Califia); Joe Dante, Johanna Went, *SPK, Flipper,* Physical Modification of Women, and more.

$8.00 each.

Louder Faster Shorter — *Punk Video*

One of the only surviving 16mm color documents of the original punk rock scene at the Mabuhay Gardens. 20 minute video featuring the AVENGERS, DILS, MUTANTS, SLEEPERS, and UXA. (This video is in US NTSC VHS FORMAT.)
$20.00

Search & Destroy:

Incendiary interviews, passionate photographs, art brutal. Corrosive minimalist documentation of the only youth rebellion of the seventies: punk rock (1977-78). The philosophy and culture, BEFORE the mass media takeover and inevitable cloning.

♦ #1 Premiere issue. Crime, Nuns, Global Punk Survey.
♦ #2 Devo, Clash, Ramones, Iggy, Weirdos, Patti Smith, Vivienne Westwood, Avengers, Dils, etc.
♦ #3 Devo, Damned, Patti Smith, Avengers, Tom Verlaine, Capt. Beefheart, Blondie, Residents, Alternative TV, Throbbing Gristle.
♦ #4 Iggy, Dead Boys, Bobby Death, Jordan & the Ants, Mumps, Metal Urbain, Helen Wheels, Sham 69, Patti Smith.
♦ #5 Sex Pistols, Nico, Crisis, Screamers, Suicide, Crime, Talking Heads, Anarchy, Surrealism & New Wave essay.
♦ #6 Throbbing Gristle, Clash, Nico, Talking Heads, Pere Ubu, Nuns, UXA, Negative Trend, Mutants, Sleepers, Buzzcocks.
♦ #7 John Waters, Devo, DNA, Cabaret Voltaire, Roky Erickson, Clash, Amos Poe, Mick Farren, Offs, Vermilion & more.
♦ #8 Mutants, Dils, Cramps, Devo, Siouxsie, Chrome, Pere Ubu, Judy Nylon & Patti Palladin, Flesheaters, Offs, Weirdos, etc.
♦ #9 Dead Kennedys, Rockabilly Rebels, X, Winston Tong, David Lynch, Television, Pere Ubu, DOA, etc.
♦ #10 J.G. Ballard, William S. Burroughs, Feederz, Plugz, X, Russ Meyer, Steve Jones, etc. Reprinted by Demand!
♦ #11 The all photo supplement. Black and White.

$4.00 each.
SEARCH & DESTROY COMPLETE SET
Issues #1-11 only $39.00.

FLASH PUBLICATIONS

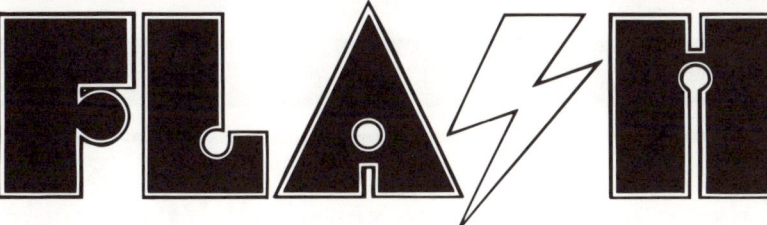

CHARLES GATEWOOD PHOTOGRAPHS: The Body & Beyond
Beautiful hardbound signed and numbered collectors' edition of Gatewood's finest work. 64 pages, 50 amazing duotone photographs. **$49.95**

Charles Gatewood's PRIMITIVES: Tribal Body Art & The Left-Hand Path
Elegant hardbound signed and numbered collectors' edition, 64 pages, with 39 intense tattoo and piercing photographs. **$49.95**

Sidetripping by Charles Gatewood and William S. Burroughs
Rare first edition copies of the 1975 underground classic exposing American sex, violence, and high weirdness. Softbound, 80 pages, 52 duotone photographs. **$19.95**

Flash Video Complete Illustrated Catalog
22 unusual documentary videos not available elsewhere: Erotic Tattooing & Body Piercing, Painless Steel, Weird San Francisco, Weird Amsterdam, Weird Thailand, more. **$5.00**

Photo: Charles Gatewood

AGE STATEMENT REQUIRED — CA RESIDENTS ADD SALES TAX

Order directly from:
FLASH PUBLICATIONS, Box 410052, San Francisco, CA 94141

BOOKS DISTRIBUTED BY RE/SEARCH

Body Art

From England, a glossy 8½ x 11" magazine devoted to tattoo, piercing, body painting, tribal influences, pubic hairdressing, *et al*. Outstanding explicit Color/B&W photographs, instructive text—a beautiful production. Approx. 48 pgs.

$17.00 EACH

- **ISSUE #1:** Finally back in print! Mr Sebastian, Scythian Man.
- **ISSUE #2:** Pubic Hairdressing, Out of the Closet, Shotsie.
- **ISSUE #3:** Africa Adorned, Tanta, Nipple Jewelry.
- **ISSUE #4:** Tattoo Expo '88, Tribal Influence, Male Piercings.
- **ISSUE #5:** Female Piercings, The Year of the Snake.
- **ISSUE #6:** Body Painting, Celtic Tattoos.
- **ISSUE #7:** Female Nipple Development, Plastic Bodies.
- **ISSUE #8:** Tattoo Symbolism, Piercing Enlargement.
- **ISSUE #9:** Tattoos, Nipple Piercing, The Perfect Body.
- **ISSUE #10:** Amsterdam Tattoo Convention, Cliff Raven.
- **ISSUE #11:** Ed Hardy, Fred Corbin, Beyond The Pain Barrier.
- **ISSUE #12:** Tattoo Expo '90, Genital Modifications.
- **ISSUE #13:** New Orleans Tattoo Convention 1990.
- **ISSUE #14:** Krystyne Kolorful, Paris Tattoo Convention.
- **ISSUE #15:** The Stainless Steel Ball, Bodyshots: Richard Todd
- **ISSUE #16:** Tattoo Expo '91, Indian Hand Painting, Nail Tattoos.
- **ISSUE #17:** Body Manipulations, Women Talk Piercing, Expo '91
- **ISSUE #18:** National Tattoo Convention '92 & Tattoo Expo '92

Please list an alternate title for all Body Art selections.

PopVoid #1: '60s Culture. edited by Jim Morton

Edited by Jim Morton (who guest-edited *Incredibly Strange Films*). Fantastic anthology of neglected pop culture: Lawrence Welk, Rod McKuen, Paper Dresses, Nudist Colonies, Goofy Grape, etc. 8½ x 11", 100 pp.
$9.95

TattooTime edited by Don Ed Hardy

- ◆ **#1: NEW TRIBALISM.**
This classic issue features the new "tribal" tattooing renaissance started by Cliff Raven, Ed Hardy, Leo Zulueta & others.
$10.00
- ◆ **#2: TATTOO MAGIC.**
This issue examines all facets of Magic & the Occult.
$10.00
- ◆ **#3: MUSIC & SEA TATTOOS.**
Deluxe double book issue with over 300 photos.
$15.00
- ◆ **#4: LIFE & DEATH.**
Deluxe double book issue with fantastic photos, examining trademarks, architectural and mechanical tattoos, the Eternal Spiral, a Tattoo Museum, plus the gamut of Death imagery.
$15.00
- ◆ **#5: ART FROM THE HEART.**
All *NEW* issue that's bigger than ever before (128 pgs) with hundreds of color photographs. Featuring in-depth articles on tattooers, contemporary tattooing in Samoa, a survey of the new weirdo monster tattoos and much more!
$20.00

Halloween by Ken Werner

A classic photo book. Startling photographs from the "Mardi Gras of the West," San Francisco's *adult* Halloween festivities in the Castro district. Limited supply. Beautiful 9x12" hardback bound in black boards. 72 pgs. Black glossy paper.
$11.00

SPECIAL DISCOUNTS

Special Deluxe Offer (Save $80!) Complete set of RE/Search serials plus reprints and complete set of Search & Destroy.

Offer includes Re/Search #1 & 3 tabloids, #4/5 Burroughs/Gysin/Throbbing Gristle, #6/7 Industrial Culture Handbook, #8/9 J.G. Ballard, #10 Incredibly Strange Films, #11 Pranks!, #12 Modern Primitives, #13: Angry Women, #14: Incredibly Strange Music, Vol. I, Search & Destroy Issues #1-11, The Confessions of Wanda von Sacher-Masoch, Freaks: We Who Are Not As Others, The Atrocity Exhibition, Torture Garden, the Willeford Trilogy and Me & Big Joe.
Special Discount Offer: $215 ppd. Seamail/Canada: $235. AIR Europe: $322. AIR Austr./Japan: $361.
FOR *Bob Flanagan, Super-Masochist*: ADD ONLY $10!

PRICES FOR THE SPECIAL DISCOUNT OFFERS INCLUDE SHIPPING & HANDLING!

Special Discount Offer (Save $45!) Complete set of all RE/Search serials

Offer includes the Re/Search #1 & 3 tabloids, #4/5 Burroughs/Gysin/Throbbing Gristle, #6/7 Industrial Culture Handbook, #8/9 J.G. Ballard, #10 Incredibly Strange Films, #11 Pranks!, #12 Modern Primitives, #13 Angry Women and #14 Incredibly Strange Music, Vol. I.
Special Discount Offer Only: $125 ppd. Seamail/Canada: $135. AIR Europe: $191. AIR Austr/Japan: $215.
FOR *Bob Flanagan, Super-Masochist*: ADD ONLY $10.

Special Reprints Offer (Save $20!) Complete set of all RE/Search Classics

Offer includes the Willeford Trilogy, Freaks: We Who Are Not As Others, The Torture Garden, The Atrocity Exhibition, and The Confessions of Wanda von Sacher-Masoch.
Special Discount Offer: $58 ppd. Seamail/Canada: $60. AIR Europe: $85. AIR Austr/Japan: $96.

Subscribe to RE/Search:

REGULAR SUBSCRIPTION:
You will receive the next three books published by RE/Search which will include either our numbered interview format serials or Re/Search classics. **$40.** Overseas/Canada: **$50.**

INSTITUTION SUBSCRIPTION:
Sorry no library or university subscriptions. Please place individual orders from this catalog.
SUBSCRIPTIONS SENT SURFACE MAIL ONLY! NO AIRMAIL.

Do you know someone who would like our catalog? Write name & address below.

NAME

ADDRESS

CITY, STATE, ZIP

PLEASE SEE PREVIOUS PAGE FOR SPECIAL DISCOUNTS

♦ ♦ ♦ ORDER FORM ♦ ♦ ♦

HAVE YOU ORDERED FROM US BEFORE?   circle one   YES   NO

NAME

ADDRESS

CITY, STATE, ZIP

VISA   MasterCard

Order by mail or phone: Phone orders may be placed Monday through Friday, from 10 a.m. to 6 p.m. Pacific Standard Time.
Phone #415-362-1465

Check or Money Order Enclosed (Payable to RE/Search Publications) or

VISA/MasterCard #

Exp. Date   Signature:

**MAIL TO: RE/SEARCH PUBLICATIONS
20 ROMOLO ST., #B
SAN FRANCISCO, CA 94133**

TITLE	QUANTITY	TOTAL

Subtotal	
CA Residents (add 8½% Sales Tax)	
Shipping/Handling (except Special Discounts)	
Add $3 UPS (Continental U.S. only)	
TOTAL DUE	

SHIPPING & HANDLING CHARGES
First item $4. Add $1 per each additional item. For UPS add an additional $3 (flat rate per order). You must give a street address—no PO Box addresses.

INTERNATIONAL CUSTOMERS. For SEAMAIL: first item $6; add $2 per each additional item. For AIRMAIL: first item $15; add $12 per each additonal item.

ATTENTION CANADIAN CUSTOMERS: WE DO NOT ACCEPT PERSONAL CHECKS EVEN IF IT IS FROM A U.S. DOLLAR ACCOUNT. SEND INTERNATIONAL MONEY ORDERS ONLY! (available from the post office.)

SEND SASE FOR CATALOG (or 4 IRCs for OVERSEAS)
FOR INFORMATION CALL: (415) 362-1465

PAYMENT IN U.S. DOLLARS
ALLOW 6-8 WEEKS FOR DELIVERY

AUG, 1993

Mine is the bittersweet tale of a sick little boy who found solace in his penis at a time when all else conspired to snuff him out, or, at the very least, fill his miserably short life span with more than its share of pain, discomfort and humiliation. The penis seemed to thrive on whatever shit the rest of the body was subjected to and rose to the occasion of each onslaught, soaking it up like a sponge, or, to be more succinct, the corpus spongiosum became full of itself and my stupid prick danced in the spotlight of sickness and suffering. That first swat on the ass from the obstetrician's skilled hands not only started my diseased lungs sputtering to life, but it also sent a shock wave through my sphincter, up my tiny rectum, and straight into the shaft of my shiny new penis, which ever since then has had this crazy idea in its head that pain and sex were one in the same.

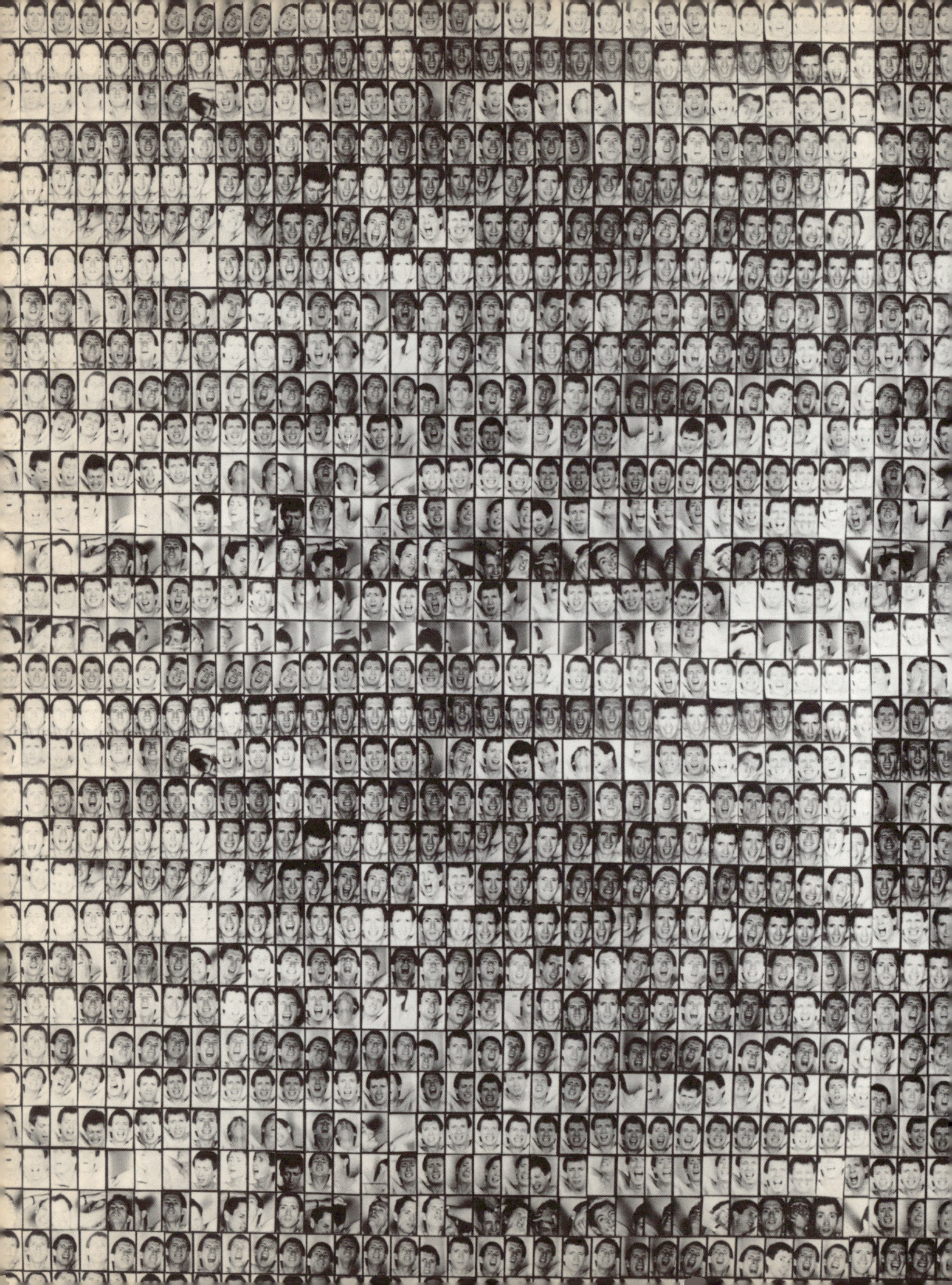